MEDIA, AUDIENCES, EFFECTS

An Introduction to the Study of Media Content and Audience Analysis

PAUL J. TRAUDT

University of Nevada, Las Vegas

PEARSON

Boston   New York   San Francisco
Mexico City   Montreal   Toronto   London   Madrid   Munich   Paris
Hong Kong   Singapore   Tokyo   Cape Town   Sydney

Series Editor: *Molly Taylor*
Series Editorial Assistant: *Michael Kish*
Marketing Manager: *Mandee Eckersley*
Senior Production Editor: *Annette Pagliaro*
Editorial Production Service: *Walsh & Associates, Inc.*
Composition Buyer: *Linda Cox*
Manufacturing Buyer: *JoAnne Sweeney*
Cover Administrator: *Kristina Mose-Libon*
Electronic Composition: *Galley Graphics*

For related titles and support materials, visit our online catalog at www.ablongman.com.

Between the time Website information is gathered and then published, it is not unusual for some sites to have closed. Also, the transcription of URLs can result in unintented typographical errors. The publisher would appreciate notification where these errors occur so that they may be corrected in subsequent editions.

Library of Congress Cataloging-in-Publication Data
Traudt, Paul J.
   Media, audiences, effects : an introduction to the study of media content and audience analysis / Paul J. Traudt.
       p. cm.
   Includes bibliographical references and index.
   ISBN 0-205-39567-8
   1. Mass media—Influence. 2. Mass media—Audiences. 3. Mass media—Research—Methodology. I. Title.

P94.T73 2005
302-23—dc22

                                                                    2004050598

Printed in the United States of America
10 9 8 7 6 5 4 3 2 1   08 07 06 05 04

This book is dedicated to the memory of John D. Gibbs, former Vice President and General Manager of KQV radio in Pittsburgh, Pennsylvania. John epitomized the best of American broadcasting and truly believed that stations should serve the "public interest, convenience, and necessity." He inspired all who worked with him for over thirty years in commercial and public radio. It was my privilege to join John on the faculty at Duquesne University in the late 1980s. He was that rare combination of gentleman, professional media practitioner, valued academic colleague, dear family friend, and fellow fly fisherman. I am a better person for having known him.

CONTENTS

CHAPTER THREE

Qualitative Media Effects Research   30

PART II   Issues in Media Effects Research

CHAPTER FOUR
Media and Health   43

CHAPTER FIVE
Tobacco and Alcohol Advertising   54

CHAPTER EIGHT

Race and Ethnic Stereotyping 91

CHAPTER NINE

Sex and Gender Stereotyping 104

CHAPTER FIFTEEN

Television and Presidential Politics   **185**

PREFACE

This book is about media, audiences, and what is commonly referred to as *media effects*. The idea for this book has been percolating for over 25 years, since the time I was an undergraduate speech communication major studying broadcasting in what was then the Department of Speech and Dramatic Arts at the University of Colorado, Boulder. There my courses included media production and industry practice, interpersonal communication, persuasion, and rhetorical theory, as well as courses in journalism and advertising taken across the "Quad" in the journalism school. The seminal ideas for this book are drawn from a well-worn work still in my library, *The Early Window: Effects of Television on Children and Youth* (Liebert, Sprafkin, & Davidson, 1982). Actually, I am now in possession of my fourth or fifth copy because the work, though now dated, ends up in some student's library on a regular basis. Such is the work's unique and appealing nature. *The Early Window* was used by one of my professors in a "Media and Society" or "Media Effects" course and thus began my introduction to the study of media, audiences, and effects.

The current book, though expanded in scope and approach, draws its inspiration from those three authors and their well-worn text. *The Early Window* introduced readers to the field of media effects research by highlighting key studies in the areas of television and violence, advertising, and portrayals of sex and sexuality. The current book draws from that approach to provide a more recent snapshot of the field of media, audiences, and effects across these same and a larger range of issues. In addition, the current work provides those of you who are mostly new to the field tools for understanding and critiquing original media effects research.

We all know that people ascribe great power to the media. Soon you will see how mass communication researchers generally acknowledge the unrealistic nature of simple cause-and-effect approaches to the study of media and human behavior. Mass communication processes and effects are a challenge to study and assess. Still, policy makers and leaders in government, education, religion, and other institutions often embrace these simple cause-and-effect approaches in their efforts to regulate and control media content and, ultimately, attempt to influence media impact on personal attitudes and behaviors. Closer to home, you have probably been part of everyday conversations where you or other family members or friends attributed great power and influence to the mass media and new communications technologies. However, you were probably unfamiliar with the theories and techniques often used to explain such processes. Chances are, you have pointed to others as most susceptible to these media influences. This **third-person effect** is a popular mass communication theory and one studied by mass communication researchers. Because of these circumstances, a primary goal for this book is to provide a framework for you to understand how researchers approach the study of media effects and to begin to understand what contemporary mass communication theory and research does and does not tell us about the relationship between media and human thought and behavior. Another goal is the simple fact that many of you who are reading this book may become future leaders who will influence policies in an effort to regulate and control media industries and content. Regardless of future professional goals, most of you will or already have responsibilities in considering the role mass media play in your lives and in the lives of others. With that in mind, an additional goal of this book is to provide basic training in how to understand and critique mass media effects research, to better understand the role media play and do not play in our everyday lives.

Some books on media effects have been organized by a history of evolving mass communication theories and research. Other books have been purely topic driven, focusing entirely on one issue such as media violence, or news, or advertising, and so on. Other media effects books are narratives based solely on the reporting of study after empirical study. Such approaches may be suitable for those audiences with more advanced knowledge and training in the area of media effects, but are not practical when the simple goal is to introduce you to the broad field that is theory and research on mass communication effects. The current work strikes a balance among these previous approaches and provides the reader with basic questions to ponder when thinking about various media effects topics, a core sample of current research for those various topics, a summary of what we know based on these and other research findings, follow-up questions and activities, and finally a listing of suggested readings.

ORGANIZATION OF THE BOOK

The book is organized into two major parts. The first part presents three chapters designed to introduce you to the topic and range of approaches to media effects research. Chapter 1 provides an introduction to the study of media and audiences, provides underlying concepts, and defines key terms of use for the remainder of the book. Chapter 2 introduces the reader to the underpinnings of media effects research based on social science approaches. Many of the studies summarized in the second part of this book reflect the traditions and procedures used in the social scientific study of media, audiences, and effects. Chapter 3 provides a similar introduction to social research anchored in qualitative research methods. Qualitative studies are also included in the second part of this book. Together, the first three introductory chapters are designed to provide baseline understanding for how researchers go about the business of systematic inquiry in the world, the world of systematically observing and interpreting media content and audience attitudes and behaviors. Further, the first three chapters are also designed to provide you with some basic criteria in order to read, interpret, and assess the value of media effects research, including those studies summarized in the second part of this book.

The second part of the book contains twelve issues-oriented chapters. Each chapter begins with an introduction and series of questions that are pertinent to each chapter's core—a presentation of recent research findings organized by topic and methods of inquiry. The majority of these findings are from academic journal articles published since 1990. Two key databases were used when searching for these articles. The first was ComAbstracts maintained by the Communication Institute for Online Scholarship. This database provides information on journal articles published in the communication discipline. The second database was the Cambridge Scientific Abstracts Database Internet Service, providing access to articles published across a broad range of disciplines, including economics, education, marketing, psychology, and sociology. These databases provided access to a broad range of research on media, audiences, and effects. As you will soon see, the practice of media effects research spans many academic disciplines, including communication, journalism and mass communication, speech, political science, psychology, sociology, education, as well as race, ethnic, and gender studies. This range of interdisciplinary study is reflected in the research reported in various chapters. In some cases, key studies predating 1990 have been included. Chapter 4 focuses on media and health, and includes one section on eating disorders and another on preventive health care. Chapter 5 introduces readers to the topics of tobacco and alcohol advertising. Chapter 6 extends the previous chapter discussion to more specific focus on children and advertising. Chapter 7 presents research literature examining relationships between television and education. Specific sections within this chapter address academic achievement and television as a tool for instruction. Chapter 8 reviews the topic of race and ethnic stereotyping and the mass media. Chapter 9 provides similar treatment of topics related to media portrayals of sex and gender stereotyping. By way of natural extension, Chapter 10 reviews recent literature on television sex and sexuality, and pornography. Chapter 11 visits the substantial body of empirical study having to do with children, television, and violence. Chapter 12 focuses on another specific type of television content, music videos. Chapter 13 addresses the increasingly robust field of research on video games. Finally, Chapters 14 and 15 review recent literature on television news and presidential politics respectively.

Intended as a stand-alone work, this book is designed for use by those of you taking introductory mass media and society or media effects courses typically taught in schools or departments of communication, journalism, or mass communication. This book also serves as a reference work, a starting point for those of you interested in media effects in general, or for a particular topic covered in the current work. Health-care professionals can find the literature summarized in multiple chapters useful. Teachers and school administrators spanning primary to secondary levels of education can use the work as a reference for research and findings on topics related to media, children, adolescents, and teens.

My professors in graduate school taught me to approach the field of media effects with a very healthy dose of skepticism. Indeed, there is much that we still do not know about the relationship between media and human behavior, even after many years of systematic inquiry. Many of the relationships we do find between media, audiences, and effects are small or are confounded by other factors. Hopefully, as you work your way through this book, you will adopt your own set of critical standards about what we do and what we do not know when it comes to the many relationships between media, audiences, and effects. This book will have been successful if even one of you takes up the cause of adding to our understanding of how we engage a world increasingly characterized by the integration of print and electronic media, and how that experience informs our perception of ourselves and our actions toward others.

REFERENCES

Liebert, R., Sprafkin, J., & Davidson, E. (1982). *The early window: Effects of television on children and youth.* New York: Pergamon.

ACKNOWLEDGMENTS

This book was not an individual effort. Many people provided different kinds of support. I would like to thank Dr. Raymond W. Alden, III, executive vice president and provost at the University of Nevada Las Vegas for approving and members of the Faculty Senate Developmental Leave Committee in recommending me for sabbatical in order to write this book. Many of the chapters herein include summaries of research reported in international or small-circulation journals and Vicky A. Hart, Head of Document Delivery Services, and her very efficient staff at the UNLV Libraries were extremely helpful in acquiring these sources.

My new friends at Allyn and Bacon provided extremely helpful guidance throughout the entire process of proposing, writing, revising, and publishing. My sincere thanks go to Molly Taylor, Acquisitions Editor for Communication, and Michael Kish, Editorial Assistant, for their guidance, collegiality, and enthusiasm during the entire project.

A number of colleagues in the field of mass communication theory and research provided comments during various stages of writing. My thanks to Linda Kean (East Carolina University), John L. Sullivan (Muhlenberg College), S. Shyam Sundar (The Pennsylvania State University), and Tracy R. Worrell (Michigan State University) for their helpful and thoughtful reviews.

Three of my colleagues at UNLV also deserve recognition. Dr. Lawrence J. Mullen was a valued resource for the occasional journal article because of his extensive office library. Drs. Gary W. Larson and Dolores Valencia Tanno were always on the sidelines urging me forward throughout the long project.

Finally, I would like to thank my wife, Susan Molen Traudt, who has been urging me to write this book for more than twenty years. This book would never have been written without her unwavering conviction and support.

CHAPTER ONE

INTRODUCTION TO THE STUDY OF MEDIA EFFECTS

People ascribe great power to the media. Hardly a week passes without reports in newspapers or electronic news sources that blame the media as the cause of specific behaviors or for the ongoing decline in society's values and morals. Politicians at the highest levels predictably convene hearings and urge further research on media effects with the advent of every new media technology, or in response to potential voters' claims that the latest pop culture diva has overstepped the bounds of good taste and is leading the nation's youth to demise and doom. Educators rail against time spent with entertainment television, interactive video games, and related distractions in the face of declining academic performance and scores on national standardized tests. Physicians and health-care professionals decry the clear and self-apparent evils between watching television commercials and obesity on the part of youths. Parents blame cable television programs for serving up examples of antisocial behavior readily adopted by their unruly children. You no doubt recognize these patterns and can provide your own shopping list of numerous examples. To be sure, there are plenty of voices eager to target the media for much of what ails society. Unfortunately, those same voices rarely employ evidence drawn from media effects research to support their claims. Sadder is the virtual lack of informed debate between those who point fingers at the media and those audiences to which they preach.

A primary purpose in writing this book is to provide you with a set of useful tools for becoming an informed participant in the larger media effects debate. What characterizes the relationship between how we think and behave and our media use? How would we go about studying those relationships? How are questions about human behavior and media content studied by researchers? What does the research literature say about the relationship between our use of media and our perceptions, attitudes, and behaviors? Are these relationships powerful or weak? To what extent are these perceptions, or attitudes, or even behaviors accounted for by exposure to media content? What are the common outlets for such research literature? How do you begin to read and understand if this research is worthwhile?

Perhaps most important of all, why should you care about media, audiences, and effects? This last question can be answered in a number of ways. Chances are you are reading this introductory chapter surrounded by some combination of print, electronic, and Internet media. There may be a copy of the campus or metropolitan daily newspaper on your breakfast counter or coffee table. You may have read a story or two as part of your morning ritual of awaking, working out, eating, and preparing for work or school. You might have scanned the headlines to see if any major international or domestic story was worthy of more in-depth reading in order to satisfy your interests and desire to stay in tune with what is going on in the world, even if those events do not always affect you directly. Maybe you do not read a morning newspaper. Perhaps radio fulfills similar functions in place of newspaper content. Or you may be reading this chapter accompanied by television in the background. Perhaps you have a cable news network channel on screen but have muted the sound in order to *feel* as though you are monitoring news events while attempting to get a handle on the initial ideas presented in this book. Maybe you are trying to do two things at the same time. Perhaps you are reading this chapter with your favorite music video channel onscreen in the background with the audio just loud enough so that you can use your remote control to crank up the sound if one of your favorite artists or songs appears. Instead of video music as a source, you might be plugged into a headset, listening to one of your favorite compilation CD-ROMs mixed down from Internet file sharing. Maybe you are trying to concentrate on reading this chapter but are keeping an eye or ear tuned to your networked computer's pop-up window telling you that a friend has sent you e-mail. In all likelihood you are doing some combination of all of these right now as you read this chapter, perhaps even enhanced by your mastery of the range of communication options afforded by today's cellular telephone technologies.

Media consumption typical of the fairly complex patterns characterized in the previous paragraph does not happen in a vacuum distinct from other social behaviors or everyday behaviors. We have, in contemporary society, come to integrate many forms of mass media into our everyday lives without even thinking about how we navigate such pathways. This development has extremely compelling results we should consider. On one hand, the fact that we readily adopt various forms of media into our daily lives means that we generally also engage the content of those media without serious consideration. Therefore, an important component of many chapters is the systematic analysis and reporting of patterns and trends in media content. You will soon see that the major mass media tend to be fairly consistent in their portrayal of character types and behaviors. They do not represent as robust or diverse channels of communication as you may first imagine. Potentially, as other research in these same chapters will demonstrate, repeated exposure to such portrayals can lead to the formulation of attitudes and behaviors in tune with those media depictions. The result can be a form of shared cultural experience. Therefore, it becomes important for you to understand media content in order to personally assess the nature of this shared experience between you and those you know and even do not know. Concurrently, our understanding of trends in the content of major media also allows us to formulate ideas about *what we do not read, see, or hear in these same media.*

At this point in your reading, you might be thinking about some important questions. For example, what are the benefits in the ways that the media portray certain things as they do? What might be the motives behind the way that they portray some things but seem to omit portrayals of other things? Are there any potential negative outcomes given such portrayals? What are these negative aspects? Correspondingly, are there any positive outcomes to such depictions? Maybe such depictions have neither positive nor negative implications, or perhaps only for certain members of the intended audience? How would we know which members of the audience are affected and which ones are not affected? What about media portrayals and their potential effects in terms of larger societal functions? What are the implications for members of your family, for your extended social network, for your community, or for society at large? These are but a handful of the range of questions one might keep in mind when reading about how various mass communication researchers have studied media, audiences, and effects.

MASS MEDIA: MEMORIES OF A NOT-SO-DISTANT LANDSCAPE

To talk about media content presumes some knowledge of the larger goals of organizations that support the production of that content. The mass media are those organizations that disseminate content to audiences. Traditionally, the mass media disseminated original or acquired content to large audiences. In fact, most of you would have had a pretty good handle on what was meant by the term **mass media** if this book had been written in the mid-1970s. At that time, the mass media were easily delineated into three major categories: print, broadcast, and cinematic. Print media meant books, magazines, and newspapers. Broadcast media meant radio and television. The recording industry, dominated by prerecorded disk record and magnetic tape cassette at the time, depended on the radio medium for exposure and promotion. Cinematic media meant feature and other films exhibited at single-theatre movie facilities and a declining number of drive-in theaters. One thing all these mass media had in common, as the name implies, was the distribution of the same information to many different readers, listeners, or viewers. For example, tens of millions of copies of *Reader's Digest* were read by readers via mail subscription or newsstand sales. Most of you reading this chapter have probably never seen a copy of this once vastly popular magazine, but you probably need only talk to older members of your family to discover the role this publication once played in American life. In addition, teenagers and young adults were listening to their favorite musical artists courtesy of prerecorded record disks and audiotapes and a growing FM stereo-radio-broadcast industry. Three major broadcast television networks dominated the prime-time program landscape. With this type of traditional mass media delivery system, the same message was disseminated the same way to many different audience members. An additional condition with traditional radio and television broadcast media was that audience members had to attend to the same message at the same time because of programming schedules determined by the industry.

TODAY'S EVOLVING MEDIA LANDSCAPE

Today, the majority of you who are reading this book probably do not remember the media industries of 1975, but are more familiar with the evolving media landscape. Each of the major mass media previously described has evolved in 25 or so years, making those traditional print, broadcast, and cinematic distinctions less clear. Millions of copies of *Readers Digest* continue to be sold via subscription and news-stand sales, but to an aging older-adult population. Chances are you subscribe to one or more magazines targeted to your age, gender, and interest group, but you might be reading magazines or supplemental content online. Local market-broadcast radio still serves to support the sale of prerecorded music, but only as a supplement to niche cable network programming services such as MTV and VH1. These local broadcasts also now compete with digital music programming services provided by cable and satellite television services. Unknown and the most promi-nent musicians alike can now record and market performances via Internet websites and without the services of recording companies. Illegal swapping of music files via Internet tools has evolved to tighter controls and licensed music shareware pro-grams. Most of you reading this chapter have become keenly aware of what you can and should not do in terms of sharing Internet music files and chances are that more and more of you are paying a subscriber fee for access to such opportunities.

Major motion picture production studios no longer pump out hundreds of movies each year, but play a principal role in the creation of 20 or so pictures, thus placing incredible importance on frequent blockbuster hits. The result has included a trend toward sequels and recycling successful narrative formulas. Movie exhibi-tion is no longer the exclusive domain of single-screen theaters, but multiplexes where the range of theatergoer demographics is served each hour by different venues. Distribution rights are negotiated long before the first scenes are cast and shot, and extend beyond theater exhibition to include pay-per-view, cable-movie channels, and videocassette and DVD rentals, to say nothing of merchandising for everything from fast foods to children's sleepwear.

Broadcast television no longer dominates the television scene. Multichannel programming services provided by cable or satellite delivery industries compete for audiences by providing increasingly enhanced digital tiers, ancillary program-ming services, and high-speed Internet connections. Remote control devices pro-vide multiplatform access to video services. Households are acquiring larger and larger television receivers including high-definition components integrated with home-theater systems. Interactive television is one example of an umbrella term used to describe many different technologies and programming services. Some of the more popular services taking shape include so-called smart television program-ming guides. Typically afforded via cable or satellite television, these advanced services provide television viewers with multiday advanced program search tools. Software driven, these services also have built-in pattern recognition and can learn a television viewer's program preferences, scan future program offerings, and make suggestions regarding future viewing and recording. Another portion of the interactive television industry finding some measure of economic success are personal video recorders, or PVRs. These are set-top boxes with increasing amounts of digital memory capacity that allow the television viewer to prerecord over a day's worth of television programming for playback at a later date, thus eliminating the need for videocassettes and magnetic tape media. Playback on PVRs often features the opportunity to skip commercials or other program interruptions, a feature of great concern to advertisers. PVRs now compete with increasingly affordable digital-video-disk recorders. Other interactive television features, such as personalized advertising services or marriages between Internet and traditional television services, remain elusive. Prototypes have been expensive, unable to pique considerable audience interest and generate viable revenue streams.

MASS MEDIA DEFINED

These evolving developments make more difficult efforts to define mass media in clear and simple terms. To be sure, mass media such as books, newspapers, magazines, television, radio, recordings, and movies remain, but they have all evolved in terms of ownership trends, message packaging, and audience consumption patterns. One may still read the paper and attend to very little else. However, every reader comprehends the potential for multimedia multitasking in typical, everyday media settings. We all know individuals, or may ourselves be the kind of audience member who watches two or more television channels concurrently while talking on a cell phone or, with increasing frequency, using our wireless laptop to interact with other viewers at a network television's website. These evolutions in the mass media landscape will only continue. Those of us who claim membership in the baby-boomer generation can see a vast difference in the way we use media, compared to the way younger generations use media. Predictably, multitasking and media usage will continue.

These trends, afforded by changes in technological delivery of media content and governmental deregulation of U.S. media, have serious implications for media effects research. For example, you will soon come to realize that a dominant portion of research on media effects has focused on the television medium. One would think that research on the relationship between television content operationally defined as violent and attitude or behavioral change would attend to the nuances of television's technological evolution. However, you will note after having read a number of chapters, the specific study of television effects continues to treat television as a largely ubiquitous beast, without regard for such things as to whether television audiences differ in terms of access to broadcast or cable television, remote control and playback recording devices, program guide services, and so on. For now, *let us define* **mass media** *as the range of print, electronic, and filmic opportunities* *supported by multiple platforms for presentation and consumption.* Such a definition indeed oversimplifies a complex set of variables generally glossed over in actual research, and the issue will be revisited in select chapters as a means for suggesting avenues for future inquiry.

MASS COMMUNICATION

Almost 100 years ago, mass communication was conceived as a process where one message could be sent by one communicator to many audience members with similar and predictable results. Since then, most media effects researchers have long abandoned any notion of the potential for mass media messages to have direct, immediate, and uniform effects on targeted audiences. One of my former colleagues argued, "We cannot think of the mass media message as something created by the journalist, author, or television or film director. We must also think of the message as something created by each member of the audience who exposes himself or herself selectively and in a unique sequence" to each message (Becker, 1983, pp. 7–8). Stated over two decades ago, the statement has even more power today, particularly in light of the changing media landscape and highly personal nature by which individuals engage content. Borrowing from my former colleague's description, we can frame the following definition: **Mass communication** *is the process by which individual audience members engage and give meaning to media contents.*

The definition allows for a range of potential actions on the part of audiences. For example, one can see that major advertisers still use network and cable television in order to generate awareness of a client's brand and, ideally, induce purchase behaviors on the part of targeted consumers comprising part of the larger audience. However, those of us who are exposed to an advertiser's message can engage the communication in a range of different ways. Some of us may not see the television commercial because we walk away from the television receiver, or because our personal-recording device allows us to skip over commercials, or because we just despise commercials and hit the mute button or change channels using our remote control device. Those of us who may actually see and hear the television commercial might tune it out because we don't match the basic demographic profile of the targeted audience, or we are already brand loyal to a competitor's product or service, or we may have a general distrust of all television advertising. Some members of the television audience may actually like advertisements and find them enjoyable, even if they do not pursue the advertiser's intended course of action resulting in a purchase of goods or services. Then there are actually those individuals within the viewing audience who are receptive to the information and appeals used by the advertiser in their commercial but who for some reason never quite get around to trying the product or who decide to stay loyal to a competitor's brand. Finally, within this range of individual audience member possibilities, there are those audience members who attend to the commercial, agree with the persuasive appeals used by the advertiser, and who change their shopping behaviors the next time they are at the store. Perhaps you can think of other outcomes given exposure to a television advertisement. Hopefully, you are also beginning to understand that *there can be no one media effect.* As in this case involving advertising, what is one audience member's aggravation is another's entertainment and maybe even persuasive message. A number of chapters in this book report findings from research on advertising content, consumer attitudes, and behaviors. Those of you interested in studying public relations, advertising, or integrated communication strategies can learn how different audiences respond to different types of persuasive appeals found in such communication. Still others of you interested in younger audiences will learn that children engage television's efforts to persuade in qualitatively different ways as a function of cognitive and physical age.

THE INTERPLAY BETWEEN MASS COMMUNICATION AND OTHER COMMUNICATION SPHERES

Mass communication processes do not occur independent of other forms of communication. Unfortunately, we tend to forget that mass communication is part of the larger sphere of communication processes and effects. Part of this tendency is a reflection of how the academic discipline of communication is often organized. Contemporary academic programs of communication often include faculty who teach and do research in interpersonal, small group, organizational, and mass communication. Often these programs include rhetoricians who study persuasion and public discourse from one or more critical perspectives. Journalism, advertising, and public relations may or may not be part of these programs. Just as viable are programs where journalism and mass communication are taught in one unit, with other areas of communication taught in a separate unit. Regardless of the organizational structure, the net effect can be one where the study of mass communication is seen to be separate or distinct from other areas of communication. Nothing could be further from reality.

The use of mass media includes a rich interplay with the social world. We often partake of media content in the company of others. For example, who among us has not attended a movie theater in the company of friends or family members? Research has shown that we use previous experiences with media content in our interactions with others. For example, we might share a favorite television program in common with a close friend and review highlights with each other after the most recent episode. We could be doing a number of things to sustain and deepen the friendship through these actions. We could be reinforcing our friendship bonds, or displaying our competence as program critics, or celebrating our favorite character's actions, or showing off our expertise in series history by sharing memories of past episodes. All of these things are possible, and you can probably generate some additional ways that we use media experiences to fuel our interactions with others on an everyday basis. Of course television and electronic media are not the only forms where we may do such things. Many of us read the morning or afternoon newspaper to satisfy the need for information about the world, but we also share that information with others in our familial and work settings to inform as well as to reinforce our importance as a member of that group.

Everyday talk, of course, can also be used to fuel media consumption. Who among us has not learned about a new television program, a recommended book, or recorded music from others in our social sphere? More important is the manner by which we engage and make meaning of our mass-mediated experiences. As much of the research reported in consequent chapters illustrates, how we interpret media messages is largely dependent on a combination of factors including the accumulation of experiences drawn from past social interactions, including those interactions spent in paired, small group, organizational, and mass-mediated settings. These past social interactions help frame our interpretation of media content we engage. As experiences in these social spheres change, so too can our interpretation of media content change. Many media effects studies, including those reported here in later chapters, do not address the function served by other communication spheres. You should keep this important fact at the forefront when thinking about what we do and do not know from these previous studies and, perhaps, what could be included as part of the effort in future research.

MODELS AND MASS COMMUNICATION STUDY

Models are often text or graphic representations of communication processes. Models are often used as representations of more complex theories or ideas. Concurrently, one of the problems with models is that they oversimplify complex processes, including human communication processes. Many books on communication theory include a progression of models from very simple linear to more complex, multidimensional representations. Typical among linear models represented is the now-aged Source-Message-Encoding-Medium-Decoding-Receiver (S-M-E-M-D-R) model used to represent both interpersonal and mass-mediated forms of communication. Concurrent with modern-day discussions of this type of linear model is recognition of the outdated nature of such a linear representation.

Many books on mass communication use the pebble-in-the-lake metaphorical model. As an avid outdoorsperson I too will use this metaphor, but with some personal extensions. When I was a much younger and foolish fisherman, I often approached the shoreline of pristine high mountain lakes above the timberline and the first thing I would do is look for a good-sized rock to heave as far as I could out into that lake. At the risk of spooking fish and angering other high-country anglers, I was creating my own model of mass communication. I was the mass media organization, my rock was the message, and the surface of the lake was my medium or vehicle for conveying that message, the transfer of motion energy from a descending rock into a viscous liquid surface exemplified by outward, rippling waves. How far my message could travel was determined by a number of factors. The more powerful my arm and the bigger the rock, the bigger the initial impact of my message. The bigger impact of my message resulted in the potential for my message to ripple far and wide. If the wind was calm and the surface of the glacial lake was smooth as glass, then my message could conceivably ripple to every inch of the lake's shoreline. However, should my rock throwing excite an entire troop of scouts to throw their own rocks, then I have competing noise in terms of how far and clear my message might travel. Or, say I chucked the same rock into a fast-flowing stream or river. One might note that my rock makes something of a splash but fast-flowing currents rapidly suppress any consequent wave motion. The stream or river's flow quickly resumes its normal pattern and pace. Again, my message encountered a cluttered and competing message environment, making any efforts on my part to communicate both challenging and potentially unsuccessful. You probably understand given your own experiences with rocks and water that today's media landscape has few isolated and idyllic ponds, but many competing attractions for the potential rock thrower.

So far, we've used the foolish-fisherman-with-rock-at-lake metaphor to portray two of the three components of a successful mass communication triad, mass media organizations and their intended messages. Mass communication can be seen as the interplay between institutions, messages, *and* audiences. One influences the others. For example, the publisher of *Rolling Stone* may be passionate about a particular political perspective and choose to influence the editorial content of each month's issue. As a subscriber, you may agree or disagree with the publisher's views. However, if too many subscribers to *Rolling Stone* disagree and stop their subscriptions, then advertising revenues decrease because the publication can no longer charge as much for advertising. The editor can either go on expressing certain views in the face of declining circulation, or tone down the strength of certain political views and regain a loyal, and paying, subscriber base. To be sure, most audience feedback in mass communication is delayed and indirect, but it can be a compelling factor in determining what messages we continue to see and hear.

CONSOLIDATION, CONGLOMERATION, AND MESSAGE HOMOGENEITY

Even if audiences can influence media content, that function is severely affected by changes in ownership structure brought on by media economics and deregulatory practices over the past quarter century. These changes have radically affected all sectors of the media. For newspapers, there are fewer and fewer major metropolitan dailies. Major U.S. cities with more than one competing daily newspaper are almost nonexistent. Fewer newspaper chains own the remaining papers, with a majority of those chains relying more and more on wire copy services for journalistic content. The result is fewer papers printing more of the same material, regardless of geographic locale. The effect is compounded by the growth of so-called national newspapers such as *USA Today* and the *Wall St. Journal.*

The book industry shows consolidation of ownership trends similar to that of the newspaper industry, resulting in fewer and fewer new titles being published by fewer and fewer publishers, who are less willing to take a chance on unknown authors. Magazines, always an extremely expensive venture to launch, have carved out niche markets in an effort to cater to the most economically lucrative readership.

The result has been a clustering of magazines targeting the same audience demographic while other audiences are underserved.

Recent developments in the radio industry have included deregulation of station ownership and increasing reliance on homogenized program services. Traditionally, radio broadcasters were limited to owning two dozen or so radio stations across the United States. In more recent times, deregulation of the radio industry has allowed owners to grow, with some now owning more than 1,000 stations. This consolidation of ownership has allowed companies to become more efficient in terms of how they do business. For example, instead of having each station program its own radio play list, programming can be centralized and made more uniform across each station. As a result, two or three major radio corporations each own a half dozen or so radio stations in major metropolitan markets, with each competing against the others for the most viable female and male listening audiences.

Why should you, as a student of media, audiences, and effects, care about such things as media consolidation of ownership and homogenizing or *sameness* in major media? The effects of consolidation are many, and have implications for future media effects research. On one hand, a reduction in the number of newspapers and book publishers means that message diversity is also reduced. That outcome has direct and important implications in terms of the opportunity for you to gain different perspectives on the same story or event from different sources. Most of us would like to think that the media provide us with a range of different perspectives on the same topic. As we will see in consequent chapters, content analyses of newspapers and magazines tend to show that messages are consistent and fairly narrow in scope, regardless of topic or issue. The result is a newspaper audience across the United States reading the same story filtered through few gatekeepers. The potential for you and me to read diverse stories about the same topic, or to read stories unique to the regions in which we live, becomes more and more difficult. There are also important economic implications for those of you reading this chapter intent on pursuing careers as authors or as journalists. The fewer newspapers there are, the fewer opportunities there are for different reporters working on different newspapers in the same town covering the same story. A majority of newspapers rely on wire service copy for regional, national, and international news, often without employing significant local reporter staffs.

In real terms, the actual number of radio and television stations and cable television channels has expanded; however, more and more of these stations are owned by fewer and fewer corporations. The consolidation of ownership in electronic media has resulted in emphasis on programming targeting economically viable audience segments, particularly females 18 to 44 years of age. Despite the technological range of station and channel possibilities, much of what is heard and seen is predictable and constantly recycled. This homogeneity of electronic programming content does little to serve audiences regarded as beyond the fringe of economically viable targets. This is not to say that younger generations do not have access to evolving and original forms of music. However, you may not have known that younger generations are, largely for the first time, listening to increasing amounts of recycled music, writers, and performers who served two or three earlier generations. Research shows that music plays an important role in adolescent socializing and development. What are the effects of recycling music from previous generations? One could speculate that social issues and musical content relevant to previous generations of music listeners may not mesh with the attitudes and beliefs held by younger generations. This particular issue has received scant attention in the research literature, but you can probably see the potential difficulties of recycling music with messages that may be inconsistent with younger generational needs in such areas of socialization and role models.

MEDIA EFFECTS: A PROBLEMATIC TERM

So far in this chapter, the reader has been introduced to the argument that individual audience members are unique in that they bring a personal set of filters to the mass media experience and that these differences are a function of prior life experiences. To be sure, audience members uniquely engage media messages from a matrix of prior experiences. And, as has been argued, these prior experiences are a unique blend of mass-mediated and socially constructed meanings. However, the reader should also allow for the potential for shared experiences with mass media. Part of this is a function of the original purpose of mass communication processes. Back in the days of few and major mass media, many individuals encountered the same message as a function of few media channels of communication. More recently, a similar phenomenon is possible, given the homogeneous nature of media messages despite so many potential outlets for exposure.

Media effects are never absolute or total, so the word *effect* is something of a misnomer, used by many because of its economy and convenience as a label encompassing a complex and varied field of theory and research. As you will note in individual topic chapters, the results from key and influential studies never demonstrate in absolute terms a total and lasting relationship between the exposure to media content and consequent attitude or behavioral changes. Many scholars have traced the history of media effects research. Some of these works are provided as suggested readings at the end of this chapter. Viewed as a whole, these works suggest that approaches in theory and research to the study of media effects evolved over much of the twentieth century. In the early 1900s, media effects were seen to be uniform and absolute. This perspective gave way by the beginning of World War II to a belief that audience perception of media messages, particularly those intent on persuading large groups in society, was contingent on a number of factors, including message characteristics, environmental conditions, and individual psychological differences on the part of audience members. By the 1970s, mass media researchers embraced the notion that individuals had needs and desires, some of which could be satisfied by means of mass media consumption. Still other researchers argued that heavy consumption of media content, particularly television, could result in audience adoption of a media-centric view of the world. Finally, other scholars have argued that media effects, though subtle, provide the undergirding fabric for much of how society functions. Many of these perspectives will be reviewed in forthcoming chapters in this book. However, what all these approaches have in common is what they say about a simplified notion of **media effects.** Early theory and research in the past century clearly embraced the notion that the mass media had an immediate, direct, and identical effect on audience members. Mid-twentieth-century theory and research realized that a number of factors mediated any power of direct effects. Thus a common perspective still shared by many engaged in mass media theory and research is that audiences *do to the mass media* rather than the other way around. As we will see, some research in the past 25 or so years has returned to a more absolutist, direct, but subtle effects model, suggesting that media are extremely powerful tools for persuading, even if audiences may be unaware of such powers.

TECHNOLOGY, INNOVATION, AND TRENDS IN MEDIA EFFECTS RESEARCH

An upside to the evolving marriage between old and new media is the potential for improved media effects research. Such developments have potential for improving mass communication theory and research, both research used by industry practitioners intent on measuring patterns of use, as well as with mass communication scholars and researchers more interested in questions about attitude and behavioral changes. For example, precise methods for reliably measuring who is watching television programming, when they are watching programming, and why they are watching remain elusive for such organizations as Nielsen Media Research and Arbitron. You may know that Nielsen is largely responsible for generating industry ratings data on television audience viewing, while Arbitron provides similar audience listening ratings data for the radio industry. Self-administered paper-and-pencil quarter-hour diaries of viewing or listening, long the means for collecting such information, have given way in some instances to electronic data-gathering techniques designed to provide more accurate measures of television and radio behavior. However, these data only provide marketers with demographic information concerning who is watching or listen to what, when, and for how long. The answers provided to marketers on behalf of Nielsen and Arbitron, or their counterparts in the print-media realm, do not begin to address the heady issue as to who or why people engage the media as they do, or any consequences as a result of having seen or heard media messages. Some researchers believe that evolving technologies, still in testing phases, will allow for more valid methods for answering both basic and more complex questions surrounding media, audiences, and effects.

THEORIES, RESEARCH, AND METHODOLOGY

Good media effects research is theory driven, though sometimes the underlying assumptions for a particular study may not be readily apparent. Chapters 2 and 3 provide readers with an overview of the two predominant approaches underlying most media effects research. Before we delve into those approaches, you should have a working understanding of what is meant by such terms as theory, research, and methodology. A **theory** is a body of beliefs, rules, or principles generally thought to be true. In addition, a theory allows one to predict outcomes with a certain degree of certainty. As we will see in the next two chapters, there are two central approaches to theory building: deductive and inductive. **Deductive thinking** incorporates a hard and fast set of rules or principles and applies those conditions to new situations with an eye toward predicting outcomes. Working from the opposite direction, **inductive thinking** assesses contexts and new conditions, gathers data, and only then hones rules governing social phenomena. You can probably recognize your own use of both deductive and inductive approaches to tasks and problem solving. The process is often a mixture of the two. For example, we often incorporate a deductive approach to principles and practices in everyday life. Many of us know from years of experience that when driving a car, certain roadside symbols predictably communicate pending road conditions ahead. These signs are **denotative** in nature, meaning that there is little ambiguity in terms of their culturally shared meaning among trained and licensed drivers. Some signs tell us what to do, some signs warn us of possible conditions, and other signs inform us of opportunities ahead. So, in a large way, we incorporate a theory of traffic rules based on a cultural system of denotative rules we share with others. Most driving, therefore, is a process of deductive thinking. Our theory of driving is based on a combination of rules and principles we know to be true.

We all realize, however, that some theories do not always apply to all situations. For example, I lived for a number of years in southwestern Pennsylvania. Anyone who has ever lived in or around the city of Pittsburgh knows that residents in that area have their own unique method for interpreting some traffic laws. Pittsburgh is a city with major rivers bisecting the urban landscape. It is also a city with thoroughfares coursing along narrow creeks and runs. Much of the traffic flowing around that city in a given day is limited to travel on narrow two-lane roads interconnecting major intersections. Often the traffic lights at these intersections do not have left-hand turn arrows. I noticed shortly after arriving in town that one to two drivers in left-hand-turn lanes would quickly make left turns in advance of approaching traffic, when both directions had the green light. Further, I noticed that opposing drivers expected you to tromp on the gas and make the left turn by waving you into the intersection. Over the years, in order to help with easing traffic congestion, Pittsburgh drivers learned to modify standard traffic laws for left-hand turns and they can be quite vocal when newcomers to the region don't pick up on these modified rules, on Pittsburgh's unique theory of urban navigation. For newcomers, driving in Pittsburgh is a frustrating process because they approach the process deductively. When those conventional rules do not work, they gather data in order to formulate new rules for driving in southwestern Pennsylvania. Drivers new to the scene must engage in a process of inductive thinking in order to create a new set of rules about driving Pittsburgh's narrow thoroughfares.

Good research is theory driven regardless of the procedure being deductive or inductive in approach. Good research is also **empirical,** in that it engages observations about the physical or social world in a systematic way. Therefore, research is any form of systematic inquiry in the service of advancing theory. The tools used to collect data in any form of systematic social inquiry are its **method** or **methodology.** Methods in media effects research include content analyses, experiments, surveys, and a range of qualitative field methods. The next two chapters spend a good deal of time showing how methodology serves to advance our understanding of mass media theory and research.

SUMMARY

Upon reading this chapter, you should be familiar with the following key points:

- Media represent the potential for a vast interplay of personal experiences unique to each audience member's information and entertainment needs.
- Media communication and interpersonal communication processes are intertwined.
- Consolidation and deregulation of U.S. media has important implications in terms of message diversity (or lack thereof) and economic opportunities for practitioners.
- While most media effects are not total or absolute, trends in media content provide the potential for shared audience experiences.
- Evolving communications technologies make the study of media effects more challenging as well as show potential for increasing the reliability of data collection techniques.
- Media effects research is a systematic process utilizing deductive or inductive approaches based on theory and appropriate methods.

REFERENCES

Becker, S. (1983). *Discovering mass communication.* Glenview, IL: Scott Foresman.

ACTIVITIES

1. Keep a diary of your media consumption for a 24-hour period, being sure to log all media activities including viewing television, listening to music, reading the newspaper, and so on. Then compare your diary to those of others. How many different media are used? What is the average number of media used? What medium gets used more than others? How long? Are there any discernable patterns to media use?
2. List the title and artist of the last five pieces of prerecorded music you purchased or downloaded. Compare your list to others. Note any overlaps. Jot down why you like to listen to that particular artist or song. Then compare your reasons to those in your class who also indicated a preference for that artist or song. What do the

results suggest to you in terms of media effects? Can there be one common effect, from a particular mass media message? Can there be more than one?

3. This chapter mentioned traffic rules and regulations as a form of shared theory. What are some other everyday theories used by members of society?

QUESTIONS

1. Some mass communication researchers distinguish between active and passive or lean-back and lean-in behaviors. For example, most of us who watch television do so in a relaxed, lean-back mode, but when we use a computer for surfing the Internet, we are engaging in lean-in behaviors. To what extent does this difference influence the way you think about media effects?

2. This chapter defined mass communication as the process by which individuals engage and actively give meaning to media content. Do you think it is possible for media content to be uniformly interpreted by audience members? Provide examples to illustrate your view.

3. Is communication via the Internet a form of mass communication? Be sure to provide examples to help illustrate and test your response.

ADDITIONAL READINGS

Bryant, J., & Zillmann, D. (Eds.). (2002). *Media effects: Advances in theory and research* (2nd ed.). Mahwah, NJ: Lawrence Erlbaum.

Lowery, S., & DeFleur, M. (1995). *Milestones in mass communication research: Media effects* (3rd ed.). White Plains, NY: Longman.

CHAPTER TWO

QUANTITATIVE MEDIA EFFECTS RESEARCH

This chapter deals with what is often referred to as **quantitative** research. Hopefully, you will soon come to know that the term quantitative is somewhat limited in describing this type of research. Certainly, assigning numbers to observations can be a significant part of this type of inquiry, but a more accurate term for the process is **social science,** and its practice can be called **social scientific research.** We can better understand the language of social science by breaking down some of these terms into their component parts.

BASIC ASSUMPTIONS, DEDUCTIVE APPROACHES

Social scientists generally engage in the process of deductive thinking discussed in the previous chapter. They believe that the world can best be understood through systematic observation. For mass media researchers, this means that the world of media content can be systematically sampled and observed. Social scientists also believe that human beings, no matter how unique, share certain beliefs and behaviors. Again by extension, mass media researchers using social scientific methods believe that audiences can engage and react to media content in similar ways, thus revealing some larger and observable characteristics about the nature of human behavior. All social scientists use **quantification** in the practice of systematic observation. Quantification is the practice of converting observed behaviors into numbers that can then be systematically analyzed using a range of mathematical tools generally known as statistics.

THEORIES, THEORETICAL CONSTRUCTS, VARIABLES

Social science proceeds deductively from theory, to theoretical constructs, to variables, and finally to the careful measurement of those variables. As was briefly discussed in Chapter 1, a theory is a set of rules or beliefs that generally hold water, stand the test of time, and allow one to predict outcomes. We can use one of the more famous theories and methods used to this day to demonstrate this deductive process. Professor Albert C. Bandura argued beginning in the mid-1960s that a variation on classical operant conditioning, what he termed **modeling theory,** could be used to explain the relationships between children, television, and learned behaviors, particularly violence (Bandura, 1977). His theory of modeling predicted that children could learn violent behaviors given the appropriate set of visual and verbal cues. Further, Professor Bandura argued that such learning could take place despite differences in positive or negative reinforcements. You may begin to see that Professor Bandura's **theoretical constructs** included things such as environmental cues (televised portrayals of violence), reinforcement contingencies (televised positive or negative reinforcement for modeling portrayals of violence), and learned behaviors (successful modeling of learned violent behaviors). He then proceeded to create variables that could be used to manipulate and measure these constructs. What are variables? **Variables** are organized sets, groupings, or classes of observations. You are probably familiar with a number of variables in everyday life even if you did not know them by their social science label. For example, the variable called *sex* is a common measure in social science research. Researchers often define the variable sex based on biological differences between males and females. You can probably think of many other variables used in social science research, including those used in media effects research. Professor Bandura's variables stemmed directly from the theoretical constructs used to explain his larger theory of learning; specifically things like environmental cues, reinforcement contingencies, and learned behaviors. Environmental cues were carefully defined models used to teach violent behavior. In Professor Bandura's case, an adult was the role model for these televised cues as he pummeled the inflatable "Bobo Doll" clown with various play tools and shouted violent verbalizations. Reinforcement contingencies were also carefully conceived and constructed so as to be able to predict different outcomes on the part of children who viewed different types of reward or punishment received by the adult model. Some children viewed the adult being rewarded for his antisocial behaviors, while others saw the perpetrator being punished. Finally, this experiment provided an opportunity for children to reenact the very behaviors they observed. Professor Bandura and his colleagues decided in advance what would constitute a child's learning of violent behaviors prior to observing each child's postexposure behaviors.

Social scientists follow these kinds of carefully prescribed plans in the conduct of analyzing media content, testing human subjects under experimental conditions, or when using surveys. The result, in the best traditions of social science, is theory-informing methods of inquiry, in order to further advance our knowledge about the world. The famous studies conducted by Professor Bandura are a good example. Initially, he and his colleagues set out to test some very basic principles about how children learn to model behaviors, including antisocial behaviors. In time, both theory and method were refined in order to explore the complex layers of how children learn and model behaviors.

Finally, this discussion about theory, theoretical constructs, and variables would not be complete without mentioning some differences in the ways variables are used in social science research. Often, social science research examines differences between two or more variables. For example, one might look at differences between females and males and differences in watching television news. In essence, we are examining how one variable influences the outcome of another variable. In this particular example, the variable used to represent females and males, or sex, is the **independent variable.** The variable used to measure watching television news is the **dependent variable.** Independent variables are those variables that we manipulate or control to predict the presence or outcome of the dependent variable. In the sex and news example, sex is the independent variable and watching television news is the dependent variable. Here, we would be predicting differences in television news watching as a function of the sex of the respondent. Returning to Professor Bandura's Bobo Doll studies, the independent variables included verbal and physical violent behaviors exhibited by the adult confederate in the televised depiction. Other independent variables included positive and negative reward contingencies manipulated in various versions of the experiment. The dependent variable was the observed behaviors displayed by children who were exposed to both modeled behaviors and one of the reinforcement conditions. You can probably begin to see that *how* the social scientist operationally defines variables has direct bearing on how corresponding research is conducted.

Replicability and Reliability

One of the hallmarks of good social science research is that it must be replicable. **Replicability** is the ability to duplicate the methods and procedures of a previous study, in order to assess similar or different outcomes. Social science assumes trial-and-error procedures. To do so requires that sufficient detail concerning the original study's procedures be provided. There are times in this book when particular studies on media, audiences, and effects are recommended for you to read. Hopefully you will read some of these original studies. One of the things you should keep in mind when reading such research is this question: "Does the researcher provide a description of method and analysis in sufficient detail to replicate the study?" Should such information be missing, the author of the original work will sometimes provide means for additional correspondence in order to provide additional methodological details. Replication is important for another reason. Typically, one study does not a theory prove. The idea behind social science is that good theories stand the test of time. That is, good theories can be tested again and again, thus refining our understanding of the theory's power to predict. Good documentation of research methods leads to our ability to replicate each other's research, toward this larger goal.

    Reliability has to do with the quality of measures used to collect data for our variables. A measure that is reliable produces the same kinds of observations from study to study and from researcher to researcher. Some measures in social science research are more reliable than other measures. For example, a common measure of media exposure is a respondent's estimate of the amount of television he or she views. Could you with a certain degree of certainty say how many television programs your viewed during the previous day? Chances are you could, even though most of us would find the question somewhat suspect because of the fact that we often use remote-control devices to watch more than just one television program during a particular time. Even so, an estimate of yesterday's television viewing would seem a fairly reliable measure. However, most media researchers who use the theoretical construct of media exposure in their research are not interested in a variable operationally defined to assess the previous day's television viewing. They are usually more interested in some larger and longer estimate of time spent with television, usually a week or longer. Perhaps you can begin to see how operationally defining variables so that they are reliable may not be as easy a task as it first seems. Social scientists often use computer-based methods to statistically determine the internal consistency of operationally defined measures.

Noninferential and Inferential Statistics

Professor Bandura's program of research was intent on exploring and confirming the component parts of modeling theory in greater and greater detail. He was not interested in inferring, in generalizing his results to a larger population of pre-adolescent children. He was intent, through repeated experiments, in confirming and furthering our understanding of the cognitive processes of learning and memory. He was not intent on generalizing his results to a larger population of children or adolescents who did not participate in one of his experiments. Therefore, Professor Bandura employed **noninferential statistics.**

For years I have been teaching undergraduates and graduate students that one of the ways to think about noninferential and inferential statistics is to remember this statement: *A statistic is to a sample is to a parameter is to a population.* Consider for a moment each key word in this phrase. Returning to our study of sex and television news, imagine that we interviewed 25 females and 25 males for our study. One of the females in our sample indicated that she did watch television news. Her response represents a **statistic** in our sample. In social science, a statistic is a numerical representation of an observation. But statistics alone are not useful, because we always want to take the next step and group statistics for a particular **sample** in meaningful and logical ways so as to be able to describe the characteristics of that sample. What we really want to do in our study is report the accumulated statistics for our sample. So, let us continue to imagine that 65 percent of females in our sample watched television news, compared to 45 percent of males interviewed. Now we are learning some useful information about the sample of 50 individuals included in our study. At this point we are also only engaging in research employing noninferential statistics because we make no attempt to extend the findings of our sample to some larger portion, a **parameter,** of population. However, what if we drew the sample with some confidence that the sample was representative of a subset, a parameter, of a larger population? What if we were to systematically sample both females and males between the ages of 18 to 49 such that every person meeting those criteria (sex and age range) had an equal opportunity of being included in our sample? Then the statistical characteristics of our sample could be used to generalize to the larger parameter of females and males 18 to 49 years of age. In such cases, we would be engaging in **inferential statistics.** We would be

extending the results of our systematic sample to a group within the larger population. Some statistics can be used for both noninferential and inferential studies, some
cannot. The differences are taught in entry and advance level courses in social
science research design and statistics courses.

Inferential Statistics and Probability

How do we know if differences in females' and males' preferences for television
news are real and not just a function of chance or error? How do we know if two or
more variables are truly related in meaningful ways? The accuracy of prediction is
generally reported in terms of mathematical probabilities. The most common way
this is done in research reports is by means of a **probability level.** No research is
perfect, and social science research attempts to account for this error potential
mathematically. Error in research can be the result of a number factors, including
sampling procedures, sample size, the range of potential responses for a given
variable, and measure reliability. Most research reports include indicators telling
you if results are statistically significant. The most common way this is done is to
state the standard or actual probability level for any statistical outcomes. The
standard way this is done is to report whether results meet the standard criteria
established among most social science researchers. So the next time you read a
research report, look for the simple equation "$p \leq .05$." Stated in lay terms, one would
read this as "The probability is less than or equal to point zero five." What does this
mean? If a calculated probability level is less than or equal to .05, then we would
expect to find similar results at least 95 out of 100 times. Those odds are generally
seen as acceptable outcomes in the social sciences. Another way to think about a
probability level of .05 is as follows. If we were to repeat a media effects study, 95
out of 100 times we would expect to find similar results to the ones generated as a
function of real differences or interactions between message contents, experimental
conditions, or survey-generated data and not because of spurious chance. Most
social science research uses this probability level when reporting the statistical
significance of results. The same criteria are generally used when reporting media
effects research incorporating social science approaches (see Box 2.1).

Sampling

There are, in keeping with noninferential and inferential statistical procedures, two
different purposes in sampling. You will recall that with noninferential statistical
procedures we are interested only in describing results for our specific sample.
Experiments such as those used by Professor Bandura are a good example. We do
not extend our findings to any larger parameter or population with inferential
statistics. In contrast, sampling takes on a different level of importance when
utilizing inferential statistics. You may recall that inferential statistics are used to
make generalizations to the larger parameter or population from which the sample
is drawn. In such cases, how the sample is drawn takes on extreme importance.

There are many suitable textbooks on sampling, and there are too many
different sampling techniques to mention in this chapter. However, readers of media

■ ■ ■ ■ ■

BOX 2.1

UNDERSTANDING CORRELATION COEFFICIENTS

Correlation statistics are commonly used to compare relationships between two or more variables. For example, the variables *income* and *education* are often compared using correlation statistics. Researchers will typically report two important pieces of information when using such statistics: a **probability level** and a **correlation coefficient.** We already know about probability levels from earlier reading in this chapter. There are many variations on the basic correlation statistic, but one of the most common used in media effects research is the **Pearson product moment correlation,** usually represented by the symbol r. Correlation coefficients contain two pieces of useful information. The first piece of information is found in the magnitude of the coefficient. Theoretically, coefficients can range from 0.00 to 1.00. A coefficient of 0.00 would indicate that there is no relationship between two or more variables. A coefficient of 1.00 would indicate that there is a perfect one-to-one correspondence between two or more variables. For example, in the case of income and education level, a coefficient of 1.00 would indicate that with every increment of income or education level, there was an equal and corresponding increment of the other variable. In practice, the actual computed coefficient between these two variables is often around .65. What does this mean? Is this important? There are generally accepted standards for interpreting a coefficient's magnitude (Koenker, 1961). A correlation of .00 to .19 represents a negligible or chance relationship, .20 to .39 a slight relationship, .40 to .59 a fair degree of relation-

ship, .60 to .79 a moderate to marked relationship, and .80 to 1.00 a highly dependable relationship. So our correlation coefficient between income and education level of .65 can be interpreted as a moderate relationship. Further, because the relationship is positive, one can infer that with the increase in one of the two variables, for example income, that there will be a corresponding increase in education level. If the statistical outcome of the two variables was negative, as in –.65, then one would interpret the relationship between the two variables as moderate and negatively related. That is, the presence of one variable, such as education level, would mean a decline in income. Be sure not to confuse a correlation coefficient with a simple percentage. In our earlier example, the correlation coefficient between income and education of .65 does not mean that 65 percent of the relationship between income and education is explained by these two variables. There is a way, however, to estimate such percentages. Social scientists use the something called **the coefficient of determination** for this purpose. The coefficient of determination is very simply calculated by squaring the correlation coefficient. Returning to our previous example, the square of .65 is .42, meaning that 42 percent of income is explained by education or vice versa. Finally, as this example illustrates, most correlation statistics cannot predict the direction of influence. We do not know if education level influences income, or if income influences education level. We only know that they are related.

effects literature can apply some general criteria to their examination of any study utilizing sampling as part of its methodology. First, good reporting of social science research includes reporting about how samples were drawn and generated. One of the first questions you can ask when reading such reports is if enough information was provided in order to allow you to duplicate the sampling procedure if you were motivated to do so. Remember, no research is perfect, and very often the shortcomings of sampling in any study are based on practical reasons. These reasons can include such things as inaccessibility to the ideal sampling pool, institutional or bureaucratic obstacles to accessing ideal sample pools, or limited funding. For example, imagine that you were interested in studying the impact that digital cable television services might be having on audience viewing and corresponding financial contributions to local public television stations. Your examination of previous research literature suggests that telephone surveys might be the best way to go. Clearly, your primary target population would be digital cable television subscribers. The most logical source for a master list of local-market subscribers would be your local cable system operator. But perhaps corporate policies for the parent cable corporation prohibit the release of subscriber information to even the most well-intentioned media effects researcher. What would one do in such a case? With adequate funding, you could hire a company to randomly generate telephone listings within the cable-service area, thus creating a potential list of both listed and unlisted numbers. However, the first thing you would have to do when talking to people who answer their phone is determine if they had digital or even the more basic cable services. You can begin to see the time and energy required to find qualified respondents for your survey. Sampling is not as easy as it first appears, and many factors can contribute to shortcomings in the final sample used by social scientists in their pursuit of knowledge. Another common criticism of social scientific research is the overreliance on university or college students as a readily available subject pool for data collection. Many of you who have read even a handful of original social science studies understand how students in higher education represent a readily abundant, if not overstudied population.

So far in this chapter, we have examined some of the underlying principles of social science research. The remainder of this chapter turns to an overview of the three most common research methods used by social scientists when studying media effects. In their order of presentation, these are content analyses, experiments, and surveys.

CONTENT ANALYSES

Content Analysis Defined

A common criticism of mass media effects research is that some researchers assume cause-and-effect relationships between media content and audience attitudes or behavioral changes without first systematically documenting what is in print, what is broadcast over the air, what is piped through cable or a high-speed Internet connection, and so on. Logic dictates that we understand the nuts and bolts of media content before we ascribe its potential to teach, influence, harm, and so on. So a good place to start in media effects research is with content analysis. **Content analysis** in media effects research is the systematic observation of elements in print, electronic, cinematic, and other media, usually by documenting the frequency with which such elements appear. Say you are a journalist interested in the ways that newspapers referred to the campaign in the last U.S. presidential election. Or perhaps you are interested in whether there are differences in the amount of wire copy included in various newspapers characterized by differences in size of markets served. Maybe your passion is broadcast radio, and you are interested in whether music programming differs across communities as a function of ownership conglomeration. Maybe you are interested in both the frequency of and differences in portrayals of physical violence in prime-time television dramas. Finally, suppose you were interested in the number of different visual elements used by cable news networks as part of their typical newscast. These types of research interests are best answered by means of content analysis.

Assumptions about Content Analysis

Readers and critics of content-analytic studies assume some reasonable and logical method of sampling. Why should you assume this? Because properly conducted content analysis allows the researcher to extend findings based on a sample of newspapers, television programs, and so on to a larger population of the same kinds of content. How would you go about this? Let us return to the first example mentioned in the previous section. Imagine that you are interested in how print journalists covered the most recent U.S. presidential election.

The first step, as is the case with any good research, would be to conduct a study of the previous research literature related to the topic. One would find that there is a considerable body of content-analytic literature examining press coverage of U.S. presidential races. One would also discover that a number of these previous studies incorporated similar if not the same theoretical constructs and operationally defined variables and measures, thus lending the qualities of reliability and replicability to these previous and your own proposed study. You would also discover some clues as to how to draw a sample for your own study. Most of these previous researchers conducted their sample of selected newspapers during the major campaign season, say from Labor Day until the eve of the November election. To be sure, stories about presidential campaigns predate Labor Day, but most researchers attempt to strike a balance between reasonable sample windows in the face of typically limited research funding. Further examination shows that some studies included every issue of one or more newspapers included in the sample for that intensive campaign period, while others randomly selected days within each week. Still other studies included only major newspapers from major population centers while others opted for a cross section of large, medium, and small markets while yet others chose to examine only the major daily newspapers from a particular region or state. Remember, your specific interest will dictate actual methods. Good content analytic studies will incorporate a reasonable blend of techniques developed by previous studies with a keen eye toward current research goals and objectives.

The job has hardly begun once techniques for actual newspaper sampling have been determined. What remains is even more critical, the sampling techniques for actual newspaper content. Again, those previous studies will be useful in helping you in your own design. Sometimes, content analysis of the newspaper attends only to stories in certain sections of the newspaper or stories containing certain headlines or photographs. Given our previously stated goal to study presidential campaigns, we might further break down our selection of story content to include all newspaper copy that mentions one or both major political party campaigns. One can see that great care must be taken when designing sampling and content selection parameters for good content analytic designs and that a good deal of trial and error can be avoided by relying on examples provided from previous research.

Reading and Critiquing Content Analyses

Content analyses in media research remain an extremely important tool in systematically documenting various forms of media messages. Readers feel a certain level of innate comfort with the technique. But how do you as a relative novice to such approaches know when a study is an actual content analysis? Often, the title of the work will provide a clue. Many content analytic studies will include some indication of the method in their titles. Another common technique is for researchers to include something like "Depictions of" or "A Content Analysis of" in the title of their work.

What criteria should the reader keep in mind when reading and analyzing a content analysis? For starters, it is important to determine whether the current research is based on previous research. As we've already seen, good content analyses are often based on previously tested approaches. Do the variables used in a content analytic study seem to be generated from previous research, or do they just seem to pop out of thin air? Do the variables seem to make sense? Are they easily understood? Did the researcher provide clear definitions for each measure used to represent a variable? Thinking back to our presidential campaign study, was it clear what the researcher meant by isolating newspaper headlines in terms of such commonly used categories to organize themes such as "horse race" or "candidate qualifications" issues?

The practice of **coding** is an important component of content analytic studies. Coding is the process where one or more researchers examine and assign the same meaning to an identical piece of media content. You can begin to see how important clear operational definitions of variables, based on larger theoretical constructs, become when performing content analyses. Typically, content analytic reports include detailed description as to how measures were coded, how coders were trained, and how coders were tested to assess mutual levels of agreement. Usually, but not always, more than person is responsible for coding the sample of media content. This is done to reduce the potential for single-coder bias. Does the study report something often referred to as **intercoder reliability** in its procedures or methods section? Intercoder reliability is typically reported as a mathematical product known as a coefficient. For example, a calculated and reported coefficient of 1.00 would represent perfect agreement on a coded item between two or more coders. Theoretically, intercoder reliability can range from absolutely no agreement to perfect agreement. In practice, minimum acceptable levels of intercoder reliability in media content analyses are .80 or higher. You should look for this important component when reading content analyses of media content. A reported coefficient less than .80 could suggest a less than valid theoretic construct, a poorly defined variable, or inadequate training of coders.

Readers should also keep in mind sampling techniques used by researchers who report results from content analytic designs. Are all aspects of sampling reported in the journal article or book chapter? Is the sampling period included? Does the rationale used in supporting sampling strategies make sense? As with all research, the reader should be sure to examine whether any and all questions posed by the researcher are systematically answered by means of data collection and reporting of results. Finally, most researchers summarize their current efforts by assessing both the strengths and shortcomings of the present study. Does reporting in the current content analytic study include recommendations for future research?

EXPERIMENTS

Experiments Defined

There are two basic types of experimental research, laboratory and field. A laboratory-based experiment has the advantage of controlling most if not all environmental factors, thus ensuring that only those factors introduced by the researcher can be measured for consequent effect on attitudes or behaviors. Bandura's previously mentioned Bobo Doll studies are a good example of laboratory-type experiment in media effects research. In contrast, a field experiment does not take place in a laboratory, and thus forces the researcher to relinquish considerable control in when and how a media message is exposed to a targeted sample member. For example, a form of field experiment occurs regularly when a national brand company sends bulk mail to thousands and thousands of residences, only the bulk mail may differ from region to region or from zip code to zip code. Some mailers may be characterized by the same headline or copy appeal but are printed in different colors. Other mailers may use different copy in the written appeals. Responses to the bulk mailings are tracked according to region or zip code. Any perceived differences in consumer responses can be attributed to various communication techniques used and tracked through the field experiment. One can see how this form of the experimental method is quite common in the field of advertising.

Assumptions about Experimental Approaches

As you may have already realized from earlier sections of this chapter, one of the fundamental assumptions of the experimental method is that every potential subject for study has an equal chance of being included in the study. Another fundamental assumption of the approach is that subjects selected for the study are randomly assigned to various experimental conditions comprising the study's design.

Experimental methods in media effects research are often criticized based on concerns about differences between audiences in experimental settings versus those same audiences in everyday situations. Put simply, most people do not consume media content in a laboratory. As we recognized in the first chapter, audiences use media content within the context of a range of behaviors at home, at work, while transporting, at play, or within a myriad of these and other activities. All the same, an effective counterargument to such concerns deals with the fundamental goal of most research using experimental methods. For example, a good deal of experimental methodology has been incorporated to isolate the complex cognitive mechanisms seen to surround human perception. In later chapters you will see how experiments have been used to isolate various cognitive mechanisms seen to relate to attention, memory, and recall given our exposure to certain kinds of media stimuli. To such ends, experimentation is an important tool. As we have already seen in Professor Bandura's use of experimentation, the method is also used to gauge the potential for learning and producing a range of positive and negative behaviors. Usually, these kinds of studies demonstrate short-term effects from exposure to certain kinds of media. One of the criticisms leveled at such approaches, indeed one often noted by its very practitioners, is the suspect nature of experimental methods to demonstrate the media's potential to produce and sustain long-term effects.

Reading and Critiquing Experiments

Those of you new to the concept of experiments in media effects research can still apply a number of criteria when assessing the value of such studies. Some of these criteria are similar to those used in assessing content analyses. Is the study systematically derived from a previous, existing body of research? Does the research include the description of theory, theoretical constructs, and operational definitions for key variables? Are these components generated or evolved in a logical pattern from previous research? There are also questions unique to experimental research designs that you can ask. How about the sampling techniques used? Does the study adequately randomize the opportunities for subjects to be included in any one particular treatment group for consequent study? Do the stimulus materials used in each experimental condition make sense? Do the tools used to observe behaviors, or to ask respondents questions, seem appropriate given the audience being tested? This is a particularly important question when research deals with children as subjects. As we shall see in a number of forthcoming chapters, younger children may not have the cognitive capacity to understand, produce, or respond to certain kinds of tasks in experiments or other methods. Finally, does the research assess both strengths and any shortcomings of the current study? Are recommendations for future research provided?

SURVEYS

Surveys Defined

The third method widely used in media effects research is the survey. Most of you who are reading this chapter are no doubt familiar with completing surveys. A survey is a data collection device where respondents answer one or more questions posed by the researcher. There are various types of surveys, ranging from self-administered to researcher administered, from mail-type surveys to interactive surveys via computer. Surveys can contain different kinds of questions, generally falling into two main categories: forced choice and open ended. Forced-choice questions can include scales and contingency-type questions. Contingency-type questions are typically constructed to include two or more parts. How a respondent answers the first part of the contingency question determines how that person will be routed to other parts of the question or survey. For example, suppose you were conducting survey research for a public radio station. One of the contingency questions you might use is whether the respondent listens to a public radio station serving the local market. The respondent who answers yes is routed to answer more specific questions about the radio station's programming, on-air personalities, and so on. However, respondents who are not listeners are routed to the next section of the survey, perhaps one dealing with general radio listening habits.

A second main type of survey question is the open-ended item, which asks a question and provides respondents with space to answer whatever they please and regardless of how verbose they may be. Most researchers practiced in the art of survey research prefer the fixed-answer or forced-choice type of questions rather than open-ended items because the former are easier to code and analyze statistically. The latter are often used sparingly to solicit unique views from respondents and to provide sample illustrations of respondent responses in research reports.

Assumptions about Survey Research

Survey methods are popular because they can generate a good deal of data of a uniform nature from as many respondents as can be included in the sample. Survey results can be generalized to a larger parameter or population when the sample is systematically drawn. When effectively designed, researchers assume that surveys tap into a collective sense of knowledge, attitudes, or experiences on the part of respondents. Effective survey design is assured by examination of previous research literature and, when possible, by acquiring survey questions used in previous studies where those measures were shown to demonstrate reliability. One important assumption concerning survey research is that good survey research instruments tap into an existing body of knowledge on the part of respondents. Or could it be the case that respondents don't often have preexisting views regarding a topic or individual until the question is posed? For example, a common technique in political campaign survey research is to provide respondents with a list of campaign issues and ask them to prioritize those issues from most to least important. One could argue that respondents may not have possessed preexisting views on the importance of any of those issues, or they may have preexisting views on the importance of other issues not listed.

Reading and Critiquing Survey Research

Consistent with critiquing content analyses and experimental studies, assessing the value of survey research as reported in reports or scholarly articles often boils down to simple common sense. Good survey research relies on past practices in order to build a foundation for the current work. Is the work grounded in previous theory and research? Do the theoretical constructions and corresponding operational variables demonstrate validity? Does the report or journal article provide enough methodological detail so as to allow the reader to understand what kind of survey was employed in the study, what questions were asked, and how responses were coded? Are important pieces of information such as number of attempted surveys versus actual number of surveys completed? These percentages can vary widely depending on whether the survey instrument is researcher or respondent self-administered. Mailed, self-administered survey research techniques typically result in very low return rates, often less than 5 percent. Do not assume that those recipients of the survey who chose not to respond are similar to those who chose to respond. Are the results linked directly to answering research questions or hypotheses? Are the reported results meaningful? Does the larger discussion include assessment as to the current study's strengths and shortcomings? Are suggestions for future research included?

SUMMARY

After reading this chapter, you should be familiar with the following principles concerning social science research approaches to the study of media effects.

- Social scientists engage in deductive thinking and believe that human beings share certain beliefs and behaviors that can be systematically observed.
- Social science proceeds from theory, to theoretical constructs, to operational definitions of variables representing those constructs, to careful measurement of variables.
- Good social science research is both replicable and reliable.
- Non-inferential statistics tell us only about the sample being studied but inferential statistics can be generalized to well-defined parameters within larger populations.
- Error in social science is accounted for by the use of probability levels, typically at the $p \leq .05$ level.
- The three primary methods for social scientists studying media effects are content analyses, experiments, and surveys.

REFERENCES

Bandura, A. (1977). *Social learning theory.* Englewood Cliffs, NJ: Prentice-Hall.
Koenker, R. (1961). *Simplified statistics.* Bloomington, IL: McNight & McNight.

ACTIVITIES

1. Conduct a content analysis of print, electronic, or Internet related messages. Investigate how previous research has operationally defined the content in ques-

tions (e.g., media violence, sexist portrayals, types of advertising appeals, etc.). Construct the new operational definition of content, conduct a sample of targeted media messages, and code the sample. What are the general findings?

2. Find and read two or more survey method media effects studies. Ideally, these studies should relate to a topic of interest to you. Feel free to consult any of the topics chapters for examples. Note how the authors identify any theoretical anchors and define important constructs and variables. Design your own simple survey in an effort to replicate or extend understanding of these constructs and variables. Pretest your survey on a non-random sample representing the target audience. Were the results what you anticipated? Were there any surprises?

3. Generate a list of 20 research questions related to media effects. Which of these questions might best be answered by use of content analyses, by experimentation, by survey research?

QUESTIONS

1. Social scientists believe that the world can best be understood through systematic observation. Further, they assume that human beings, no matter how unique, share certain beliefs and behaviors that can be measured. Do you agree or disagree? Provide examples of your own or other's media behaviors to support your view.

2. One criticism of experimental methods in media effects research has to do with short versus long term effects. Many experiments in media effects research demonstrate that audiences learn from experimental stimuli and, given adequate environmental cues, can reproduce what they have learned. Critics of this approach argue that audiences are trying to please researchers and conduct themselves accordingly, thus creating a false impression of real-world media effects phenomena. What do you think? Why?

3. Social science approaches to media effects quantify observable phenomena. That is, assigns numbers to phenomena for consequent statistical analysis. Do you think observable phenomena related to the field of media effects are quantifiable? Can you think of times when this might be problematic? If no, why? If so, why? Be sure to use examples in your response.

ADDITIONAL READINGS

Babbie, E. (1995). *The practice of social research* (7th ed.). Belmont, CA: Wadsworth.

Berger, A. (1998). *Media research techniques* (2nd ed.). Thousand Oaks, CA: Sage.

Poindexter, P., & McCombs, M. (2000). *Research in mass communication: A practical guide.* Boston: Bedford/St. Martin's.

Reinard, J. (2001). *Introduction to communication research* (3rd ed.). Boston: McGraw Hill.

Udan, T. (2001). *Statistics in plain English.* Mahwah, NJ: Lawrence Erlbaum.

Wimmer, R., & Dominick, J. (2003). *Mass media research: An introduction* (7th ed.). Belmont, CA: Wadsworth.

CHAPTER THREE

QUALITATIVE MEDIA EFFECTS RESEARCH

This chapter introduces you to **qualitative research** in general, and specifically when used in the study of media, audiences, and effects. You will soon see that qualitative research is very different from social scientific approaches to the study of media effects. Each approach in anchored in theory and has its own appropriate methods for inquiry.

BASIC ASSUMPTIONS, INDUCTIVE APPROACHES

Qualitative researchers generally use the process of deductive thinking. Their questions and methods are framed from larger theories and constructs not unlike those used by social scientists, but the similarities end there. A fundamental assumption of most researchers using qualitative methodology is that what people say and do is a reflection of how they view the surrounding world. Therefore, understanding human thoughts and actions, for the qualitative researcher, must be embedded in observing how *individuals act and describe their actions in society*. We saw in the previous chapter how social scientists believe that human beings share certain beliefs and behaviors that can be systematically observed, and even predicted. Qualitative researchers also use methods of systematic observation, but of chief concern is the ability to capture the essence of individual expressions, actions, and thoughts in everyday life. It may help you to think about qualitative research as the *study of the lived experience.*

To study the lived experience, qualitative social researchers generally use field research procedures designed to document what people say and do. In keeping with the general inductive nature of such inquiry, qualitative researchers also use analytic techniques to isolate or delay their own interpretations of what they are observing in order to see the world from the perspective of those people being studied. You can probably begin to see that qualitative approaches to the study of media, audiences, and effects are fundamentally different than social science approaches.

Qualitative study of media content and audiences gained momentum in the 1980s and 1990s. Examples are included in the following issue-oriented chapters when they appeared in the systematic search of research literature. You will also find examples included as suggested readings at the end of this chapter. Qualitative mass media research is noteworthy for creative approaches to answering questions about how human beings interpret and use media in everyday life to help make their worlds meaningful. Such approaches often take time and require their own pace for entering the field, gaining trust with people, developing rapport, and creating and implementing data-gathering methods. Effective qualitative research generates descriptive data requiring sifting, synthesis, and interpretation. The process of qualitative research can take considerable amounts of time, even years to complete one study. Despite such challenges, many mass media researchers have turned to qualitative approaches because they recognize its usefulness in exploring fundamental questions about how everyday life with media happens. "What's going on here?" "How do people do what they do?" "What reasons do people provide when explaining their actions?" These and related questions are the domain of qualitative research.

It may be useful at this point to review some of the differences between social scientific and qualitative approaches to the study of media effects. In terms of media content, the social scientist using content analytic methods may ask questions such as "What percentages of characters presented in prime-time comedies are women?" "What percentages are men?" "What percentages of women portrayed in prime-time comedies occupy central or primary roles?" In keeping with the underlying principles of qualitative research, the questions are notably different. For example, most qualitative studies interested in media content ask people about their interpretations of such content. So the questions directing this kind of research might be similar to the following: "What do audiences think about men and women portrayed in prime-time comedy roles?" "How do they describe these characters?" "Do the descriptions provided by audience members provide for any larger conclusions?" As you may begin to understand, media researchers using qualitative methods would not use experimental or survey methods, but they very often study people who use media and typically in the natural settings in which such use occurs.

We can also compare the kinds of questions typically generated by social scientists using experiments and surveys to their counterparts who employ qualitative methods to study audiences, media, and effects. For example, a social scientist using experimental procedures may be interested in answering the following type of question. "Is brand recall affected by advertising using direct or indirect messages designed to persuade?" The qualitative researcher would ask very different questions. "How do audiences describe different types of advertising proposed for a particular campaign?" "Do these descriptions provide any larger conclusions concerning the similarities and differences between these two types of advertising?" "In terms of recall, do audience members perceive one of the two types of advertising to be more memorable?" "What parts of the advertising, if any, seem to cue recall?" Social scientists, as you now know from having read the previous chapter, also use a good deal of survey methodology in order to assess relationships between one or more independent and dependent variables. For example, social science researchers interested in relationships between playing video games and violent attitudes might ask the following types of questions: "What is the relationship between the number of hours one plays video games and violent inclinations?" "What is the relationship between playing certain kinds of video games and callous behavior on the part of male adolescents?" Qualitative researchers typically begin such inquiry with the following kinds of questions: "Who is the audience for video games?" "What kinds of games are preferred by children, adolescents, or adults?" "How do these people describe game-playing experiences?" "How do parents with children who play video games perceive any outcomes of such play?" Perhaps you now begin to see the fundamental differences underlying the types of research conducted in the previous and this chapter.

You also read in the previous chapter about the common methods used by social scientists that study media effects, or content analysis, experiments, and surveys. Qualitative research, by its very nature, has no standard set of methodological tools. Every setting in which people engage media content and use media in everyday life is unique, and calls for similarly unique utilization of a range of data-gathering tools. These qualitative tools are discussed in a latter part of this chapter. You also read in the previous chapter about how social scientists follow an established set of guidelines in the practice of their craft. These include guiding principles for such things as replicability, reliability, inferential statistics, probability, and sampling. Some of these principles have their counterpart in qualitative research and, as you may already realize, some do not. Let us take up each of these principles in turn.

As with social science approaches, good qualitative research is also replicable. You will note when reading a qualitative study examining media, audiences, or effects that care is taken to describe in detail the theoretical approaches informing the study and the methods used to gain entry into the field and to collect and analyze data. Qualitative research, by its nature, must be creative in its ability to match an appropriate set of methodological tools to each unique research setting. Documenting such approaches becomes extremely important in order to help readers understand how data were generated and analyzed, and to provide adequate description in case other researchers decide to repeat the study.

The concept of reliability is different for the qualitative research when compared to the social scientist. The qualitative researcher typically does not enter into the field with a fixed set of operationally defined variables derived from theoretical constructs. In fact, the qualitative researcher assumes that the summaries and conclusions generated from data collected during field research will be based on their interpretation of what people say and do. Therefore, the reliability of any observation made by the qualitative researcher is by its very nature subject to scrutiny, but the validity of such findings are enhanced by typical characteristics of a qualitative study. These include such things as multiple approaches to data collection; highly descriptive accounts of people, utterances, places, and things; and extended periods of time spent in the field.

Other characteristics of social science such as inferential statistics, probability, and sampling are clearly at odds with the fundamental goals of qualitative study.

Statistics, beyond mere reporting of simple frequencies and trends based on field observations, are rarely if ever reported in qualitative research. Probability and sampling in social science research can enable the generalization of results to larger groups within the population. Qualitative researchers are generally careful about extending their findings beyond the scope of individuals or groups participating in the current study, as their goal is one of thick description in order to provide in-depth understanding of how people in one particular setting describe their thoughts and actions. As we will also see in the next section, most qualitative research is informed by theory. Qualitative studies often include in their analyses conclusions relating back to those theories in order to promote our understanding of such things as media, audiences, and effects.

THEORIES AND QUALITATIVE RESEARCH

Approaches to qualitative research are informed by larger theories concerning the nature of human thought and communication. You may note in the future when reading media research using qualitative approaches that researchers often refer to one or more theories or theoretical perspectives guiding their research. Remember, theories are beliefs or guiding principles generally seen as true. The theories used by qualitative researchers propose different perspectives in understanding human thought and action. There are many from which to choose, but three of the more prominent ones are presented below in order to give you some idea about how theory informs the types of questions and methods used by qualitative researchers. These theories are **phenomenological sociology; symbolic interactionism;** and **ethnomethodology.** Each theory varies in interpretation of what it means to study the lived experience. Therefore, each has its own corresponding and acceptable set of methods for empirical work in the social world.

Those who practice phenomenological sociology believe that what people say and do is a product of how they view the world; therefore, qualitative researchers using this approach focus on language and observe and collect samples of how individuals perceive themselves with regard to that social world. These researchers pay particular attention to what people say. They then analyze those utterances to understand people's meanings and intentions. For example, imagine that you were a qualitative researcher interested in studying how contemporary families use traditional and new media in the home. One of your primary goals as a phenomenological sociologist would be to observe family members' use of media in the home, and particularly any talk accompanying such use. Since clearly a good deal of media consumption does not always include self-reflecting talk or talk with others, you would also want to conduct a series of open-ended interviews to capture how family members describe their own and each others' media use.

Symbolic interactionists also study language, but they are more concerned with understanding the *mind.* These qualitative researchers see the mind as a combination of people's perceptions of themselves, particularly perceptions of *self.*

Even further, these researchers see the self as on display for observation through each individual's presentation of *roles,* which are displayed in different settings. Put another way, symbolic interactionists look at individuals as actors putting forth roles. These roles, the theory continues, are a primary method by which we organize experiences. Identifying these roles for the qualitative researcher leads to understanding both self and mind. Qualitative researchers working within this perspective often believe that the only way to identify such processes is to experience things first hand. Therefore, those qualitative researchers who practice symbolic interactionism often assume the role of the one being studied. This method is called participant observation, and will receive more attention in a later section of this chapter. Examples of media effects research using this perspective are potentially limitless. For example, imagine that you wanted to examine what roles are exhibited in video game arcades, and how increasingly proficient game play contributed to such role-playing. The symbolic interactionist would begin by visiting a local video game arcade and establish rapport over time with other players while becoming more and more proficient at higher levels of game play. Over time, the researcher would acquire an extensive set of descriptive data based on personal experiences and interactions suitable for consequent analysis.

Ethnomethodology remains one of the more misunderstood and difficult theories to comprehend. Ethnomethodology is the study of how people do everyday life. Put another way, ethnomethodology is the study of how individuals exercise the artful practice of everyday social interaction. As with symbolic interactionism, the focus with ethnomethodology is on everyday talk. However, here, talk is seen to include glimpses into the way people maintain the normal patterns of everyday interaction. Ethnomethodologists pay attention to everyday talk by gaining access to those places where talk happens and by recording what people in those settings say. A number of possibilities come to mind when thinking about ways ethnomethodology could be applied to the study of media, audiences, and effects. Groups within society often use television as the stuff to fuel conversations. A perfect example of this is how some audiences talk about favorite soap operas in common. When people talk about characters and events in soap operas they are doing much more than sharing television experiences. They may be helping each other escape to a world distant from the realities of everyday settings. They may be sharing close bonds and reinforcing the importance of friendships. They may be conveying their value as experts when it comes to a certain type of television. You probably perform this very kind of behavior from time to time with some form of media. A perfect opportunity for such research is on the Internet in chat groups, where thousands of discussions occur on a regular basis recounting the episodes of a group's favorite television program.

Please remember that there are many different theoretical perspectives informing approaches to the study of human thought and action. Some of the readings suggested at the end of the chapter will help you learn more about these different perspectives. Ultimately, the true test of any research is whether we gain insight into the human condition after reading a journal article or similar research report.

TYPES OF QUALITATIVE RESEARCH

Qualitative research can be some combination of three data-gathering approaches: observation, interviewing, and document or artifact gathering. Each social setting under study may warrant some combination of one or all of these approaches.

Observation: From Covert to Participant Observation

Hidden observation anchors one end of the continuum of observational methods. Hidden observation is incorporated when no other method is desirable or possible. Here, people typically know that they are being observed but since the "interaction" is one-way, there is no interaction between observer and observed. Not surprisingly, this technique is also viable for using experimental methods in social science research. Hidden observation is less than ideal as a qualitative approach to social inquiry given the one-sided and nonexistent relationship between the observer and those being observed. One form of hidden observation is the focus-group interview. This technique is a popular method of data collection in the fields of marketing, television and movie program testing, and advertising. Typically, paid participants matching a target demographic, for example, females 18 to 49 years of age, will agree to use a product or service, watch a television program or movie, or screen print or electronic advertisements. Then skilled interviewers ask participants for their reactions. Clients and other researchers generally observe these group interviews from behind a one-way glass mirror where they can both see and hear these interactions. Focus group interviews often provide researchers and clients with rich information about how people perceive their products, services, or media. Such research is not truly qualitative, however, since the approach is more deductive than inductive in nature.

Somewhat further along the covert continuum is unknown observation. Unknown observation is a condition where people in their natural settings do not know the researcher's motives and do not know they are being studied. An advantage to unknown observation methods is that the qualitative researcher can feel confident about the natural order of interactions observed. You can probably think of a number of natural settings where this might be an appropriate technique to consider. For example, imagine that you were interested in examining the relationship between children and parents and advertising, with a focus on breakfast-cereal advertising. One of the things you could do would be to acquire permission to hang out in your local grocery store, complete with cart half full of groceries, and roam up and down the cereal aisle, observing and noting interactions between children and parents. The limitations of this approach may outweigh the advantages. There is no way with such approaches to explore early hunches and have those people you observe amplify initial hunches and ideas with open-ended interviewing or related techniques. In addition, the risks of discovery and alienation are always possibilities. Finally, most universities, colleges, and related federally supported organizations must observe strict guidelines on ethical social research practices. Observing people who may not want to be observed presents unique ethnical concerns for any research proposal.

Uninvolved observation enters the area between covert and known techniques in qualitative research. Typically, when people think about qualitative field study, they have in mind some stereotype similar to the role played by most uninvolved observers. With uninvolved observation, people know the researcher's identity and perhaps to some extent the purpose of the study. However, the researcher's interaction with people is limited to sharing the same physical space and little more. Uninvolved observation can be considered as a field strategy when direct involvement would conceivably alter or change the course of people's behaviors. For example, one might consider this approach as part of a collection of qualitative methods used to study how children express gender roles during play. Your uninvolved observations could be conducted during school recess, but you would probably also want to talk to children and their parents in order to advance your understanding of what you observed. Another example could involve the study of families. Perhaps you are interested in the ways that television and computer media come to play a role in the patterns of everyday family life. This could include the study of how families use such media to schedule and organize daily routines, as well as use media content in everyday family communication. Obviously, you would need to gain access into the family's home in order to conduct parts of your study, but consistent with the previous example, you would probably want to also use additional data gathering techniques to round out your growing impressions and hunches as to the larger meanings of what you were seeing and hearing.

You may remember that one of the prominent theories linked to qualitative research is symbolic interactionism and that a key component of that perspective requires that researchers need to experience things first hand. In such cases, the researcher steps over the threshold from the role of observer to one of personal experience of that being studied. Some classic studies using this technique have been conducted, including those where researchers assumed the role of auto-assembly-line workers in order to experience first hand the sociology of work in manufacturing industries. You can probably begin to think about the range of possibilities for such research. You could, with sufficient training and credentials, learn about the daily editorial policies in a local television station newsroom, as you worked side by side with professional journalists. The range is fairly limitless with this method.

Interviewing: From Researcher as Subject to Subject as Interviewer

Some form of interviewing people typically enters into the equation in all but the most covert approaches to qualitative research and, hopefully, you are beginning to understand given earlier examples that good qualitative research typically employs two or more methods of data collection.

When the researcher is the participant observer, then the researcher's own perceptions and thoughts about such things as work in the newsroom, life on the road with an up-and-coming-alternative-music band, or expertise in playing video games become a major source of data collection. However, good qualitative research, even that guided by the theory of symbolic interactionism, requires additional types of data to help our understanding of what things mean. Interviewing is very often a way to do this. Sometimes there are people who have special expertise about the thing we are studying. Every setting has its experts, whether they are assistant managers in grocery stores, family members, newscasters, or other video game players. There are many situations involving audiences, media, and effects where researchers have neither the time nor resources to hang around for months on end hoping to observe key behaviors and hear key communication between people. Here is where the role of people as informants plays an important role. Central to most good qualitative research is the ability to identify individuals in your study who can by virtue of professional expertise or other abilities provide you with important information or with connections to other people with additional information. These may be those very store managers, parents, children, or newsroom workers previously mentioned who can share their personal views about customers, television in the home, expert video game play, and so on.

Documents and Artifacts

We live in a world of paper and digital documents. Documents can play a very important role as data in qualitative research. More traditional forms of documentation have included personal letters, business correspondence, and annual reports. These documents have often been at the core of qualitative research on organizational communication. Since most media are today part of large organizations, this form of data collection remains an extremely viable tool. Obviously, documents also fulfill important roles in other kinds of media effects research. Print media such as newspapers and magazines remain a valuable and rich source of data for both qualitative and quantitative analyses of content. The Internet is an increasingly important and readily accessible source of text and document information for a potentially unlimited range of qualitative studies. For example, we noted earlier how some research has examined the way some people use popular television soap operas to negotiate personal and group roles in everyday life. Chat group communication about soap operas is of itself a rich and easily accessed source of data for such study.

Cultural artifacts are those material things we use and display on an everyday basis. They are a reflection of what we consider important in our lives, and can be noted and explored by qualitative researchers as an extension of people's personal values. For example, I have a framed picture of John Belushi in my home office. The picture is a scene from the movie *Animal House,* where the actor is wearing a sweatshirt emblazoned with the word "College." If you were conducting a media inventory in my home as part of a qualitative study, you would probably feel compelled to ask me about that picture. I would tell you that the picture represents many things to me. For one, it reminds me of one of my all-time favorite movies, an exaggerated and extremely stereotyped depiction not that different from parts of my own undergraduate college experience back in the early 1970s. It also reminds me of a favorite comedic actor and weekend television rituals surrounding the group viewing of *Saturday Night Live* with close friends. The word "College" on Belushi's sweatshirt also has special meaning, because it is both a reflection of the abundance of obscure institutions of higher learning and, at the same time, of all universities and colleges, regardless of notoriety. I would probably go on with a few more examples if you were actually interviewing me about this cultural artifact, but you probably see the value in studying such things. In the case of this John Belushi picture, I was able to provide you with information so as to help you form some ideas about how I surround myself with some things to remind me of pleasant media experiences, pleasant personal experiences, and perhaps commentary on the nature of the profession of which I am a part. Together, these things begin to tell you something about me as a person, and the role media play in my everyday existence.

Using Qualitative Methods and Collecting Data

As you can imagine, most qualitative media effects research generates some combination of observation notes, interview transcripts, as well as relevant documents and artifacts. These are typically used in different combinations and at different times during field study. For example, let us imagine that we are interested in an ethnomethodological approach to the study of families. Specifically, we are interested in how each family member defines and maintains their role in the family and how, if any, media used in and outside the home are used in such role maintenance. Remember also that the emphasis on such research for the ethnomethodologist is on talk, both on naturally occurring talk and on family member's talk about how they do what they do as family members. Okay, how would you start? Would you begin by hanging out with family members when they all sit down to watch some television together on a Saturday night? Thinking about your own family or situation, you probably realize that this would produce a potentially uncomfortable situation for all involved. Chances are you have multiple television receivers throughout your own household and finding the family gathered to do anything together would seem a rare occurrence. In keeping with the flexibility afforded by qualitative research methods, you might start by getting your feet wet and simply try to schedule one or more informal interviews with each family member. The purpose of these interviews would be to get acquainted, try to establish a baseline level of trust and rapport, and set about gathering some basic and nonthreatening information from each family member. You might ask each family member to describe himself or herself or, perhaps more effective, have each family member describe how a best friend or acquaintance might describe them. You might gently pursue some preliminary baseline data about family schedules and individual media profiles including what media they use, what types of content they typically engage within those media, and when they might be using such media. This preliminary set of interviews helps to establish individual patterns of media use, plus any overlapping patterns with other family members. Ideally, interviews are recorded for later transcription, in order to capture any insights and growing trends in data. From these initial interviews, and as rapport is established, schedules can be established for opportunities to observe family gatherings, including events where media are involved. This may also be a good time during initial data collection to observe potential documents and artifacts.

As time passes, fieldwork moves more and more away from pure description and data collection to early stages of data analysis. If we recall the basic questions directing our research, we are most interested in returning to the larger question of how it is that family members define their roles as individuals and as family members as a function of media use—either in terms of actual patterns of media use independent of media content, or as a function of engaging media content to serve unique and personal communication goals. Typically, at some point in time you would return to one-on-one interviews in order to talk about your initial ideas and to ask family members to confirm, extend, or disconfirm your growing hunches (see Box 3.1).

Methods of Qualitative Data Analysis

Analysis of qualitative data typically occurs using some method of critically examining bits and pieces of field data in order to generate more complex patterns and themes. This process is called a lot of different things in the literature, and some of these sources are provided in the readings suggested at the end of this chapter. Regardless of what the process is called, the mental act of qualitative data analysis typically involves some effort to examine and reexamine data in order to discover initial patterns and themes. Typically, the perspectives informing qualitative data analysis are described in journal articles and reports, just as they are by social scientists. The outcome of such analyses typically includes the isolation of key themes or labels seen to explain a range of social or behavioral phenomena observed. For example, some qualitative studies have examined select audience perceptions of certain types of television portrayals. Results from such studies typically explain these audience perceptions within a framework of key themes or explanatory labels expressed independently, but shared by those people you are studying. For example, some of my own qualitative research has examined the methods by which individuals use television remote control devices when watching television. Data were collected using a combination of methods. First, open-ended interviews were conducted to determine when the person being studied typically watched television. Additional information was gathered in order to determine the type of electronic inputs and outputs on the person's television receiver and the range of operations afforded by their remote control device. Then each individual being studied used a videocassette recorder to tape the output of one of her or his television sessions, thus recording every result of remote control activity. This videotape provided the substance of consequent open-ended interviews, where both the person being studied and the researcher co-viewed the videotape, pausing and stopping frequently, to explore the interplay between programming content and remote control strategies. The analysis revealed a limited set of remote control "repertoires" or strategies used by all people studied, regardless of gender or programming preferences.

Analysis of qualitative data is enhanced by abundant data generated by different methods. Qualitative researchers sometimes call this process **triangulation.** The more one knows about a particular form of behavior from different angles such as observation, interviewing, and document gathering, the better one feels

■ ■ ■ ■ ■

BOX 3.1

QUALITATIVE METHODS AND CONTENT ANALYSIS OF MEDIA

Did you know that qualitative research methods could also be used to study media content? For example, social science approaches have used different categories to sample and label music video content. Categories such as performance versus story and reality versus fantasy have been used to help label and organize music video content. However, these categories may or may not have meaning for those who watch music videos. Qualitative research methods could be used to develop potentially more meaningful categories of use to researchers. One way to do this would be to select a sample of popular videos based on ratings information provided by music video organizations. These videos could be viewed by small groups of the typical target audience for such television, specifically adolescents and young adults. As a qualitative researcher, your job would be to tell people in these groups that you want them to watch each music video after which you will ask a series of questions. Remember, the goal of most qualitative research is to gain perspective into the world of audience members, so you would want to be careful to structure your questions so as to generate as many original ideas from these research participants. So you would probably start off by asking people in the group to talk about their reactions to the video, and you would want to listen carefully in order to note any important statements worth pursuing in the way of follow-up questions. Good qualitative research involves a fair amount of watching, listening, and careful probing. You would often find yourself asking things like "Anything else?" "Are there

any other reactions to this video?" Of course, your list of general probing questions would be designed to seek people's understanding of the basic differences among most music videos. So you would definitely want to ask some questions like "How is this video similar to other music videos?" "How does this video differ from other videos?" "Are there other videos like this one?" "What do these videos all have in common?" Of course, these are only very general questions you could ask. Your research interests may be more focused on issues like gender portrayals in music videos and your questions would be designed to probe into those areas of inquiry as well. "What about the way women are portrayed in this video?" "What about the way most women are portrayed in most videos?" "What would you say these videos say about relationships between men and women?" In time, and after considerable interviewing with a number of groups of people, you would begin to see patterns emerge in the answers you were generating. Qualitative research is a process where initial investigations give way to increasing levels of analysis, even while field research often continues. You might find, in the case of this research on music videos, that your preliminary questions generated important information, only to find that people's answers also led you to realize that other questions needed to be answered. So you might go back to these same groups, or you might interview new groups in order to further understand how audiences interpret the content of music videos and make that information meaningful in their everyday lives.

about drawing larger conclusions from such behavior. Computers have also helped add analytic power to the examination of qualitative data. Since the mid-1970s and the advent of increasingly affordable desktop computing, an increasing array of computer-assisted data analysis techniques have become available to qualitative researchers. These tools allow for the management of larger quantities of data and increasingly powerful methods of examining patterns and trends.

Reading and Critiquing Qualitative Research

As you have seen, qualitative research methods are particularly well suited for documenting what people think about media in everyday life. What are some of the criteria you can use when reading media effects studies using qualitative methods? First, good reporting of qualitative research is just as accessible in its use of language as social science research. Does the researcher introduce the reader to underlying philosophical assumptions driving the current inquiry? Are references to key philosophical works cited and referenced? Are there any studies related to the current effort included in a review of literature? Are field research methods reported? Is the process of data analysis documented? Are software applications identified if used in the process of assisting with data analysis? Does the report include examples of dialogue, interview text, or related data samples to help illustrate key analytic points? This last item is very often the hallmark of such research. Is analysis reflective of the particular philosophical underpinnings that anchor the study? Does the report include a section assessing both strengths and shortcomings of the current study, and are suggestions provided for ways to bolster future efforts? Did you learn something of value as a result of reading the report or article?

SUMMARY

Having read this chapter on qualitative media effects research, you should be familiar with the following ideas:

- Qualitative researchers use deductive approaches in social inquiry.
- Qualitative researchers believe that what people say and do is a reflection of how they perceive the world. As a result, qualitative researchers use research methods designed to capture those perceptions.
- Qualitative researchers, like social scientists, use theories to direct the scope and nature of their work. These theories include phenomenological sociology, symbolic interactionism, and ethnomethodology.
- The three basic methods in qualitative research are observation, interviewing, and analysis of documents and cultural artifacts.

ACTIVITIES

1. Generate a list of 10 questions having to do with mass media and audience attitudes or behaviors. For example, you might ask questions like "What is the relationship between the number of hours a child spends watching television and his or her academic achievement?" or "Do young women incorporate magazine depictions of ideal body types into their everyday comparisons of self and others?" Once you have generated the 10 questions, go back and try to determine which

questions would best be answered utilizing social scientific or qualitative research methods.

2. Visit a public place where people actively use mass media. For example, you might visit a computer-game arcade, a sporting event with large-video-screen playback capacities, or a movie theater. Conduct a pre-fieldwork assessment of the setting. Be prepared to report on such things as the types of preliminary research questions you might ask when doing research in setting, the type or types of qualitative research methods you might employ (e.g., participation observation, use of informants, etc.), and the types of data collection methods you might use (e.g., interviewing, note taking, use of documents and cultural artifacts, and so on).

3. Secure permission to visit a day school or preschool in your vicinity. Observe children playing during recess. Can you discern if their play incorporates mass media experiences? If so, what kinds of experiences are incorporated? How? If not, what characterizes the content of the children's play? In either case, what does this tell you about media effects?

QUESTIONS

1. Qualitative researchers believe that what people say and do is a reflection of how they perceive the world. Does this belief differ from the fundamental assumptions of social science research discussed in the previous chapter? What are the differences? What are the similarities? Be sure to use examples of media effects in your response.

2. Some critics of qualitative social research methods argue that entering into the natural world of people disrupts everyday life in such ways to render any findings suspect. Proponents of qualitative research techniques argue that all research is intrusive and that the longitudinal nature of their particular craft overcomes any potential disruptions and is sensitive to assessing any influence the researcher might have on the field setting. What are your views on this issue?

3. Many examples of qualitative research depend on some combination of observations and interviews. Provide three reasons for why you think this is so.

ADDITIONAL READINGS

Berg, B. (2004). *Qualitative research methods for the social sciences* (5th ed.). Boston: Pearson/Allyn and Bacon.

Berger, A. (1998). *Media research techniques* (2nd ed.). Thousand Oaks, CA: Sage.

Denzin, N., & Lincoln, Y. (Eds.). (1994). *Handbook of qualitative research.* Thousand Oaks, CA: Sage.

Grodin, D., & Lindlof, T. (Eds.). (1996). *Constructing the self in a mediated world.* Thousand Oaks, CA: Sage.

Lindlof, T. (Ed). (1987). *Natural audiences: Qualitative research of media uses and effects.* Norwood, NJ: Ablex.

Lindlof, T., & Taylor, B. (2002). *Qualitative communication research methods* (2nd ed.). Thousand Oaks, CA: Sage.

Philo, G. (Ed.). (1999). *Message received.* Essex, England: Longman.

Schwartz, H., & Jacobs, J. (1979). *Qualitative sociology: A method to the madness.* New York: Free Press.

Spradley, J. (1979). *The ethnographic interview.* New York: Holt, Rinehart and Winston.

Taylor, S., & Bogdan, R. (1984). *Introduction to qualitative research methods* (2nd ed.). New York: John Wiley & Sons.

■ ■ ■ ■ ■

CHAPTER FOUR

MEDIA AND HEALTH

This chapter features two areas of media effects research under the broader topic of media and health. The first area has to do with mass media images and eating disorders. The second area deals with the mass media and the worldwide HIV/ AIDS crisis.

EATING DISORDERS

Sources estimate that approximately one out of every 100 U.S. female adolescents have anorexia, and 4 percent of college-aged females suffer from bulimia. Though predominantly a female disease, estimates suggest that 10 percent of all anorexics or bulimics are males (Anorexia Nervosa and Related Eating Disorders, 2003). Critics and researchers often point to the mass media as a significant factor in causing such diseases. They argue that mass media images continually emphasize *thinness* as a requirement for female attractiveness. Further, these critics and re- searchers often argue that people's repeated exposure to such images contributes to low self-esteem or worse, eating disorders. What do you think have been the predominant mass media images about body image? Do you think those images have changed over time? Do you agree or disagree with those critics who argue that there are connections between these images and perceptions of one's own body? Do mass media images of body type influence eating disorders?

The first part of this chapter reviews recent literature on mass media images and factors contributing to eating disorders, often referred to in the health commu- nities as **eating disorder symptomatology.** Findings from social science media effects research are included in this analysis and are organized according to method, including content analytic, experimental, and survey-research approaches. No qualitative studies were discovered in the search for research articles for this topic.

Often, survey-type studies report the percentage of a dependent variable accounted for by the presence of one or more measured independent variables. When this happens, you will note that I have included this percentage in the presentation of results. These kinds of findings are key in our ability to summarize the importance of some studies. A summary of key findings is provided to help you understand what we do and what we do not know about the relationship between media portrayals of body image and audience attitudes or behaviors. You are also encouraged to consult sections of Chapter 9 on sex and gender stereotyping and Chapter 10 on sex and sexuality for related discussions pertinent to this topic.

Content Analyses

Petrie and colleagues (1986) performed a content analysis of *GQ* and *Esquire* magazines in order to determine messages about male attractiveness. The researchers noted how previous research documented changes in media depictions of female beauty and thinness as a predictor of increases in female eating disorders. Petrie and colleagues wanted to see if there were similar changes in the male depictions of beauty in men's magazines. The sample consisted of every other issue of the two publications over a 32-year period, with alternate months selected for every other year. Results indicated a consistent message about male ideal body types over the 32-year period. A second phase of the study examined articles or advertising in the same publications. Articles or advertisements containing weight loss, beauty, fitness, or health themes were included for analysis (p. 588). The researchers concluded that findings "suggest that over the course of the last three decades, males have been exposed to an increasing number of articles and advertisements encouraging them to use products aimed at improving physical fitness and health" (p. 591), though their study did not show differences in over 32 years of magazine portrayals of male body types. Wilson and Blackhurst (1999) conducted a descriptive analysis of prominent themes in magazine advertising for foods targeting women. The researchers concluded that such advertisements encourage dieting and emphasize low-fat or nonfat foods as the only option for dieters.

Experiments

Prabu and Johnson (1998) measured audience perceptions of how media affect others in terms of eating disorders, an extension of the **third-person effect** theory. Their study dealt with a number of hypotheses examining various relationships between the assumption that respondents would perceive the potential effect of media on eating disorders to be greater on others than on themselves. The researchers found support for their primary hypothesis that perceived effect of the mass media is seen as greater for others than for self. Results indicated a "robust third-person effect . . . widening . . . with social distance" (pp. 51–52), meaning that there was a tendency to attribute more media influence to those persons less well known. King, Touyz, and Charles (2000) recognized that mass media were not the single cause of women's eating disorders. Their study set out to assess any relationships between media influences on eating disorders and individualized perceptions of body dissatisfaction. The researchers found, "The high body shape concern group performed as expected, showing inaccuracy via underestimation for the thin celebrities . . . and inaccuracy via overestimation for the heavy celebrities" (p. 345). They concluded that results supported the idea that women with concerns about their own body appear to overestimate thinness in female celebrities and therefore are more susceptible to media portrayals of thinness.

Surveys

Harrison and Cantor (1997) employed **social learning theory** to examine relationships between media exposure and eating disorders. They argued that the prominence in mass media of thin body images combined with incentives for social acceptance "help make the modeling of delayed-reward behaviors (such as dieting to lose weight) more feasible" (p. 44). The authors hypothesized that consumption of media portraying thinness and fitness themes would be positively associated with eating disorder symptoms, dissatisfaction with one's body, and efforts to achieve thinness. Both male and female undergraduate students were studied. For female respondents, results showed that media consumption was positively related to eating disorder symptoms in women for magazines but not for television. In this study, media consumption accounted for 6 percent of the presence of eating disorder symptoms. Television, not magazines, was seen to be a predictor of body dissatisfaction (4 percent). In contrast, magazine consumption predicted efforts to achieve thinness (3 percent). For male respondents, magazine consumption was related to endorsing thinness and personal dieting (5 percent). Also for males, overall television and magazine consumption was not a significant predictor of the importance of thinness. Cusumano and Thompson (1997) argued that "social pressure" could fuel the "individual's need to conform to body shape standards" (p. 701). The researchers used surveys to measure relationships between five constructs: magazine media exposure, awareness of society's emphasis on physical appearance, internalization of this emphasis on appearance, eating disorders, and self-esteem. No significant relationships were found between exposure to magazine portrayals of ideal body types and "measure of body satisfaction, eating disturbance, self-esteem, and one's own actual degree of obesity" (p. 714). Awareness of society's emphasis on physical appearance and internalizing this emphasis was a predictor of eating disorders and self-esteem. In this study, these variables accounted for between 8 and 18 percent of those factors contributing to eating disorders and self-esteem. Magazine exposure was not significant. Jane, Hunter, and Lozzi (1999) examined relationships between disorders and media exposure in Cuban American women. Survey respondents provided demographic information, and completed a media exposure scale, an eating attitudes test, and a series of questions designed to assess participation in Cuban-ethnic behaviors. Results indicated that respondents who reported "close identification with Cuban identity and activities" were less inclined toward eating disorders (p. 215). There was no statistical relationship between media exposure and eating inclination toward eating disorders. The authors concluded that higher degrees of identification and involvement with Cuban Hispanic cultures might serve as "mitigating factors in the predisposition and development of eating disorders" (p. 216). Paxton, Schutz, Wertheim and Muir (1999) explored whether female adolescents in the same social cliques shared similar concerns about their bodies, dieting, and binge eating. A number of scale-type survey instruments were combined to measure body image concerns, eating behaviors, friendship networks, feelings of acceptance by others, body height and weight, pressure from parents to be thin, and pressure from media to be thin (pp. 257–259). Results showed that body weight and height, anxiety, parental pressures, and media exposure were significant predictors of body image concern. In this study, these five variables contributed to 56 percent of the body image dependent variable (p. 260). Cusumano and Thompson (2000) measured student awareness of media promotions of thinness; student adoption of media portrayals of thinness for personal standards of attractiveness; importance of media as source of information about attractiveness; comparison of one's body to mediated ideals; and perceptions of media pressures to adopt media standards. The researchers found that factors such as media pressure accounted for 32 percent of female and 10 percent of male internalization of feelings about body image and thinness.

In the first of a series of studies, Harrison (1997) examined relationships between college-aged female interpersonal attraction to media personalities and eating symptomatology. Results indicated that interpersonal attractiveness to thin and provocative media personalities helped to predict eating disorder symptomatology compared to attraction to average and heavy media personalities where no links to eating disorders were found. These factors contributed from 7 to 12 percent in helping to predict eating disorders (pp. 491–493). Harrison concluded, "young women's patterns of disordered eating, including both attitudinal and behavioral tendencies, are related not only to the types of media they expose themselves to, but also to the way they perceive and respond to specific mass media characters" (p. 494).

In a second study, Harrison (2000a) attempted to measure links between media effects and eating disorders on the part of both female and male adolescents. The researcher found for females that "overall television viewing positively predicted bulimia, and interest in body-improvement television content positively predicted anorexia, drive for thinness, and body dissatisfaction. . . . There were no significant interactions between grade and television exposure" (p. 131). The factors contributed, respectively, 4, 2, 3, and 11 percent in predicting either bulimia or anorexia. The author also found that exposure to fat-character television portrayals was a predictor of bulimia for females. Results differed slightly for males, in that television viewing was not a predictor of eating disorders. However, "there was a significant positive relationship between exposure to fat-character television and body dissatisfaction for 6th grade, but not for older males" (p. 131).

In a third study, Harrison (2000b) turned her attention to grade-school children and assessed relationships between exposure to television characters, fat stereotyping, and eating disorders. She argued that that television exposure would be positively related to fat stereotyping, preference for lean body standards, and eating disorders. Second and more specific was her suggestion that attraction to thin-bodied television characters would also be positively related to fat stereotyping, preference for lean body standards, and eating disorders (pp. 620–621). Results for male children indicated a relationship between television viewing and fat-girl stereotyping. Television viewing contributed 4 percent to this stereotyping (pp. 627–628). In addition, "Television viewing failed to predict the perceived importance of good looks, but for males it positively predicted the importance of thinness. For females [interpersonal attractiveness] to average-weight female characters negatively predicted the perceived importance of both thinness and good looks" (p. 628), with these factors contributing from 3 to 8 percent in helping to predict the dependent variable (p. 630). Finally, television viewing was a significant predictor of eating disorders (4 percent) for both females and males. Harrison concluded that the results from this study lent support to the argument that there is a relationship between viewing television and eating disorders.

Summary

Some key questions were posed at the beginning of this section to help focus your attention on the findings reported in various studies. Keeping in mind those questions, we can summarize the results from research as follows:

- Physical images of women and men in mass media continue to emphasize beauty and thinness themes. If anything, there has been an increase in emphasis on editorial content and advertising promoting physical fitness, health, dieting, and special foods.
- There appears to be more content analysis of print than electronic media messages, perhaps in part due to the more durable nature of printed media.
- Experiments show evidence to support the claim that individuals believe that media images about beauty and thinness have a greater effect on others than on themselves. Consistent with this perspective, other experiments have shown that women who are dissatisfied with their own bodies tend to distort media images of others.
- Survey research in this area demonstrates increasing reliance on a standard array of eating disorder symptomatology scale-type measures. These measures are showing repeated statistical reliability when used in some combination with other measures designed to assess media exposure.
- Some survey research has demonstrated relationships between media variables and eating disorder symptoms such as dissatisfaction with one's body or efforts to achieve thinness. The statistical relationships demonstrated in these studies generally account for 10 to 20 percent, and over 50 percent in one study reported here, in helping to account for such eating disorder symptoms.
- Some research has also demonstrated relationships between media variables and actual eating disorders such as anorexia and bulimia. The statistical relationships demonstrated in these studies generally account for less than 10 percent of the total picture in helping to account for eating disorders.

Where do we go from here? One way to start would be to encourage more content analyses, particularly since so much work performed of late focuses on print media. More content analyses of television programming are needed, particularly for more popular and mainstream reality, drama, and comedy genres. What do we know from the range of experiments and surveys conducted? Taken together, these studies suggest that certain types of media exposure may help influence self-perceptions of thinness, fatness, and body satisfaction. We are less sure of how such media exposure may influence actual eating disorders such as anorexia or bulimia. Both types of study indicate that media variables play a minority role in helping to predict either symptoms leading to or actual eating disorders. There may be a number of reasons for this. For example, one problem may be in the way researchers currently measure theoretical constructs such as eating disorder symptomatology or media exposure. While such measures have demonstrated utility when used by researchers, they may still lack validity in terms of really measuring what they are designed to measure. So one of the problems may lie in the design and defining of key independent and dependent variables.

Another problem may lie in the fact that researchers have yet to tap into one or more of the important factors contributing to how we feel about our selves, our bodies, and why such feelings sometimes lead to dangerous behaviors such as eating disorders. Is the problem one of imprecise measurement, as so many of these previous researchers suggest, or are our fundamental notions about the role media play in the development of perceptions of body-based self esteem inadequate, underdeveloped, or misdirected?

Compared to many other areas of media, audiences, and effects, study in this area of the field remains relatively new. Few scholars have systematically set upon a course for programmatic and constantly refined approaches to the problem. Additional years should provide the opportunity to collectively analyze methods and findings so as to assist with future research. Some of the previous research reported here suggests that cultural, ethnic, geographic and racial factors may play a role in eating disorders in general. Current research findings really only begin to shed light on the potential for fruitful avenues of future research in this important area (see Box 4.1).

PREVENTIVE HEALTH CARE

Health Promotion, Disease Prevention, and the Media

You are no doubt acutely aware of the worldwide HIV/AIDS epidemic. The United Nations estimates that 42 million people are afflicted with the HIV/AIDS virus, of which over three million are children and young adults under the age of 15 years. Over three million people died of the virus in 2002. Here in the U.S., almost 900,000 adult or adolescent cases of HIV/AIDS had been diagnosed, with over 150,000 of these cases reported for females (UNAIDS, 2002). What has been the role of mass media in attempting to turn the tide on this terrible affliction? What have been some of the images about HIV/AIDS prevention in such media? Can mass media be used to promote HIV/AIDS prevention? Or are messages concerning disease prevention and health promotion mostly superficial, as some critics argue (Phillips & Jones,

■ ■ ■ ■ ■

BOX 4.1

EATING DISORDERS AND MEDIA: THE DEBATE CONTINUES

Using any popular Internet search engine, one can find hundreds of websites about eating disorders and the mass media. Some of these websites are sponsored by professional health-care communities that provide important information for those interested in learning more about eating disorders. Other websites are sponsored by individuals or interest groups with strong opinions about these terrible health problems. Even a quick survey of many of these sites show that most blame the mass media, and television in particular, as a major cause of eating disorders such as anorexia and bulimia. These claims are based on some of the same studies summarized in this chapter, research suggesting that the mass

media play, at best, contributing roles. Few websites honor the language and conclusions found in most of these studies. One exception is the United Kingdom's Eating Disorders Association. This group noted, "People generally have a predisposition to eating disorders and while television images can influence people's thinking they are not the root cause" (BBC News, 2002). Remember, as a student of media, audiences, and effects one of your goals is to become a more informed consumer of research methods and findings, so as to make informed and accurate conclusions about what we do and do not know about important topics such as the relationship between the mass media and eating disorders.

1991)? When have mass media been used to positive effect in altering attitudes toward health or disease prevention and detection? The second portion of this chapter provides some answers to those questions. Results from one content analysis, one experiment, and two surveys are reported. No qualitative studies were found for this particular topic.

Content Analyses

Myrick (1999) compared public service announcements produced by the Center for Disease Control (CDC) in 1991–1992 and 1995, part of a larger federal government AIDS prevention campaign. This researcher found that "initial PSAs represented women as deceptive and responsible for the transmission of HIV to men" whereas in "the most recent PSAs, the use of . . . more positive representations of women offer significantly enhanced messages of empowerment, but a consideration of context remains absent from the message" (p. 60).

Experiments

Vaughan, Rogers, Singhal, and Swalehe (2000) examined the effectiveness of a radio soap opera as an HIV/AIDS prevention strategy in Tanzania. The authors found that "an entertainment-education radio soap opera . . . stimulated adoption of HIV/AIDS prevention behaviors in the treatment area of Tanzania from 1993–1995, and then throughout our study area from 1995 to 1997" (p. 96). They summarized their findings by arguing that media employing entertainment-education strategies are viable methods for combatting the worldwide AIDS health crisis (p. 98).

Surveys

O'Keefe, Hartwig Boyd, and Brown (1998) documented channels of health care information most preferred by individuals. The researchers found that "interest in preventive health information is a significant predictor of learning and persons who see themselves in good health and who worry about illness learn more from magazines and newspapers" (p. 32). In addition, "younger adults and lesser educated report more learning from television, reversing the findings for print" (p. 32). These independent factors contributed from 12 to 23 percent to the dependent variables. Bradner, Ku, and Duberstein Lindberg (2000) used data from the National Survey of Adolescent Males to assess how men aged 21 to 26 acquire information about AIDS and other sexually transmitted diseases. Results showed television was the most prominent source for information about AIDS and STDs (pp. 34–35). Results also showed, "after controlling for a host of social, demographic and other traits . . . that black or Latino men are much more likely to get information about reproductive health, suggesting that minority youth have been targeted for prevention efforts" compared to white male counterparts (pp. 36–37). Television, overall, was the most common source of prevention information.

Summary

Based on these few studies, some preliminary conclusions can be drawn about the relationship between health-related messages and AIDS/HIV prevention:

- The mass media appear to be an effective means for promoting health and disease prevention behaviors.
- The higher the importance the information has for individuals, the greater the potential for media influence.
- Printed disease prevention information appears to be of greater use with older, literate populations, while younger individuals tend to prefer electronic media.
- Media and interpersonal channels of communication appear to work together to create an effect larger than their separate parts when used in communication campaigns designed to promote healthy behaviors or prevent the spread of diseases.
- When reported, print and television media appeared to contribute from 10 to 20 percent of a person's interest in learning about ways to prevent disease.

An intriguing aspect of research in this area is the opportunity to work with large samples of people. Funding is generally abundant, both domestically and internationally, for health-related research. Governments or world health organizations provide much of this funding. The United States, with its abundant and diverse media industries, makes difficult any effort to isolate the impact of one, or a handful of communication strategies designed to inform and persuade audiences about public health. In contrast, research in emergent Third World or Second World nations often affords the opportunity to test the effectiveness of one or more message strategies within a less media-rich environment.

Message salience, or the relevance a message has within the larger framework of an audience member's everyday life, may help explain some of the stronger statistical associations demonstrated in this particular area of theory and research. Clearly, concerns about one's health, or practices leading to the prevention of avoidable diseases, or proactive behaviors leading to the increased likelihood of a healthy life, resonate in strong ways with audiences, regardless of geographic or cultural origin. Issues surrounding our mortality have a way of gaining our attention, and the high salience audience members give to health-related messages may help to explain why this area of research has been productive in demonstrating somewhat stronger statistical relationships between media and certain factors compared to the previous section's research on eating disorders.

Some areas of media effects research are sufficiently mature to have a number of studies focus on the same or related questions over time. When an area of media research is relatively mature, there is the opportunity for researchers to conduct what are known as **meta-analyses.** Meta-analyses are summaries of other studies, often including statistical analyses of the results reported in those previous studies. These studies are extremely useful, and provide an opportunity for us to further summarize what we know, and point to what we do not know within a particular area of media effects research. Myhre and Flora (2000) reviewed the findings of 41 previous studies examining HIV/AIDS prevention campaigns. They found that a majority of these previous studies identified the target for such campaigns as the general public and examined the effectiveness of using one or more media channels as part of the campaign. Three-quarters of the 41 studies analyzed campaign message content, two-thirds examined campaign theme, and almost two-thirds provided some estimation of audience exposure to the prevention campaign. The authors also summarized the common effort to assess prevention campaign outcomes, including attitudinal and, in fewer instances, behavioral changes (pp. 36–39). Myhre and Flora's analysis provides a useful start for those readers interested in studying specific prevention campaigns for sexually transmitted diseases, and prevention campaigns in general.

REFERENCES

Anorexia Nervosa and Related Eating Disorders, Inc. (2003, November). *Statistics: How many people have eating disorders?* Retrieved November 12, 2003, from http://www.anred.com/stats.html.

BBC News. (2002, May 31). *Television link to eating disorders.* Retrieved December 4, 2002, from http://news.bbc.co.uk/1/hi/health/2018900.stm.

Bradner, C., Ku, L., & Duberstein Lindberg, L. (2000). Older, but not wiser: How men get information about AIDS and sexually transmitted diseases after high school. *Family Planning Perspectives, 32,* 33–38.

Cusumano, D., & Thompson, K. (1997). Body image and body shape ideals in magazines: Exposure, awareness and internalization. *Sex Roles, 37,* 701–721.

Cusumano, D., & Thompson, K. (2000). Media influence and body image in 8–11-year-old boys and girls: A preliminary report on the multidimensional media influence scale. *International Journal of Eating Disorders, 29,* 37–44.

Harrison, K. (1997). Does interpersonal attraction to think media personalities promote eating disorders? *Journal of Broadcasting and Electronic Media, 41,* 478–500.

Harrison, K. (2000a). The body electric: Thin-ideal media and eating disorders in adolescents. *Journal of Communication, 50*(3), 119–143.

Harrison, K. (2000b). Television viewing, fat stereotyping, body shape standards, and eating disorder symptomatology in grade school children. *Communication Research, 27*(5), 617–640.

Harrison, K., & Cantor, J. (1997). The relationship between media consumption and eating disorders. *Journal of Communication, 47*(1), 40–67.

Jane, D., Hunter, G., & Lozzi, B. (1999). Do Cuban American women suffer from eating disorders? Effects of media exposure and acculturation. *Hispanic Journal of Behavioral Sciences, 21,* 212–224.

King, N., Touyz, S., & Charles, M. (2000). The effect of body dissatisfaction on women's perceptions of female celebrities. *International Journal of Eating Disorders, 27,* 341–347.

Myhre, S., & Flora, J. (2000). HIV/AIDS communication campaigns and prospects. *Journal of Health Communication, 5*(Suppl.), 29–46.

Myrick, R. (1999). Making women visible through health communication: Representations of gender in AIDS PSAs. *Women's Studies in Communication, 22*(1), 45–65.

O'Keefe, G., Hartwig Boyd, H., & Brown, M. (1998). Who learns preventive health care information from where: Cross-channel and repertoire comparisons. *Health Communication, 10,* 25–36.

Paxton, S., Schutz, H., Wertheim, E., & Muir, S. (1999). Friendship clique and peer influences on body image concerns, dietary restraint, extreme weight-loss behaviors, and binge eating in adolescent girls. *Journal of Abnormal Psychology, 108,* 255–266.

Petrie, T., Austin, L., Crowley, B., Helmcamp, A., Johnson, C., Lester, R., et al. (1996). Sociocultural expectations of attractiveness for males. *Sex Roles, 35,* 581–602.

Phillips, G., & Jones, J. (1991). Medical compliance. *American Behavioral Scientist, 34,* 756–767.

Prabu, D., & Johnson, M. (1998). The role of self in third-person effects about body image. *Journal of Communication, 48*(4), 37–58.

UNAIDS. (2002, December). *Table of UNAIDS/WHO global and regional HIV/AIDS estimates end-2002.* Retrieved November 12, 2003, from http://www.unaids.org/en/resources/epidemiology.asp.

Vaughan, P., Rogers, E., Singhal, A., & Swalehe, R. (2000). Entertainment-education and HIV/AIDS prevention: A field experiment in Tanzania. *Journal of Health Communication, 5*(Suppl.), 81–100.

Wilson, N., & Blackhurst, A. (1999). Food advertising and eating disorders: Marketing body dissatisfaction, the drive for thinness, and dieting in women's magazines. *Journal of Humanistic Counseling, Education and Development, 38,* 111–122.

ACTIVITIES

1. Visit a local bookstore's magazine rack. Note how the covers of various magazines are typically organized so as to target particular readers. Choose one of those groupings for further analysis. Note the type of activity emphasized by the magazine grouping (e.g., men's health, female teen fashions, heavy-metal music, and the like). Describe the physical characteristics of persons displayed on the cover in terms of some of the constructs used by previous researchers discussed in this chapter. What, based on your field research, is the cumulative message this

grouping of magazines projects to the target readership? Compare your findings to those similar studies conducted by peers.

2. Consult website or newspaper reports to determine the top ten prime-time television programs according to the Nielsen Television Index. List the principal characters or participants in those programs as well as some basic demographics for each (e.g., approximate age, gender, role, marital status). Then rate the body type for each character or participant according to whether you feel it portrays a thin, average, or overweight body type. Compare your findings across all television programs analyzed. What can you conclude about television's portrayal of body type based on this analysis? What can you conclude about any character trends associated with character body type?

3. You have a track record in devising communications campaigns designed to effect attitudinal and behavioral changes in the area of public health. The federal government has just announced that it will entertain bids for a huge federal grant designed to increase awareness and prevention of communicable diseases on college campuses. Create a one-page proposal, highlighting the message(s) you would employ, the channels of communication you would use, and the ways you would measure the success of your campaign proposal. Be sure to cite relevant studies to help support your claims.

QUESTIONS

1. Where do you stand on the issue of media influences on eating disorder behaviors? Do you believe that media portrayals cause eating disorders, are part of a myriad of causes contributing to eating disorders, or have little or no influence on eating disorders? Be sure to cite relevant research to support your view.

2. Previous research has shown that media can be effectively employed to effect positive health-care outcomes for such things as preventing communicable diseases. Research also shows that media can often be more effective than traditional channels of health-care communication, such as that between doctor and patient. Are there any health-care issues where doctor-patient communication might be more effective than using various mass media approaches?

3. Social science approaches tend to predominate research approaches in the area of media and health. Why do you think this is?

ADDITIONAL READINGS

Champeau, D., & Shaw, S. (2002). Power, empowerment, and critical consciousness in community collaboration: Lessons from an advisory panel for an HIV awareness media campaign for women. *Women & Health, 36*(3), 31–50.

Garner, D., Garfinkel, P., Schwartz, D., & Thompson, M. (1980). Cultural expectations of thinness in women. *Psychological Reports, 47*, 483–491.

Hollander, D. (1993). Publicity about Magic Johnson may have led some to reduce their risky behavior, request HIV testing. *Family Planning Perspectives, 25*, 192–193.

Hurley, J. (Ed). (2001). *Eating disorders: Opposing viewpoints.* San Diego: Greenhaven Press.

Tinsley, B. (2003). *How children learn to be healthy.* New York: Cambridge University Press.

CHAPTER FIVE

TOBACCO AND ALCOHOL ADVERTISING

This chapter deals with the relationship between advertising and two forms of consumer behavior: smoking and drinking beer, wine, or distilled spirits. The chapter is organized in three main sections. The first section introduces the topic of tobacco advertising and smoking. The second does the same for alcohol advertising. A third, very important section covers the topic of advertising bans for tobacco- and alcohol-related products.

TOBACCO ADVERTISING

In 1995 the U.S. Food and Drug Administration established guidelines in an effort to curb child and adolescent tobacco consumption. At the same time, the medical community, including the American Medical Association and the American Academy of Pediatrics, launched communication campaigns to warn children and adolescents about the dangers of tobacco-related products. Two years later, R. J. Reynolds withdrew its "Joe Camel" character from all advertising. The same year marked the beginning of landmark court settlements by states' attorney generals wherein major players in tobacco industry agreed to pay billions of dollars in order to offset Medicaid costs steming from tobacco-related diseases and to promote antismoking campaigns. In 1999, 46 states' attorney generals agreed to the "Master Settlement," a $406 billion agreement with the tobacco industry to fund Medicaid costs. Part of the settlement included the creation of the American Legacy Foundation to help coordinate communication efforts to control tobacco (Centers for Disease Control, 2003a). Meanwhile, approximately 4,000 U.S. adolescents under the age of 18 smoke their first cigarette each day. Over 46 million Americans smoke or use tobacco products, and over 80 percent of those who are adults started smoking before they were 18 years of age (Centers for Disease Control, 2003b). What have been some of the prominent strategies in tobacco advertising? What do you think are some of the prevailing influences in a child's or adolescent's decision to begin smoking or use other tobacco products? What about the billions of dollars being poured into various antitobacco communication campaigns and related strategies? What parts of these campaigns appear to be effective? This part of Chapter 5 reviews some of the research conducted in an effort to answer these and other questions. Results from content analyses, experiments, and survey research are reported. No qualitative studies were found for this particular topic in the chapter. A summary of this research is provided.

Content Analyses

Krupka and Vener (1992) provided a history of tobacco and alcohol marketing. This study does not include original data, but may be of interest to those of you interested in further reading on the topic. Stoddard, Johnson, Sussman, Dent, and Boley-Cruz (1998) examined billboard placement and visual content in four regions of Los Angeles over a four-year period. Billboards were content-analyzed for representations of gender, age, and ethnic representation. Results showed a greater number of billboards in African American and Hispanic neighborhoods compared to white neighborhoods during the four-year study (p. 139). Billboards in African American neighborhoods "contained a significantly . . . greater proportion of ads with youthful characters, whereas White neighborhoods had a greater . . . proportion of older characters" (p. 141). African American depictions were more common and Caucasian depictions less common in African American neighborhoods compared to all other regions. Male depictions were less common in African American neighborhoods and female depictions were less common in Hispanic neighborhoods compared to all other regions (p. 142). The authors concluded that billboard advertising is "significantly higher in all minority neighborhoods" compared to Caucasian regions (p. 143). Basil, Basil, and Schooler (2000) examined what they claimed were magazine advertising industry efforts to curb smoking cessation during fourth and first quarters of the calendar year, a period of time when many people are considering New Year's resolutions such as smoking cessation. Results indicated "there was a higher proportion of cigarette ads appearing on the back cover of popular magazines in January and February than in the rest of the year" (p. 169). The authors argued that results pointed to the potential for the tobacco industry to offset New Year's resolutions with an increase in cigarette advertising in order to reinforce current smoking habits.

Experiments

There has been considerable use of experimental methods in order to test peer and parental influences on an adolescent's decisions to begin smoking. Some of this research has found that peers and parents are influential. Results from other research have been less conclusive. Males (1995) examined parental influences with 320 junior high school students who first completed a survey designed to assess parental smoking status, student's smoking status, student's interest in future smoking, and demographics. Students then saw a live, antismoking presentation on the part of a public speaker whose cancerous larynx had been removed and consequently completed the same survey to measure any effects from the presentation. Results showed that "children of smoking parents were twice as likely to have tried cigarettes, three times more likely to have smoked within the past week, and 2.5 times more likely to indicate future intent to smoke" (p. 228). The researcher concluded that tobacco advertising counted for little, if any, of an adolescent's decision to begin smoking in light of such strong parental influences (p. 230). Beltramini and Bridge (2001) examined the effectiveness of one school's antismoking campaign targeting youths in grades five through seven in two separate samples. In phase one of their study, 259 students were administered the survey instrument prior to antismoking training (p. 269). Seven weeks later, the same students were administered the same version of the survey to measure any differences in responses to questions. A control group of students were also administered the survey twice, without experiencing the antismoking information. Results showed that students participating in the antismoking campaign demonstrated "a significant positive increase in their understanding of the role of tobacco advertising" and a 24 percent decrease in student expressed desires to initiate smoking (p. 271). The authors argued that antismoking campaigns have a positive, if not short-term, impact on youths and smoking initiation. Henriksen, Flora, Fieghery, and Fortmann (2002) examined the effect of retail tobacco advertising on adolescent perceptions of cigarette accessibility, peer acceptance of smoking, and tobacco-control policies. A total of 385 students were randomly assigned to one of four experimental conditions and read fictitious news stories and viewed corresponding pictures of point-of-purchase retail counters and convenience store windows (pp. 1776–1777). The type of display advertising and story context was manipulated in the experimental design. Results showed that "student exposed to retail tobacco advertising perceived significantly easier access to cigarettes from stores" (p. 1780). In addition, students exposed to a picture showing a storefront "saturated with tobacco advertising believed that more students smoked" and "perceived significantly more approval for smoking" (p. 1781). Finally, respondents who were exposed to cigarette-rich advertising also expressed less interest in tobacco controls (p. 1781). Box 5.1 gives an example of research examining smoking initiation and eating disorder behavior discussed in the previous chapter.

Surveys

Tellervo, Uutela, Korhonen, and Puska (1998) examined the impact of media and interpersonal factors on smoking cessation in one region of Finland. The project was part of a larger, multidecade effort on the part of the Finnish government to reduce incidents of cardiovascular disease. Results were reported for the years 1989 to 1996 and were based on responses generated from 1,694 surveys of adults aged 25 to 64 years of age (p. 107). Results indicated that exposure to mass media messages about health were "significantly related to smoking cessation for men only" (p. 114).

■ ■ ■ ■ ■

BOX 5.1

STUDY FINDS LINK BETWEEN WEIGHT CONCERNS AND SMOKING INITIATION

There may be a link between eating disorders and smoking initiation. A recent study by Tomeo, Field, Berkey, Colditz, and Frazier (1999) published in *Pediatrics* found small relationships between children's concerns about weight and smoking initiation. Over 16,000 9- to 14-year-old children were surveyed. Nine percent of those participating in the survey had already tried smoking plus an additional 6 percent were considering cigarette smoking. A number of factors were found to be related to these behaviors, including concerns about being overweight, exercising to control weight, purging, and dieting. The findings from this study are interesting because they provide a potential link for future research on media, eating disorders, and tobacco-related behaviors. Ironically, some of the earlier tobacco advertising during the 1920s and 1930s targeting women emphasized the weight-controlling properties of smoking cigarettes.

Interpersonal communication about health increased the likelihood of smoking cessation on the part of both men and women (p. 114). Pierce, Choi, Gilpin, Farkas, and Berry (1998) interviewed 1,752 adolescents who indicated that they had never smoked in 1993 and again three years later in an effort to determine if tobacco promotion was a factor in smoking initiation. They measured adolescent receptivity to tobacco promotions, demographics, and exposure to people who smoke (p. 512). Results indicated that "the percentage of [tobacco] experimentation attributable to tobacco advertising and promotional activities is 34.3%" (p. 514). Unger, Cruz, Schuster, Flora, and Johnson (2001) assessed the impact of pro- and antismoking marketing efforts on 5,870 eighth graders in 1996 and 1997 as part of a large, state-sponsored study of schools in 18 different California counties (p. 15). Surveys were designed to assess student perceptions of and exposure to pro- and antitobacco advertising pervasiveness, current smoking status, and demographics. Results indicated that "established smokers perceived that both protobacco and antitobacco marketing were more pervasive" and "protobacco billboards, which were perceived to be most pervasive by never smokers" (p. 18). In addition, "perceived pervasiveness of protobacco marketing was higher" than antitobacco efforts (p. 18). The independent variables were seen to contribute no more than 5 percent to student perceptions. Gidwani, Sobol, Gortmaker, DeJong, and Perrin (2002) analyzed U.S. nationwide survey data originally collected in 1979 and thereafter in order to assess whether increased adolescent viewing of television was a causal factor in smoking initiation. A total of 592 individuals surveyed annually from 1979 through 1992 were sampled (p. 506). Variables included for analysis were smoking initiation status, hours spent viewing television, ethnicity and family composition, and respondent's and mother's intelligence measures. Results indicated that "youth[s] who watched

>5 of television per day were 5.99 times more likely to initiate smoking behaviors . . . than those . . . who watched 0–2 hours per day" (p. 506).

Summary

Here are some of the things that we can summarize from this body of research:

- The tobacco industry uses a number of advertising strategies in their attempts to persuade niche-market segments to try a new product or service or switch loyalties across existing brands.
- Results from experiments remain inconclusive. Some research finds support for the positive effect of counter-attitudinal messages regarding smoking. Other studies appear to find support for point-of-display advertising to help diffuse existing antismoking sentiments on the part of adolescents. Those crafting these experiments often note the inherent methodological weaknesses of such research. Short-term effects, artificial testing conditions, and small sample sizes are among their concerns.
- Some survey research includes nationally supported and funded projects to study the effects of tobacco advertising on large segments of the population, particularly in California and Scandinavian countries. Results from these studies are mixed. Some of this research points to the influence of interpersonal communication in decisions to initiate or cease smoking behaviors. Other research suggests that advertising messages and related persuasive appeals may influence adolescents, though tobacco advertising often accounts for very small percentages of overall decision making.

After years of funded study, both domestic and abroad, the small body of research reviewed propels one to the conclusion that results remain inconclusive regarding the relationship between advertising designed to promote tobacco use and actual consumer behaviors. Critical in any future research is continued effort to study smoking initiation when it is most likely to occur—during childhood and adolescent years. Research with children and adolescents, as other chapters will also demonstrate, is extremely difficult. Since most children don't smoke, and since most adolescents included in programs of research have either not smoked or have only experimented with smoking, questions put to people in these age groups tend to explore future intentions and actions. Put another way, most of this research involving younger populations relies on the young person's ability to respond to the question "Do you ever think you will begin smoking?" Perhaps you have been asked this question and answered with a sense of deep conviction. Or perhaps you were unsure of how to respond. Peer pressures, the artificiality of research settings conducted in schools, and other factors all have the potential to influence our responses to such health and lifestyle questions at any point in time. Clearly, this is an area of inquiry badly in need of more of those longitudinal studies so often called for by researchers. Part of such longitudinal research, it seems, should include qualitative life studies of families, including those who do and who do not have parents and older siblings who smoke.

ALCOHOL ADVERTISING

The second section of this chapter reviews similar questions relative to the promotion of alcohol. The National Institute on Alcohol Abuse and Alcoholism estimates that the average U.S. citizen aged 15 years or older consumes annually over two gallons of beer, wine, or spirits. These figures are holding steady and reflect something of a slight downturn over the past decade. Still, over 31 percent of all traffic fatalities in 2000 were attributable to driving under the influence of alcohol. Almost 30 percent of all U.S. male and 24 percent of female students reported in 2000 having tried alcohol and "more than a few sips" by their thirteenth birthday. More alarming, for the same year, over 13 percent of teenagers reported driving a car after having consumed alcohol and over 30 percent reported having been driven in a car by someone who had been drinking (National Institute on Alcohol Abuse, 2003). What do you think about alcohol advertising and audience effects? What about the special case involving children and adolescents? What are prominent seasonal trends in alcohol advertising? What kinds of reactions do audiences experience when exposed to alcohol advertising in experimental settings? When do children first learn and understand the goals of marketers who promote alcohol through advertising channels? These and related questions are addressed in the following content analytic, experimental, and survey approaches. Noteworthy is the inclusion of one qualitative study in this area. Again, a summary of key findings is provided to help promote your understanding of what can be generalized from this research. Readers are encouraged to consult Chapter 6 on children and advertising for related information.

Content Analyses

Scott, Denniston, and Magruder (1992) provided an exploratory critical reading in support of their claim that the industry "targets and promotes to inner-city African-American youth using themes of sex, hedonism, and violence" (p. 450). They analyzed television and radio advertising lyrics and cited violation of federal guidelines, use of controversial celebrities, and associations of product with "violence that is so prevalent on inner-city streets" (p. 461). They provided accounts of how community activist groups were able to halt such advertising practices through coordinated efforts. Snyder, Milici, Mitchell, and Proctor (2000) summarized U.S. alcohol industry advertising regulations and practices during the mid- to late 1990s. This portion of their article provides useful background to those interested in the legal and policy aspects of this debate. A second part of their article analyzed network television, network and local radio, national and local magazines, national and local newspapers, and outdoor advertising schedules for 1997 (pp. 899–900). Results showed that 70 percent of all alcohol advertising was spent for television,

■ ■ ■ ■ ■

BOX 5.2

AMERICAN MEDICAL ASSOCIATION AND LIQUOR ADVERTISING

The American Medical Association has increased efforts in recent years to influence television executives to curb the airing of alcohol-related advertising until after 10 o'clock in the evening. They are also asking for such advertising to be removed from any programming attracting a portion of underage viewers. Finally, they are asking these same television executives to cease airing advertisements containing cartoon characters, mascots, or other images perceived to appeal to younger audiences. The AMA notes how younger audiences are exposed to over 100,000 beer advertisements before they are 18 years old. The AMA argues that such practices legitimize youth alcohol consumption as a rite of passage, and ignore the realities of statistics about youth and drinking, including excessive drinking, automobile deaths, sexual assaults, and sexually transmitted diseases (American Medical Association, 2003). You might keep this issue in mind when reading further in this chapter about what mass communication researchers tell us in terms of the relationship between our exposure to alcohol advertising and audience attitudes and behaviors.

followed by magazines with 22 percent. In terms of product category, 71 percent of advertising was for beer, followed by 19 percent for distilled spirits. Television was the overwhelming choice for beer and wine distributors, with distilled spirits favoring magazines, consistent with regulatory or industry practices (p. 900). Finally, alcohol advertising expenditures were seasonally concentrated during second and end of fourth quarters (see Box 5.2).

Experiments

Does discussion about alcohol advertising increase adolescent formation of counter-attitudinal arguments? Slater, Rouner, Murphy, Beauvais, Van Leuven, et al. (1996) used experimental methodology to answer this and related questions and constructed 18 separate video segments containing beer and nonbeer commercials, comedy, and sports programming. They tested 82 students 12 to 18 years of age who were shown videos and asked to complete survey items after viewing each commercial. Results indicated that students who had completed alcohol education training or who had participated in alcohol education discussions used counterarguments for alcohol advertising on a significantly greater basis than those students who had not received such training. The researchers concluded that alcohol education in schools could generate effective counter arguments to alcohol advertising. In related research, Austin and Johnson (1998) tested 246 third graders who first completed a survey and then viewed videotape designed to introduce children to advertiser techniques. The videotape was followed by a discussion designed to reinforce the video's message followed immediately by the screening of television commercials for beer or soft drinks. Results showed that the media literacy training did increase children's understanding of advertising's intent. "Understanding of [advertising's] persuasive intent positively predicted perceived realism and less positive social norms for alcohol used" (p. 341), with understanding contributing 20 percent to perceived realism and 12 percent to social norms for alcohol. Results, the authors argued, "suggest that third graders already have established beliefs about alcohol and alcohol portrayals on television" and that such attitudes are amenable to change given media literacy efforts (p. 345).

Does advertising emphasizing lifestyle images over product attributes influence adolescent decisions to consume alcohol products? This question was asked by Kelly and Edwards (1998) in their study of 1,058 seventh, ninth, and eleventh graders in three separate U.S. communities (p. 50). Students completed an alcohol-use survey and then viewed three pairs of advertisements, answering additional questions for each pair. Results showed that "Image advertisements were, on average, preferred by participants over product advertisements for all pairs presented" (p. 53). Male and female respondents who indicated intentions to drink in the future preferred image advertising in all grade levels, except for female eleventh graders (p. 54). Overall, the authors argued that the findings lent support to the claim that adolescents prefer alcohol advertising emphasizing lifestyle images. Cassisi, Delehant, Tsoutsouris, and Levin (1998) measured heart rate, skin conductance, and exposure to alcohol and nonalcohol print advertising. Heart rate and skin conductance have been shown to be reliable measures of attention. Prior to viewing print advertisements, 46 university students filled out surveys to assess demographic and alcohol consumption habits. Visual stimuli were 19 print advertisements for various alcoholic beverages matched to an identical number of nonalcoholic beverage advertisements. Results showed that "Light social drinkers demonstrated significant reductions in heart rate to alcohol and nonalcohol slides" (p. 271). Moderate drinkers did not exhibit a similar pattern. In addition, "Moderate social drinkers demonstrated significant increases in skin conductance from baseline to the alcohol and nonalcohol slides" (p. 272).

Does gender inform adolescent perceptions of alcohol advertising? Andsager, Austin, and Pinkleton (2002) argued that male and female adolescents would perceive alcohol advertising using different types of appeals in different ways (p. 250). They had 578 ninth and twelfth graders watch video clips of four alcohol advertisements and four alcohol warning public service announcements. Students then completed surveys designed to assess each message for humorous, persuasive, trustworthy, and memorable (p. 253). Results showed that females found messages appealing to group values more memorable than males did. Males found messages using appeals to the individual's values more memorable. The authors argued that findings demonstrated gender differences in perceiving advertisements.

Surveys

What do younger children know about television beer advertising and drinking and does that knowledge relate to any future intentions to consume alcohol? Grube and

Wallack asked these questions of 468 fifth and sixth graders in northern California. In addition, one parent of each student completed a survey. Measures in the study included estimates of television viewing, alcohol advertising awareness, knowledge of beer brand marketing and advertising copy strategies, general beliefs regarding alcohol, future intentions to drink, perceptions of parental views of and behaviors involving drinking, and demographics (p. 255). Results showed that awareness of alcohol advertising was "related to increased knowledge of beer brands" and "to more positive beliefs about drinking" and "was *indirectly* related to intentions to drink as an adult" (p. 257). These three factors helped explain, respectively, 14 percent, 22 percent, and 5 percent of advertising awareness. In addition, "Children who expected to drink more frequently as adults had more favorable beliefs about drinking" and believed that peers approved of drinking and that their parents drank more often (p. 257). These three factors helped explain 10 percent, 7 percent, and 7 percent of expectations to drink more frequently. Connolly, Casswell, Zhang and Silva (1994) conducted a six-year longitudinal study of 667 13-, 15-, and 18-year-old New Zealanders (p. 1257). Television advertising restrictions were significantly relaxed during the years the study was conducted. Independent variables included respondent's age, recall of mass media messages urging moderation, recall of mass media messages about alcohol, amount of television viewing, and demographics. The dependent variable was amount of alcohol consumed. For 15-year-old male respondents, results showed that "number of commercial advertisements recalled ... was significantly associated with the maximum amount of beer consumed at age 18 years" (p. 1259); with advertising recall contributing to 10 percent of beer consumption. For females, "the average of the times spent watching television at ages 13 and 15 years was positively related to the average occasion amount of beer consumed at age 18 years" (p. 1259), in this case with television exposure explaining 17 percent of beer consumption. Are television alcohol advertisements, favorite beer brands, actual beer consumption, and respondent admissions of aggression related to drinking interrelated? Casswell and Zhang (1998) studied this question using 630 New Zealanders who were surveyed at age 18 and then again at age 21 (p. 1209). Data were collected by means of surveys as well as interviews. Results showed that "young people who expressed certain positive attitudes to alcohol by their brand allegiance and their liking for alcohol advertising would be those who drank larger volumes of beer and experienced more alcohol-related aggression at a later age" (pp. 1214–1215). Positive attitudes toward alcohol and liking related advertising helped predict 57 percent of beer drinking and aggressive behaviors at age 21. The same authors and an additional colleague examined the relationship between television alcohol advertising and drinking behavior on the part of youths 10 to 17 years of age (Wyllie, Zhang, & Casswell, 1998). In-home surveys were administered to 500 respondents in three of New Zealand's largest cities. Results indicated that "The strongest relationship in the model was from peer behaviour to current frequency of drinking" (p. 368). In addition, "Liking of the beer advertisements, plus the peer and parental variables, explained 35% of the variance for the frequency of drinking" (p. 369).

Qualitative Research

Parker (1998) conducted in-depth interviews with nine college students to assess perceptions of five magazine alcohol advertisements. Each interview spanned more than three and less than six hours where students were asked to provide their own description of each advertisement, feelings about the advertising, and perceptions of support for marketer's communication goals (p. 101). Results showed that subjects "used the advertising medium as a projective device to transfer meanings to themselves" (p. 107) and that "themes, characters, and myths present in alcohol advertising are attractive and entertaining to students and often consistent with their life themes and self-concepts. Advertisers should be responsible, the author argued, when those attractive and highly personal components of alcohol advertisements resonate so effectively in the consumer experience.

Summary

Not surprisingly, patterns and outcomes from alcohol advertising research parallel those of tobacco advertising research. We can summarize some of those findings as follows:

- Alcohol advertising uses niche message strategies designed to appeal to diverse geographic, ethnic, gendered, and cultural tastes.
- Results from experimental methods demonstrate that counter-attitudinal messages regarding alcohol consumption can be learned and produced on cue. Many researchers using such techniques note that the effects from such training may be short term.
- Some research suggests that gender differences may play a role in how certain messages strategies are perceived.
- Image and lifestyle alcohol advertising may be a more powerful agent for conveying messages than so-called "medicine cabinet" or product-attribute strategies.
- Results based on survey research showing some relationship between alcohol advertising, demographics, and future intentions to consume alcohol are slightly higher than those for similar tobacco studies; however, the contributions media variables play in such decisions remains very small.

The case of New Zealand is interesting, and findings there suggest larger percentages of alcohol consumption accounted for by media and peer variables, with peer influences leading the way. Such results produce more questions than provide clear and conclusive results at the present time. What, if any, are the unique cultural traits endemic to New Zealand related to alcohol and, apparently in particular, beer consumption? Do New Zealand characteristics in terms of per-capita percentages of alcoholism, liver disease, and related social ills attributable to alcohol-abuse exceed those of other countries with similar advertising and marketing industries? Clearly, future research assessing these additional factors and providing comparative data across national borders must be accomplished in order to determine what role, if any, mass media play in terms of the health and social ills associated with alcohol abuse.

ADVERTISING BANS

Do advertising bans work? Do they work only sometimes under some conditions? Do they fail and, in fact, have the opposite effect than what was intended? The final section of this chapter reviews and summarizes recent research literature in this area. The study of advertising bans represents a large body of research, and includes reports of both domestic analysis of U.S. partial bans on some forms of tobacco and liquor advertising as well as a range of international analyses including study of some countries that have completely banned all forms of advertising and promotion. For example, a number of Scandinavian countries that have implemented complete bans are now fertile ground for research. Much of the research conducted in this area is by economists, who employ theoretical models of marketing and consumer demand as well as econometric data drawn from public and private sources in order to test hypotheses.

Many of these researchers find continued support for concluding that advertising increases consumption and, therefore, consequent full or partial bans of such communication decrease purchases and usage of tobaccos, wines, beers, or distilled spirits. Reviews of these arguments are plentiful (Saffer, 1998). Many other researchers continue to cite evidence for just the opposite, that bans do not decrease purchases or consumption and reviews of these are also available (Boddewyn, 1994; Laugesen & Meads, 1991). Still others have reviewed previous research and find both strengths and limitations in arguments favoring either position (Duffy, 1996). Finally, there are those who argue that a government's decision to ban advertising should be based on ethical positions, in part because of less than clear conclusions drawn from advertising theory and research (Hoek, 1999). Below is a cross-section of studies published in the past decade. They are generally economic studies, and therefore are not organized in the typical format (i.e., content analyses, experiments, surveys, qualitative) used in previous sections of this and in other chapters.

How do factors such as advertising and governmental bans affect tobacco consumption? Seldon and Boyd (1991) examined U.S. data from 1953 to 1984, including the 1971 ban on televised tobacco advertising and federally sanctioned product warning labels and antismoking commercials. Consumer, retail, and advertising data were compiled and findings suggested that "Initial health warnings seem to be heeded by consumers, but subsequent health warnings may not be too effective. Encouraging antismoking advertising and imposing partial advertising bans also seem to lower consumption" (p. 325). Stewart (1993) examined Organisation for Economic Co-operation and Development (OECD) data for 22 countries over a 27-year period between 1964 and 1990 (p. 157). Tobacco price, smoker consumption rate, disposable income, unemployment rate, as well as cultural and demographic variables were analyzed (pp. 160–163). Results showed that "When the data are analysed in as neutral and unbiased a way as possible, they do not show any negative effect of advertising bans on tobacco consumption. Indeed they suggest, but do not prove, that they may have had the opposite effect to that intended" (p. 168). Sixteen of the countries included for analysis require health warnings on tobacco advertising. Banning advertising would also eliminate these warnings, and may account for Stewart's finding. Duffy (1995) examined consumer demand in light of a complete ban on tobacco advertising in the United Kingdom. Econometric data supplied by government offices from 1963 to 1992 provided information on consumer expenditures for alcohol products and tobacco (p. 566). Findings suggested, "There is very little in our results to support the view that advertising restrictions, including complete bans, are likely to be an effective way of restraining the consumption of these products to any specific extent" (p. 575).

In comparison, Saffer and Chaloupka (2000) reexamine this argument and provided new evidence concerning differences in the effectiveness between complete and partial tobacco advertising bans. They reviewed findings from 21 previous studies, many finding no or only partial advertising influences, and concluded that much of this research suffered from problems in method. The researchers performed their own analysis of data from 22 countries including measures for per capita consumption of tobacco and type of advertising ban, pricing, income, unemployment status, time, and country (pp. 1123–1124, 1127). Results showed no relationship between bans and tobacco consumption in countries with only partial restrictions on tobacco advertising. Results also showed significant relationships between restrictions and tobacco consumption in countries with complete advertising bans. The authors argued, "This suggests that moving from a Limited Ban to a Comprehensive ban has a compounding effect, which is consistent with the theory that Limited Bans allow substitution to other media (p. 1130).

Young (1993) examined the effects of bans on broadcast advertising relative to alcohol consumption, motor vehicle deaths, and liver disease. Countries included in the analyses were very diverse in terms of advertising policies and in the amount of per-capita alcohol consumption. Results indicated, "Neither total consumption nor cirrhosis deaths appears to be related to advertising bans. A ban on all ads is associated with reduced motor vehicle fatalities" (p. 227).

How do U.S. advertising restrictions on distilled spirits influence product demand and pricing competition? Has there been a change in demand and pricing since the distilled spirits industry voted in 1997 to lift the voluntary ban on television advertising (p. 314)? Tremblay and Okuyama (2001) studied these questions in their examination of industry market data and U.S. Bureau of the Census data (p. 318). Results provided "some support for the policy concern that eliminating the ban on broadcast advertising will lead to an increase in alcohol consumption" (p. 319). The authors argued that even if no direct effect of advertising on consumption can be measured, other factors would. Increased advertising leads to increased competition. Increased competition leads to lowering of prices. Lower prices, the authors argued, would lead to increased consumption (p. 319). Saffer and Dave (2002) conducted a multicountry analysis of the relationship between alcohol consumption and advertising bans. OECD data for 20 countries spanning 1970–1995 were analyzed. The dependent variables were per-capita annual pure alcohol consumption and number of advertising bans for each country (p. 1329). Independent variables included price, income, economic value of alcohol production, and public attitudes toward bans (pp. 1330–1331). "The primary conclusion of this study is that alcohol advertising bans decrease alcohol consumption. The effect of bans may increase as the number of bans increases" (p. 1333). The authors also found evidence that increases in alcohol consumption can trigger total advertising bans (p. 1333).

Summary

Hundreds if not thousands of studies have assessed the impact of advertising bans. The small sample of studies reported here is generally representative of findings over time. What do we know from these and related studies?

- Bans on tobacco or alcohol advertising are generally ineffective as a deterrent to smoking or drinking.
- Partial or complete bans often result in a boomerang outcome or unintended effect, because elimination of advertising often also results in the removal of warnings designed to promote counter-attitudinal themes.

Other factors may play significantly greater roles in whether a person decides to initiate or continue smoking or drinking. One concept often studied in this research is **price elasticity** and demand. Price elasticity is the study of how demand for various products and services are influenced by pricing. For example, demand for cigarettes and related tobacco products has been shown to be relatively *inelastic*. As the price of cigarettes increases, often as a function of increases in so-called sin taxes, the demand for cigarettes decreases, particularly on the part of those most interested in experimenting with tobacco products, adolescents and younger adults.

To be sure, many other studies do argue for direct and causal linkages between advertising and such consumption, and often these studies are funded by such organizations as the World Health Organization (WHO) that funds considerable work in this area. The potential for such funding to influence research outcomes, indeed if only in indirect ways, cannot be ignored.

REFERENCES

American Medical Association (2003, February 24). *Break needed from alcohol ads.* Retrieved December 4, 2003, from http://www.ama-assn.org/amednews/2003/02/24/edsa0224.htm.

Andsager, J., Austin, E., & Pinkleton, B. (2002). Gender as a variable in interpretation of alcohol-related messages. *Communication Research, 29,* 246–269.

Austin, E., & Johnson, K. (1997). Immediate and delayed effects of media literacy training on third graders' decision making for alcohol. *Health Communication, 9,* 323–349.

Basil, M., Basil, D., & Schooler, C. (2000). Cigarette advertising to counter new year's resolutions. *Journal of Health Communication, 5*(2), 161–174.

Beltramini, R., & Bridge, P. (2001). Relationship between tobacco advertising and youth smoking: Assessing the effectiveness of a school-based, antismoking intervention program. *Journal of Consumer Affairs, 35*(2), 263–277.

Boddewyn, J. (1994). Cigarette advertising bans and smoking: The flawed policy connection. *International Journal of Advertising, 13,* 331–332.

Cassisi, J., Delehant, M., Tsoutsouris, J., & Levin, J. (1998). Psychophysiological reactivity to alcohol advertising in light and moderate social drinkers. *Addictive Behaviors, 23,* 267–274.

Casswell, S., & Zhang, J. (1998). Impact for liking for advertising and brand allegiance on drinking and alcohol—related aggression: A longitudinal study. *Addiction, 93,* 1209–1217.

Centers for Disease Control. (2003a, September 11). *Tobacco Information and Prevention Source (TIPS).* Retrieved November 11, 2003, from http://www.cdc.gov/tobacco/overview/chron96.htm.

Centers for Disease Control. (2003b, September 28). *Tobacco Information and Prevention Source (TIPS).* Retrieved November 11, 2003, from http://www.cdc.gov/tobacco/issue.htm.

Connolly, G., Casswell, S., Zhang, J, & Silva, P. (1994). Alcohol in the mass media and drinking by adolescents: A longitudinal study. *Addiction, 89,* 1255–1263.

Duffy, M. (1995). Advertising in demand systems for alcoholic drinks and tobacco: A comparative study. *Journal of Policy Modeling, 17,* 557–577.

Duffy, M. (1996). Econometric studies of advertising, advertising restrictions and cigarette demand: A survey. *International Journal of Advertising, 1996,* 1–23.

Gidwani, P., Sobol, A., Gortmaker, S., DeJong, W., & Perrin, J. (2002). Television viewing and initiation of smoking among youth. *Pediatrics, 110*(3), 505–508.

Grube, J., & Wallack, L. (1994). Television beer advertising and drinking knowledge, beliefs, and intentions among schoolchildren. *American Journal of Public Health, 84,* 254–259.

Henriksen, L., Flora, J., Fieghery, E., & Fortmann, S. (2002). Effects on youth of exposure to retail advertising. *Journal of Applied Social Psychology, 39,* 1771–1789.

Hoek, J. (1999). Effects of tobacco advertising restrictions: Weak responses to strong measures? *International Journal of Advertising, 18,* 23–39.

Kelly, K., & Edwards, R. (1998). Image advertisements for alcohol products: Is their appeal associated with adolescents' intention to consumer alcohol? *Adolescence, 33*(129), 47–59.

Korhonen, T., Uutela, A., Korhonen, H., & Puska, P. (1998). Impact of mass media and interpersonal health communication on smoking cessation attempts: A study in North Karelia, 1989–1996. *Journal of Health Communication, 3*(2), 105–119.

Krupka, L., & Vener, A. (1992). Gender differences in drug (prescription, nonprescription, alcohol and tobacco) advertising: Trends and implications. *The Journal of Drug Issues, 22,* 339–360.

Laugesen, M., & Meads, C. (1991). Tobacco advertising restrictions, price, income, and tobacco consumption in OECD countries 1960-1986. *British Journal of Addictions, 86,* 1343–1354.

Males, M. (1995). The influence of parental smoking on youth smoking: Is the recent downplaying justified? *Journal of School Health, 65,* 228–231.

National Institute on Alcohol Abuse and Alcoholism. (2003, September 17). *Databases.* Retrieved November 11, 2003, from http://www.niaaa.nih.gov/databases/qf.htm.

Parker, B. (1988). Exploring life themes and myths in alcohol advertisements through a meaning-based model of advertising experiences. *Journal of Advertising, 27,* 97–112.

Pierce, J., Choi, W., Gilpin, E., Farkas, A., & Berry, C. (1998). Tobacco industry promotion of cigarettes and adolescent smoking. *JAMA: Journal of the American Medical Association, 279*(7), 511–515.

Saffer, H. (1998). Economic issues in cigarette and alcohol advertising. *Journal of Drug Issues, 28,* 781–793.

Saffer, H., & Chaloupka, F. (2000). The effect of tobacco advertising bans on tobacco consumption. *Journal of Health Economics, 19,* 1117–1137.

Saffer, H., & Dave, D. (2002). Alcohol consumption and alcohol advertising bans. *Applied Economics, 34,* 1325–1334.

Seldon, B., & Boyd, R. (1991). The stability of cigarette demand. *Applied Economics, 23,* 319–326.

Scott, B., Denniston, R., & Magruder, K. (1992). Alcohol advertising in the African-American community. *Journal of Drug Issues, 22,* 455–469.

Slater, M., Rouner, D., Murphy, K., Beauvais, F., Van Leuven, J., et al. (1996). Adolescent counterarguing of TV beer advertisements: Evidence for effectiveness of alcohol education and critical viewing discussions. *Journal of Drug Education, 26,* 143–158.

Snyder, L., Milici, F., Mitchell, E., & Proctor, D. (2000). Media, product differences and seasonality in alcohol advertising in 1997. *Journal of Studies on Alcohol, 61,* 896–906.

Stewart, M. (1993). The effect on tobacco consumption of advertising bans in OECD countries. *International Journal of Advertising, 12,* 155–180.

Stoddard, J., Johnson, C., Sussman, S., Dent, C., & Boley-Cruz, T. (1998). Tailoring outdoor tobacco advertising to minorities in Los Angeles County. *Journal of Health Communication, 3*(2), 137–148.

Tellervo, K., Uutela, A., Korhonen, H., & Puska, P. (1998). Impact of mass media and interpersonal health communication on smoking cessation attempts: A study in North Karelia, 1989–1996. *Journal of Health Communication, 3*(2), 105–118.

Tomeo, C., Field, A., Berkey, C. Colditz, F., & Frazier, A. (1999). Weight concerns, weight control behaviors, and smoking initiation. *Pediatrics 104*(4), 918–924.

Tremblay, V., & Okuyama, K. (2001). Advertising restrictions, competition, and alcohol consumption. *Contemporary Economic Policy, 19,* 313–321.

Unger, J., Cruz, T., Schuster, D., Flora, J., & Johnson, C. (2001). Measuring exposure to pro- and anti-tobacco marketing among adolescents: Intercorrelations among measures and associations with smoking status. *Journal of Health Communication, 6*(2), 11–29.

Wyllie, A., Zhang, J, & Casswell, S. (1998). Responses to televised alcohol advertisements associated with drinking behaviour of 10–17-year-olds. *Addiction, 93,* 361–371.

Young, D. (1993). Alcohol advertising bans and alcohol abuse: Comment. *Journal of Health Economics, 12,* 213–228.

ACTIVITIES

1. Critics of cigarette advertising often claim that a primary goal of the tobacco industry is to get young people to take up smoking. Representatives of the tobacco industry claim otherwise. They argue that the tobacco industry does not target youths, but only attempts to target existing smokers in order to get them to switch brands. Visit your local magazine vendor and purchase one month's worth of magazines targeting younger audiences. Be sure to purchase enough magazine issues in order to feel comfortable that you have a good representation of those targeting younger women, younger men, music for younger generations, and so on. Remove all the print advertising for cigarettes or related tobacco products. Note any duplication of advertisements in the group of magazines. Then analyze various elements of the advertising. Note headlines, body copy, background and foreground objects, and any real or graphically rendered characters depicted. Summarize your findings. Do you agree or disagree that the tobacco industry targets younger audiences?

2. Advertisers employ sophisticated tools in order to deliver persuasive messages designed with specific appeals to appeal to audiences comprising gender, ethnic, racial, and cultural differences. Some of the research reviewed in this chapter suggests that antismoking and -alcohol messages can be effective in helping to influence attitudes, if not behaviors. Imagine that you were in charge of a large and well-funded antismoking or antidrinking campaign. What kinds of strategies would you employ to augment those on the part of the advertising industry? Frame your approach with attention to things like traditional and nontraditional media

channels used, seasonal considerations, media schedules, length of campaign, types of persuasive appeals, and so on.

3. Choose five countries for future study on the topic of advertising bans for tobacco or alcohol advertising. Use library and World Wide Web resources in order to tabulate the following types of information: the country's type of economic system; the country's type of media system(s) (commercial, government controlled, a mixture of both, etc.); the type of ban on advertising (i.e., full, partial, none) for tobacco and alcohol; and the results from any research conducted to assess trends in tobacco or alcohol consumption. Compare your results with others to develop a larger, more-global understanding of international efforts to regulate these types of advertising messages.

QUESTIONS

1. Various kinds of research examining relationships between tobacco advertising and smoking initiation on the part of youths suggest that, in general, advertising plays a small or nonexistent role in the decisions to take up smoking. Rather, things like influences on the part of peers and parents who smoke may be a much greater predictor of smoking initiation. What do you think? Why? Be sure to support your views with examples from the textbook and your own research.

2. Readers of this chapter may be surprised at the outcome of recent research on the study of advertising bans. As reported, what are the conclusions one can generate based on the findings from much of this research? Why is this outcome so counter-attitudinal to what most think is the case prior to engaging any of this research literature?

3. What, based on your understanding of how tobacco and alcohol advertising research is conducted, are the current strengths of such approaches? What are any limitations you see? What would you propose to shore up any limitations?

ADDITIONAL READINGS

Atkin, C. (1990). Effects of televised alcohol messages on teenage drinking patterns. *Journal of Adolescent Health Care, 11,* 10–24.

Green, L., Murphy, R., McKenna, J. (2002). New insights into how mass media works for and against tobacco. *Journal of Health Communication, 7*(3), 245–248.

Grube, J. (1993). Alcohol portrayals and alcohol advertising on television. *Alcohol Health & Research World, 17,* 61–66.

Morrison, A. (2002). Counteracting cigarette advertising. *JAMA: Journal of the American Medical Association, 287*(22), 3001–3003.

Northridge, M. (Ed.). (2002). Tobacco and the media. *American Journal of Public Health, 92*(6).

Pierce, J., Lee, L., & Gilpin, E. (1994). Smoking initiation by adolescent girls, 1944 through 1988. *JAMA: Journal of the American Medical Association, 271*(8), 608–611.

Resnick, M. (1990). Study group report on the impact of televised drinking and alcohol advertising on youth. *Journal of Adolescent Health Care, 11,* 25–30.

CHAPTER SIX

CHILDREN AND ADVERTISING

Children in the United States may be exposed to over 20,000 television advertisements annually and estimates project that those aged 4 to 12 will spend more than $51 billion on goods and services in 2006. Children also influenced more than $500 billion worth of family purchases in 2000. U.S. advertising expenditures exceeded $230 billion in 2000, averaging $2,190 per household (Center for a New American Dream). Clearly, advertisers understand the significant role played by younger consumers. This chapter examines the important topic of children and advertising.

Most of us understand that children are not smaller versions of adults. Children engage the world in qualitatively different ways than we do. Often, these differences are referred to as *stages* in development, and most psychologists and researchers who study children recognize at least four stages of cognitive development. The first stage is generally seen to range from infancy to age two. Here development is most characterized by increasing levels of physiological ability to perceive, attend, and react to external stimuli. For example, research has demonstrated that most children actually begin watching television by about 1 year of age. The second stage, between years 2 and 7, is where children increasingly engage their surrounding world in simple ways. Younger children in this age range see the entire world at face value, with limited understanding of the causes or implications of what they experience. For example, research in this area has shown that children in this stage are unable to distinguish between fact and fiction, fantasy and reality, or real and make believe. Consequently, research on television and children in this stage often shows that children are unable to distinguish between television and events in real life, or between television commercials and other types of television programming. You will note that a good deal of research reported in this chapter includes samples of children within this age range. Children aged 7 to 12 years develop an increasingly sophisticated set of cognitive tools for engaging the world around them. They are more and more capable of thinking in abstract ways, of displaying more complex logical solutions to problems, and of understanding causation and prediction. Children in this stage are capable of thinking about thought processes, often referred to as **metacognition.** Some of the more popular stage theories of cognition include yet a fourth stage, after the age of 12, where higher-order abstractions such as self-actualization, morals, and ethics are often refined.

Given this brief background, you may be asking yourself one or more questions about children and advertising. What kinds of images of children are contained in advertising in general? What kinds of images are included in advertising directly targeting children? At what age do children understand advertising? How does a child's direct experience with a product or service influence consequent perceptions of advertising? Do different kinds of advertising strategies influence children's recognition and recall of advertising? What is the relationship between children and parents and the advertising of goods and services? These and related questions are addressed in the summary of research provided in this chapter. These studies include a cross section of content analyses, experiments, surveys, and qualitative research.

CONTENT ANALYSES

To what extent did images of children in advertising change during much of the twentieth century? Alexander (1994) argued that such images influence real parent-child interactions. Six magazines published during the twentieth century were included for analysis. Results indicated that children were not at the forefront in print advertising prior to World War II, but came to be portrayed in more central roles during the postwar baby boom (p. 750). The researcher also found that "adults and children interact more intensely as the century progresses" (p. 754) in advertising depictions. Viser (1997) examined how images of children make advertising more appealing (p. 85). A total of 1,038 advertisements were analyzed from a random sample of general-interest magazines such as *Life* and the *Saturday Evening Post* over an 11-year period. Results showed significant changes in the types of appeals between pre- and post–World War II periods. Products appearing in these later advertisements were larger compared to prewar depictions and children appeared "more excited" in postwar images (pp. 95–96). The researcher argued that results demonstrated that pre- and postwar advertising reflected the times. Prewar imagery projected imagery in keeping with all-out efforts to win the war. Postwar images emphasized "domestic recovery and economic expansion" (p. 97).

Do portrayals of gender and ethnicity differ when comparing portrayals between English and U.S. children's television commercials? Furnham, Abramsky, and Gunter (1997) analyzed a total of 67 different Saturday and Sunday morning children's television advertisements aired on London's ITV network and the U.S. ABC network during two weekends in 1993. Results showed more male central figures and male voiceovers compared to females for advertising on both networks. Music was used in over 80 percent of advertisements for both countries and over two-thirds targeted boys and girls (p. 96). In conclusion, these researchers argued that the study revealed more similarities than differences when comparing children's television advertising between England and the United States. In a similar study, Browne (1998) compared gender stereotypes in television advertising between the United States and Australia. Cross-cultural research, Browne argued, fills an important gap in the study of stereotyping and perceptions of cultures (p. 83). A total of 298 advertisements were analyzed (p. 86). Overall, results showed more representations of males over females, male voiceovers versus female voiceovers, and males serving in primary character roles more often than girls (p. 87). In general, Australian television advertisements were more balanced in their portrayal of gender and less stereotypic in character roles. In conclusion, the author argued, "Certainly the numerical representations of boys and girls in the commercials are not consistent with real-world distributions" (p. 93).

How has television food advertising targeting children changed over time? Gamble and Cotugna (1999) cited how previous research has demonstrated a relationship between watching television and obesity. The researchers videotaped Saturday morning children's programming on three broadcast and one cable network (ABC, CBS, Fox, and Nickelodeon). A total of 16 hours of programming was recorded, containing 222 advertisements for food (p. 263). Of these, the majority was for breads, cereals, rice, or pastas, followed by slightly more than 25 percent for fast food restaurants (p. 263). The researchers then compared current findings to those reported by other scholars over a 25-year period. Comparisons across time showed "Saturday morning children's programming are of low nutritional value and that the types of products advertised have remained constant over 25 years" (p. 264).

What kinds of racial and ethnic relationships are portrayed in television advertising targeting children? Larson (2002) examined portrayals of Caucasian, African American, Hispanic, Native American, and Asian (AHANA) children recorded during Saturday morning and weekday afternoon programming on three broadcast and one cable network (ABC, CBS, Fox, and Nickelodeon) for seven months. The sample consisted of 595 television advertisements. Results showed over 40 percent of all commercials featuring only Caucasian children, though 57 percent featured Caucasian children and other-race children together (p. 228). Results also showed significant differences in depictions of how races were shown. Caucasian children were more often in "home/indoor" settings compared to commercials with Caucasian and other races where settings were more "other/indoor" (p. 229). In terms of interactions, Caucasian "children were more likely to feature children 'alone' " (quotes in original) and "Commercials that featured White and AHANA children together were more likely to contain 'competitive' activities" (quotes in original; p. 229). For product association, Caucasian and other-race children were more often depicted in restaurants compared to commercials for toys that more often depicted only Caucasian children (p. 230). The researcher concluded that overall representations of race in children's television commercials approaches those proportions of race in society, but she also warned that the virtual nonexistence of other-race-only commercials represents a significant underrepresentation.

EXPERIMENTS

A child's experience with advertising may be fueled by prior experiences with earlier, advertised products. Moore and Lutz (2000) employed both experimental and in-depth interviews to test the effect of "product usage experiences" on perceptions of advertising. Their approach was anchored in **cognitive developmental theory,** suggesting that children of different stages process information, including information about advertising's intent, in qualitatively different ways. Some of the key aspects of this approach were highlighted in this chapter's introduction. The researchers hypothesized that older children (aged 10–11 years) with product usage experience would have stronger brand beliefs about that product compared to older children without usage experience (p. 33). They also hypothesized that children without product usage experience, regardless of age, would be more affected by advertising (p. 34). Results showed that both older and younger children exhibited stronger product beliefs with prior usage, with younger children less so than their older counterparts. The researchers concluded that product trial and usage "yielded higher levels of confidence in brand attitudes than did advertising" (p. 40).

When do children understand advertising intent? Is there a point in the psychological development of a child when they comprehend that television advertisements are design to persuade and sell? Oates, Blades, and Gunter (2002) examined these questions based on previous research suggesting that children as young as 4 years of age were able to distinguish between television advertisements and other kinds of programming. However, the same research showed that not until ages 7 or 8 were children able to articulate advertising's persuasive intent (p. 241). Results showed 6-year-olds were unable to recall brand and "none of the six-year-olds, only a quarter of the eight-year olds and a third of the ten-year olds referred to the persuasive nature of advertising" (p. 243).

Gunter, Baluch, Duffy, and Furnham (2002) studied how memory of television advertising is affected by placement within other programming. Their work was anchored in the psychological theory of priming. **Priming theory,** which is widely used in media effects research, suggests that prior exposure to a certain type of message will influence consequent messages. The study focused on 56 students from a primary school in London. Results showed that "free recall of advertisements was better when they were placed in a cartoon programme than in a non-cartoon programme. . . . Cartoon advertisements were better recalled than non-cartoon advertisements" (p. 177). In conclusion, the authors argued that where television advertisements are placed within the larger program schedule does influence memory (see Box 6.1).

SURVEYS

A somewhat different take on the subject of children and advertising was provided by Laczniak, Muehling, and Carlson, who studied mothers' perceptions of toll-number advertising directed toward children (1995). Specifically, this study examined parental perceptions of efforts to have children use the telephone in order to incur charges on parent's monthly bill. A convenience sampling method was used to acquire 372 surveys from mothers of schoolchildren in three different U.S. locations. Results showed that mothers both familiar and unfamiliar with 900-number services expressed "extremely negative" attitudes toward such businesses.

■ ■ ■ ■ ■

BOX 6.1

INDUSTRY'S VOLUNTARY GUIDELINES FOR CHILDREN'S ADVERTISING

Advertisers have their own set of voluntary guidelines for advertising to children. The Children's Advertising Review Unit (CARU) is part of the Council of Better Business Bureaus and works in cooperation with the National Advertising Review Council (NARC), which represents the major advertising trade organizations. These guidelines, which can be found at the CARU website (www.caru.org), provide a list of specific recommendations when advertising products to children. These include avoiding the use of production techniques that could mislead children about what products can and cannot do; being sure to show products being used in safe ways and in safe places; accurate depictions of what children do and do not receive if they or their parents buy a particular product; food advertising that emphasizes "healthy" and "nutri-

tional practices" and as part of "balanced diets"; careful "age-appropriate" targeting of media advertising for such as films and videos; and avoidance of violence or sexual themes in children's advertising (Children's Advertising Review Unit, 2003).

What do you think about these voluntary guidelines? The findings reported in this chapter should help you form an opinion. For example, do you think these guidelines are realistic given what you have come to understand about the relationships between children of different ages and television? Do you think these guidelines are practiced by a majority of those whose job it is to advertise products and services to children? Can you think of specific examples of children's advertising where these guidelines have been practiced? Can you think of exceptions?

In conclusion, the authors reported, "mothers' attitudes toward 900-number advertising were overwhelmingly negative and largely unaffected by demographic factors, media habits of the family, and mothers' parental styles" (p. 114).

As we have seen in other chapters, researchers will often use meta-analysis in order to analyze a number of studies previously conducted. Martin (1997) conducted a meta-analysis of 23 previous studies on children's understanding of advertising intent. The article is valuable for readers interested in this subject because it provides information beyond the meta-analysis, including a review of U.S. television advertising regulatory policy over recent decades.

QUALITATIVE RESEARCH

One area of research in this field is the study of how children or adolescents influence family purchasing behaviors. Palan and Wilkes (1997) cited previous research demonstrating how young children make simple product requests, but adolescents use more sophisticated strategies in efforts to influence parents, often successfully. Palan and Wilkes sought to observe and document these strategies via qualitative methods. Sampling provided an estimated 70 cooperating families including 100 male and female adolescents. Researchers interviewed all family members utilizing ten basic questions. Results showed seven adolescent strategies: bargaining, persuasion, emotional, request, expert, legitimate, and directive. Results showed that the most effective adolescent strategies were those most aligned with parental strategies. "[I]n families where parents reported using reasoning strategies, the most effective adolescent influence strategy was reported as reasoning" (p. 166). For example, an adolescent would use economic arguments in cases where he or she knew cost or price would be the basis for an objection raised by parents. Ritson and Elliott (1999) examined the social uses of advertising among adolescents in northwest England. The researchers observed, documented, and analyzed the methods by which adolescents in school incorporated advertising into their daily social lives. Students in six schools were observed and interviewed over a six-month period. Results showed that advertising played a role in daily social interactions, that peers helped each other to recall and interpret advertising content, and that talking about advertising was a way for peers to reflect personal tastes to one another (p. 267). The researchers concluded that advertising could fuel a range of important daily social interactions and thus occupy an important function in culture. Moore and Lutz (2000) conducted a qualitative study of children's perceptions of product usage and advertising. They used in-depth interview techniques with 38 younger and older children. Results showed that younger children "chose to report on products of personal relevance for their daily lives and largely restricted their discussion of ads to those involving products either personally owned or sought for future acquisition" (p. 41). Younger children also assumed that "the product was as depicted . . . there was little reporting of trust or credibility concerns" (p. 42). The authors concluded that older children "approach advertising with a broadened and richer perspective" (p. 45).

SUMMARY

We can summarize recent literature examining children and advertising as follows.

- Content analyses taking longer looks back in time show that children portrayed in advertising have come to occupy a more central role in the family, in society, and as potential consumers.
- Other content analyses suggest the potential for mixed messages about equity between females and males, races, and socioeconomic classes. Some studies show that there has been progress in diversity. Others show that little has changed and that some groups of people are underrepresented or totally missing from television fare designed to persuade and sell.
- Experiments show that older children who have more experience with product categories and brands and tend to filter advertising content based on those prior experiences.

- Younger children may perceive the difference between television advertisements and other forms of programming, but they do not appear to understand advertising's intent to sell until the ages of 6 to 8 years. These findings were corroborated by one of the qualitative studies reported in this chapter.
- A meta-analysis of survey research suggests that developmental stage predicts roughly 14 percent of the child's capacity to understand advertising content.

Advertisers face considerable challenges when competing for their share of the target market. They must overcome clutter in the marketplace their message must garner the attention of the target audience, who then must engage the same message in favorable ways. Finally, the target audience must be compelled to act in such ways so as to adopt the product or service being advertised. Considerable marketing and advertising research has shown that targeted audiences often adopt a product or service because they feel a particular brand represents an extension of their own selves. Put another way, the purchasing of particular brands is often a reflection of how consumers feel about themselves. The qualitative research reported in this chapter provides a glimpse into such processes on the part of both children and adolescents. Clearly, results from these studies show that advertising messages, and by extension perhaps the acquisition of advertised products, can become a part of daily interaction rituals with important peer groups.

You will also note the different research strategies employed by researchers when conducting research with children. The range of possible methodological dilemmas when working with children can be daunting. Differences in developmental stages complicate the use of the research methods typically used to assess relationships between adult audiences and media content. For example, a study that relies on verbal-report data from younger children may produce less than reliable results. Research has shown that what younger children may think may not always be reflected in what they say because they have yet to develop more refined skills central to speech production or expanded vocabularies. Children may understand what the researcher is asking or they may not. Even when they do understand what the researcher is asking, they may not have the cognitive or physiological skills necessary for providing an answer.

Some research reported here attempted to overcome these various problems by providing alternative means for asking children questions and for soliciting their responses. Some used a technique similar to the ways things are often taught in elementary schools. **Manipulatives,** objects such as building blocks, dolls, or other toys, are used by the researcher to frame questions and by children to act out responses. Though time consuming, the best approaches to studying children assess attitudes and behaviors from as many different windows of inquiry as possible. Clearly, research on children and advertising, particularly television advertising, has achieved a certain level of understanding about the world of younger consumers, particularly older children and adolescents. A problem with most of this research, however, is the shortcomings inherent in working with younger children. Much work remains to be done to help us understand how children, particularly children aged 2 to 6, navigate the world of advertising.

REFERENCES

Alexander, V. (1994). The image of children in magazine advertisements from 1905 to 1990. *Communication Research, 21,* 742–765.

Browne, B. (1998). Gender stereotypes in advertising on children's television in the 1990s: A cross-national analysis. *Journal of Advertising, 27*(1), 83–96.

The Center for a New American Dream. (n.d.). *Just the facts about advertising and marketing to children.* Retrieved November 13, 2003, from http://www.newdream.org/campaign/kids/facts.html.

Children's Advertising Review Unit. (2003). *Self-regulatory guidelines for children's advertising.* Retrieved December 8, 2003, from http://www.caru.org/guidelines/index.asp.

Furnham, A., Abramsky, S., & Gunter, B. (1997). A cross-cultural content analysis of children's television advertisements. *Sex Roles, 37,* 91–99.

Gamble, M., & Cotugna, N. (1999). A quarter century of TV food advertising targeted at children. *American Journal of Health Behavior, 23,* 261–267.

Gunter, B., Baluch, B., Duffy, L., & Furnham, A. (2002). Children's memory for television advertising: Effects of programme-advertisement congruency. *Applied Cognitive Psychology, 16,* 171–190.

Laczniak, R., Muehling, D., & Carlson, L. (1995). Mothers' attitudes toward 900-number advertising directed at children. *Journal of Public Policy and Marketing, 14,* 108–116.

Larson, M. (2002). Race and interracial relationships in children's television commercials. *Howard Journal of Communications, 13,* 223–235.

Martin, M. (1997). Children's understanding of the intent of advertising: A meta-analysis. *Journal of Public Policy and Marketing, 16,* 205–216.

Moore, E., & Lutz, R. (2000). Children, advertising, and product experiences: A multimethod inquiry. *Journal of Consumer Research, 27,* 31–48.

Oates, C., Blades, M., & Gunter, B. (2002). Children and television advertising: When do they understand persuasive intent? *Journal of Consumer Behavior, 3,* 238–245.

Palan, K., & Wilkes, R. (1997). Adolescent-parent interaction in family decision making. *Journal of Consumer Research, 24,* 159–169.

Ritson, M., Elliott, R. (1999). The social uses of advertising: An ethnographic study of adolescent advertising audiences. *Journal of Consumer Research, 26,* 260–277.

Viser, V. (1997). Mode of address, emotion, and stylistics: Images of children in American magazine advertising, 1940–1950. *Communication Research, 24,* 83–101.

ACTIVITIES

1. Some of the research summarized in this chapter used verbal question and answer techniques with children. Other research reported in this chapter utilized toys and objects for children to manipulate, or visual scenes duplicated from television commercials, or other methods of generating responses from children. Imagine that you were interested in pursuing the question as to when it is that children understand the intent behind television advertising to persuade and sell. Discuss with other members of your group the range of possible methods that you could use to affect this goal, including specific questions or other methods of generating answers. Delegate one of these methods to each member of your group. Have each group member locate one 4-year-old and one 10-year-old child by gaining permission from parents or guardians and then administer the method to the two children. Rejoin as a gathered group once all data have been collected. Discuss your findings and reactions to various methods employed for doing research with

children. What do your collective findings say about things to keep in mind when doing any kind of research with children of various age levels?

2. Videotape at least three hours of television programming targeting children. This could include after-school programming on broadcast, cable, or satellite channels or Saturday morning programming. Note what kinds of product categories are advertised during these programs (e.g., cereals, toys, fast foods, candies). Choose one of these product categories for further analysis. Return to the first television advertisement for the product category. What is the primary appeal used by the advertiser to try to get children to purchase, or get their parents to purchase, the product? These appeals could be things like associating the product with a fun time, associating the product with being popular among peers, and so on. Upon isolating the primary appeal, note what visual or auditory elements are used to make the appeal more desirable. Now do this same analysis for every other commercial for the same product category. Compare and contrast your results when completed. What can you say about the dominant appeals used to target children for this product or service? Do these appeals differ across brands?

3. You have been asked by the chairperson of the Federal Trade Commission to draft new regulations for television advertising targeting children. Visit the Federal Trade Commission's website and other sites devoted to protecting children against manipulative advertising practices. You will note that past policies, some no longer in force, regulated such things as number of commercials per half hour of children's programming, types of production elements used to make advertisements visually appealing, language used in product disclaimers, and so on. Review the research reported in this chapter, as well as suggested readings or related sources. Write the new regulations. Share these with others for review and discussion.

QUESTIONS

1. Where do you stand on the issue of children and advertising? Do you think that television advertising targeting children is a good thing because it helps with consumer socialization, informs them about goods and services in the marketplace, or other reasons? Be sure to include examples shored up by relevant readings or research literature in your response. Or are you of the opinion that television advertising is a negative thing because it contributes to a materialistic society, creates unnecessary wants for goods and services, or for other reasons? Again, be sure to include examples drawn from relevant readings or research literature in your response.

2. Some countries completely ban advertising, including advertising targeting children. Other countries load television advertisements into their own programming block, thus never interrupting actual newscasts, dramas, comedies, or other types of programs. U.S. programming blends advertisements with other forms of programming. What, based on your understanding of the readings, do you thing represents the best policy? Why?

3. Much of the research literature reviewed in this chapter is anchored to our understanding of cognitive stages in child development. Younger children, the argument goes, are qualitatively different in the way they think and engage their

surrounding world compared to older children and still again compared to adults. Do you think that younger children should be protected from television advertising? If so, how would you protect them and who should do the protecting? If not, upon what evidence do you base your argument?

ADDITIONAL READINGS

Aidman, A. (1995). Children, television, and the market. *Journal of Communication, 45*(4), 170–173.

Almarsdottir, A., & Bush, P. (1992). The influence of drug advertising on children's drug use and attitudes and behaviors. *Journal of Drug Issues, 22,* 361–376.

Carole, M., & Carlson, L. (Eds.). (1999). *Advertising to Children: Concepts and Controversies.* Thousand Oaks, CA: Sage.

Haefner, M. (1991). Ethical problems of advertising to children. *Journal of Mass Media Ethics, 6*(2), 83–92.

John, D. (1999). Consumer socialization of children: A retrospective look at twenty-five years of research. *Journal of Consumer Research, 26*(3), 182–213.

Pecora, N. (1995). Children and television advertising from a social science perspective. *Critical Studies in Mass Communication, 12,* 354–364.

Ward, S., Wackman, D., & Wartella, E. (1977). *How Children Learn to Buy: The Development of Consumer Information-Processing Skills.* Beverly Hills, CA: Sage.

Wartella, E., Wackman, D., Ward, S., Shamir, J., & Alexander, A. (1979). The young child as consumer. In E. Wartella (Ed.), *Children Communicating: Media and Development of Thought, Speech, Understanding* (pp. 251–279). Beverly Hills, CA: Sage.

Zhang, S., & Sood, S. (2002). "Deep" and "surface" cues: Brand extension evaluations by children and adults. *Journal of Consumer Research, 29,* 129–141.

CHAPTER SEVEN

TELEVISION
AND EDUCATION

Many educators have long believed that television influences academic achievement. Critics bemoan television's negative influences. Time spent watching television, they argue, takes time away from studying or related intellectual pursuits. Others argue that television's continual stream of lowest-denominator programming creates lazy learners (LimiTV, Inc., 2000). Other organizations, such as the National Institute on Media and the Family, cite research showing how television in moderation can actually enhance learning (National Institute on Media and the Family, 2002).

What do you think about the relationship between television and academic achievement? Do you agree with critics that television is a negative influence on learning and academic performance? Or do you think that some media may actually enhance learning? Do you think all television is negative when it comes to academic performance, or would you say that some programming might be detrimental, while other may actually benefit learning and school performance? The first section of this chapter reviews recent literature addressing these and related questions. This area of study typically examines relationships between two constructs, television exposure and academic achievement. Hence, there are no content analyses to report. One experiment is summarized, followed by survey-type studies. One econometric study is also included. Results from this body of literature are then summarized.

TELEVISION AND ACADEMIC ACHIEVEMENT

Experiments

Many children use television or radio as background noise in order to facilitate studying. Some in education community argue that such background media distract from effective learning. Still other research has shown that many students do use media as background noise and argue that such sources block out other distractions and allow them to concentrate on learning tasks. Cool, Yarbrough, Patton, Runde, and Keith (1994) studied how background media influence mathematical and reading abilities. They used 21 sixth-grade students, who were randomly assigned to one of three treatment groups: television, radio, and "relative quiet" (p. 184). Results from the math experiment showed students in the relative quiet group finished more questions than the other two groups. Students listening to radio completed more questions than the television group (p. 188). Results from the reading experiment were less conclusive. The authors argued, "it does not seem that students always need to eliminate distractions from their studying environment. Whereas the present findings failed to demonstrate a facilitation effect, neither did they show that radio and TV are generally harmful" (p. 192).

Surveys

Gortmaker, Salter, Walker, and Dietz (1990) measured the influence of television on academic achievement. A total of 1,745 children were surveyed and included 6- to 11-year-olds and 12- to 17-year-olds. Measures included parent estimates of amount of time spent viewing television on the part of the younger children and self-reports from the older group. Results showed that "When television viewing is the only variable examined, there appears to be a modest but significant negative effect on mental abilities. But when other controls are added, the apparent effects become negligible and nonsignificant" (pp. 600–601). Henggeler, Cohen, Edwards, Summerville, and Ray (1991) explored the relationship between family stress levels, television viewing, and academic achievement. They used surveys to collect data from 25 third graders and their parents. The children also completed a standardized achievement test in school. Results showed "a relatively strong association between television viewing and academic competence that is independent of the child's verbal ability" (pp. 5–6). These factors helped predict 11.5 to almost 48 percent of academic performance. In addition, family stress was a significant predictor of higher levels of television viewing in the variance. The stress variable accounted for 24 percent of higher levels of television consumption (p. 6). Smith (1992) measured the relationship between lifestyle and demographic variables and academic achievement. A total of 1,208 seventh- and ninth-grade students were surveyed. Results indicated that "the interaction between parental occupation and time spent watching television had a significant effect only on growth in mathematics achievement" (p. 742).

Some research suggests that adolescents with antisocial tendencies are drawn to television programming and films containing violent, action, or adventure themes. This research will receive considerable attention in Chapter 11. Working from this premise, Aluja-Fabregat and Torrubia-Beltri (1998) hypothesized a relationship between viewing such content and low academic achievement. Self-administered surveys were administered to 470 eighth graders in Lleida, Spain. Measures included personality scales, perceptions and viewing patterns for violent filmic and television content, and academic achievement measuring the student's grades for the previous academic year. Teachers also completed a scale assessing each student's behavior. Results suggested that "more aggressive, sensation-seeking, impulsive adolescents watch a greater number of violent films . . . rate them as being less violent . . . [and] are judged by their teachers to be less socialized . . . and perform worse academically" (p. 986).

Does a student's race factor into the equation when examining relationships between television viewing and academic performance? Caldas and Bankston (1999) argued, "television affects people in situations of relative advantage and disadvantage in American society" (p. 41), and has consequences for academic performance. They used surveys to collect data from 42,041 tenth-grade students (pp. 46–47). Results showed 71 percent of African Americans scoring below the median level of proficiency compared to 33 percent of Caucasians. African American students watched on average 4.7 hours of television daily compared to 3.9 hours for Caucasians (pp. 49–50). For Caucasians, there was a negative relationship between watching television and academic achievement. As viewership increased, achievement fell, but this television measure only accounted for 1 percent in helping to predict achievement. For African Americans, there was a positive relationship between the same two same variables. As viewership increased, academic achievement fell, but again the relationship only accounted for 1 percent of the variance.

An oft-cited study in this area is one where Cooper, Valentine, Nye, and Lindsay (1999) interviewed 424 sixth through twelfth graders and one of their parents in order to assess the relationship between a number of after-school activities and academic achievement. The researchers hypothesized that time spent on homework would be the strongest predictor of academic achievement, and that television's role would be negative (pp. 370–371). Results showed that television viewing was negatively related to achievement test scores, but only contributed 2 percent to this decline (p. 374). Chief among their findings was that "after-school activities contributed to the prediction of achievement even after the student's gender, grade level, ethnicity" and other variables were controlled (p. 377). Homework was central among those after-school activities.

McCale, Crouter, and Tucker (2001) used telephone surveys to measure the relationship between television viewing and academic achievement. Data were collected from children in 198 families over a two-year period in order to measure the influence of child maturation. Results showed no significant relationship between watching television and grades. The researchers summarized their findings as suggesting "children spent more time watching television during the winter months than in the spring, lending credence to assertions that children watch television primarily when they have nothing better to do" (p. 1774). Anderson, Huston, Schmitt, Linebarger, and Wright (2001) added an extra step in their study of television viewing and academic achievement. Most research measures television exposure as a simple estimate of total time spent viewing. These researchers included analysis of the different kinds of television programming viewed by members of their sample of teenagers. Results showed that "Teen total viewing . . . was not significantly associated with high school grades for either sex" (p. 40). However, with boys, "teen violence viewing was negatively associated with grades in English, . . . science, and average grades" (p. 50). "For Massachusetts girls, . . . there were negative relations of teen violence viewing with grades" (p. 50).

At least one meta-analysis has been conducted in this area of inquiry. Razsel (2001) analyzed results from six different studies conducted between 1986 and 1998. This researcher argued that television viewing was positively related to academic achievement up to an "optimal viewing time." For 9-year-olds, this was two hours; for 13-year-olds, one and one-half hours; and for 17-year-olds, one-half hour (pp. 373–374). This same researcher suggested that future research examine the relationship between specific types of television programming and academic achievement.

Econometric Analysis

The search for current literature also produced one applied economic analysis using econometric measures more common to the study of such things as television advertising and cigarette demand. Koshal, Koshal, and Gupta (1996) examined the relationship between student math skills and television viewing (p. 920). Results indicated that "schools could supply a higher quality of mathematics skills if expenditure per pupil was increased, but the actual outcome would not materialize unless parents . . . were also willing to . . . [control] the amount of television viewing by their children" (924). These factors contributed 66 to 72 percent to academic achievement.

Summary

We can generate a number of conclusions based on this research:

- Many of the studies reported here utilized large samples of students, often statewide, and thus lend support to the strength of findings.
- Many of these same studies suffer from weak measures, particularly those assessing television exposure variables. You may recall from early chapters that simply asking individuals to estimate time spent viewing television may represent problems in reliability and validity.
- Preliminary findings suggest there may be some links between some kinds of television programming and academic achievement. Future research would do well to continue this logical and potentially rewarding area of inquiry.
- Academic achievement is dependent on a rich mixture of both positive and negative factors, including such things as parental involvement, family demographics, group and individual psychological variables, homework, peer-group influences, as well as the mass media (see Box 7.1).
- Television may have a minimal but negative impact on academic achievement.

TELEVISION AND INSTRUCTION

The second section of this chapter reviews recent discussion concerning television's potential as an educational tool in the classroom. Long touted as the magic solution to many of education's ills, television's role in classroom instruction has been

■ ■ ■ ■ ■

BOX 7.1

NATIONAL EDUCATION ASSOCIATION AND TELEVISION

The National Education Association (NEA), is the largest teacher's organization in the United States. NEA president Reg Weaver recently talked about factors he considered important in striking a balanced approach to teaching children to read. He emphasized the importance of reading to and making resources available to children and the importance of having parents "balance" reading and homework with television and computer games (National Education Association, 2003). President Weaver's recommendations would appear consistent with what you have discovered in this chapter—that academic successes begin at home where involved parents make learning a priority, ensure that homework is completed, and monitor both the content of and time spent with television and other media.

studied for over 50 years. Previous research in this area demonstrates that television will never replace the teacher in the classroom, but may be an effective instructional tool when integrated with more traditional forms of teaching. There has been a revival in examining television's role in education. The University of Southern California now offers videoconferencing to on-campus residents compatible with both Macintosh and Windows-operating computers. The development is part of a larger Internet service seen as important to future educational goals (Chronicle of Higher Education, 2003). Kozma (1991) provided an overview of theory and research examining the relationship between learners and media. This article is recommended for those of you interested in additional reading.

Microprocessors and digital communications have made interactive television technologies increasingly affordable and portable. The result, aligned with increasing demands for flexible and cheaper means of instructional delivery, has been increased use of nontraditional instruction on the part of colleges, universities, and other institutions in the public and private spheres. Have you thought about what might be the best ways to use television to teach? What are some of the aspects of television production that might enhance learning? How does our personal experience with television influence the ways we might approach the medium as a tool for instruction? Can popular entertainment television programming be used as an instructional tool? What are some of the misconceptions surrounding the use of television as a part of distance learning? These are the kinds of questions addressed in the studies reported in this section. There are few studies in this area of study containing original data. Those few are reported under the categories of experiments and surveys. Much of the work reported in this section is more anecdotal, based on nonscientific assessment of practical applications of instructional delivery systems. Other work summarizes trends in the use of television and instructions and includes recommendations for future use. The result is something of a potpourri of actual studies and critiques, not unreflective of this actual field of study, but one intended to provide readers with a taste of recent issues and approaches. A summary of this recent work is provided.

Experiments

How do visual elements projected on the television screen influence audience attention and memory? Thorson and Lang (1992) provided a theoretical framework drawing from a number of perspectives in order to ground their experimental approach. They measured how visual elements such as graphs, figures, and photographs affected viewer attention (p. 347). The audience for this testing consisted of 60 journalism majors. Results showed that students remembered more content from lectures using topic-related visual elements (p. 361).

Surveys

How effective is interactive television (ITV) when teaching basic accounting skills in academic programs in business? Pirrong and Lathen (1990) surveyed 50 students taking the same introductory course, but who were divided into an ITV lab with instructor present, or a remote ITV classroom. A third group of students were enrolled in a different section of the course. Results showed no significant differences in student performances scores across the three modes of instruction. However, "There were significant attitude differences about the ability to communicate with the instructor" (p. 53) on the part of students at the remote ITV site. This finding was balanced, however, by students at the remote site who found the remote version of the course a time saver in terms of commuting back and forth from campus (p. 53).

Other Research on Television and Instruction

Many chapters in this book discuss audience perceptions and actions as a function of watching television. Do those very perceptions influence our approaches to television when it is used as a tool for instruction? Cennamo (1993) asked that very question and probed three areas of the research literature in order to generate her own conclusions. The first conclusion was that audience members view television's imagery and symbol systems differently than they view reading materials traditionally associated with learning. While educational programming may occupy a portion of a younger child's life, we all tend to drift away from such programming fare as we mature and tend to process most televisual fare differently than we do so-called educational programming (p. 35). The second discussion focused on the cognitive effort required of television in comparison to other types of knowledge transfer. Previous research suggested that "the amount of mental effort invested in a video-based lesson may be influenced by characteristics of the media, characteristics of the task, and characteristics of the learners" (p. 37). The final area of discussion summarized research literature examining the relationship between cognitive effort and achievement. Some findings suggest a positive and linear relationship between the two constructs, while other research remains inconclusive (p. 41).

Some scholars in communication suggest using popular television programming in order to teach important communication skills and concepts. Winegarden, Fuss-Reineck, and Charron (1993) critically examined the use of *Star Trek: The Next Generation* as classroom material in order to teach persuasion, family communication, and ethics. Among the advantages are high production values, program appeal, and resource accessibility. Chief among the disadvantages were concerns about copyright violation (p. 180). The majority of the article reviewed how programming segments containing character interaction could be used as effective persuasion models of power, influence, logos, pathos, and ethos as they are practiced in televised interactions (pp. 181–182). The researchers reviewed family-interaction theory and research and discussed prominent communication patterns. They also performed an episodic analysis of *Star Trek* to show how the program provides parent-child role models (p. 184). Fulmer, Hazzard, Jones, and Keene (1992) studied the effectiveness of Western Kentucky University's distance education delivery of a pharmacology course as part of a degree program in nursing. Instructors taught in front of a real classroom as well as to the remote site classroom by means of one-way video and two-way audio technologies. Results indicated on-campus instructors needed to improve overall performance skills when working with video cameras, including eye contact and interaction style to help students at the remote-site classroom feel more involved (p. 290). Based on results, the researchers suggested that successful two-way-video instruction required detailed planning, attention to communication strategies, flexibility when technology fails, and consistency in course materials and methods of assessment (pp. 290–291). Two-way video instruction is often met with skepticism on the part of teachers using traditional methods. Musical and Kampmueller (1996) provided a set of guidelines designed to correct some of the misconceptions surrounding interactive television (ITV) and instruction. A few of their key points are summarized here. Many educators are concerned that ITV will somehow replace the person in front of the classroom. The authors noted how ITV solves the common problem of having geographic accessibility to instruction. One of the strongest and most traditional arguments favoring all forms of distance education is that one teacher can communicate with students in one or more remote settings. While students generally embrace ITV opportunities, the authors cited evidence supporting both student and instructor preferences for face-to-face forms of communication (p. 29). Another misconception regarding ITV is that students do not learn as much with such delivery systems. The type of student who signs up for an ITV course is probably the best predictor of successful or marginal learning. Students who are "more responsible, more motivated, and more disciplined" (p. 32) generally do best in such courses. Clearly, not all student learners are best suited for the self-discipline required of ITV instruction. Finally, a number of universities, colleges, and related educational institutions have moved toward ITV delivery systems because they believe the technologies will save money. The authors cited how entry into ITV system technologies can be very expensive, but that such costs may be outweighed by "the benefits they provide for students and for educational institutions" (p. 33), particularly so-called nontraditional student populations.

Summary

The diverse range of studies reported in this section makes difficult any clear summary of research. Clearly, more systematic research in this area is needed. A few comments about potential directions for future research would seem in order.

Few studies have thoroughly explored relationships between visual communication and learning. Television technologies now afford relatively inexpensive means for image rendering and postproduction. Gone are the days of simple and less than engaging "talking heads" as a primary method for teaching with television. Computer-based graphical systems allow for increasingly affordable methods for blending and layering real video with motion graphics and text so as to provide engaging television suitable for learning situations. Lacking, however, is any systematic testing to determine what visual techniques are best suited for teaching certain types of skills to young and adult learners. This is a potentially rich avenue for future research, particularly as traditional video becomes increasingly married to computer-based and Internet applications for interactive instructional delivery. For example, computer based platforms for instruction are now fully integrated with video instruction as one of a range of instructional tools. Video streaming of recorded lectures and demonstrations is a common element in web-driven applications such as WebCT, where instructors build both asynchronous (delayed time) and synchronous (real time) tools to create stand-alone online courses or parts of courses designed to complement traditional forms of instruction. Previous research from 1990 reported here often alludes to a balancing act between nontraditional learners who embrace the convenience of online course instruction but who miss the face-to-face interaction with course instructors. Future research would do well to systematically investigate whether developments such as increasingly smaller video cameras or web-cams represent one solution to this type of problem.

REFERENCES

Anderson, D., Huston, A., Schmitt, K., Linebarger, D., & Wright, J. (2001). Early childhood television viewing and adolescent behavior. *Monographs of the Society for Research in Child Development, 66*(1), 1–147.

Aluja-Fabregat, A., Torrubia-Beltri, R. (1998). Viewing of mass media violence, perception of violence, personality and academic achievement. *Personality and Individual Differences, 25*, 973–989.

Caldas, S., & Bankston, C. (1999). Black and white TV: Race, television viewing, and academic achievement. *Sociological Spectrum, 19*, 39–61.

Cennamo, K. (1993). Learning from video: Factors influencing learner's preconceptions and invested mental effort. *Educational Technology Research and Development, 41*(3), 33–45.

Chronicle of Higher Education. (2003, November 21). *U. of Southern California replaces students' long-distance with videoconferencing.* Retrieved November 17, 2003, from http://chronicle.com/prm/weekly/v50/i13/13a02902.htm.

Cool, V., Yarbrough, D., Patton, J., Runde, R., & Keith, T. (1994). Experimental effects of radio and television distractors on children's performance on mathematics and reading assignments. *Journal of Experimental Education, 62,* 181–194.

Cooper, H., Valentine, J., Nye, B., & Lindsay, J. (1999). Relationships between five after-school activities and academic achievement. *Journal of Educational Psychology, 91,* 369–378.

Fulmer, J., Hazzard, M., Jones, S., & Keene, K. (1992). Distance learning: An innovative approach to nursing education. *Journal of Professional Nursing, 8,* 280–294.

Gortmaker, S., Salter, C., Walker, D., & Dietz, W. (1990). The impact of television viewing on mental aptitude and achievement: A longitudinal study. *Public Opinion Quarterly, 54,* 594–604.

Hagborg, W. (1995). High school student television viewing time: A study of school performance and adjustment. *Child Study Journal, 25,* 155–167.

Henggeler, S., Cohen, R., Edwards, J., Summerville, M., and Ray, G. (1991). Family stress as a link in the association between television viewing and achievement. *Child Study Journal, 21,* 1–10.

Koshal, R., Koshal, M., & Gupta, A. (1996). Academic achievement and television viewing by eighth graders: A quantitative analysis. *Applied Economics, 28,* 919–926.

Kozma, R. (1991). Learning with media. *Review of Educational Research, 61,* 179–211.

LimiTV, Inc. (2000). *Parents are the developing brain's first and most important influence.* Retrieved November 14, 2002, from http://www.limittv.org.preschool.htm.

McHale, S., Crouter, A., & Tucker, C. (2001). Free-time activities in middle childhood: Links with adjustment in early adolescence. *Child Development, 72,* 1764–1778.

Musial, G., & Kampmueller, W. (1996). Two-way video distance education: Ten misconceptions about teaching and learning via interactive television. *Action in Teacher Education, 17*(4), 28–36.

National Education Association. (2003, March 2). *Pathway to the world.* Retrieved December 8, 2003, from http://www.nea.org/columns/rw030302.html.

National Institute on Media and the Family. (2002, July 17). *Television's effect on reading and academic achievement.* Retrieved November 14, 2003, from http:///www.mediafamily.org/facts/facts_tveffect.shtml.

Pirrong, G., & Lathen, W. (1990). The use of interactive television in business education. *Educational Technology, 30*(5), 49–54.

Razel, M. (2001). The complex model of television viewing and educational achievement. *Journal of Educational Research, 94,* 371–379.

Smith, T. (1992). Time use and change in academic achievement: A longitudinal follow-up. *Journal of Youth and Adolescence, 21,* 725–747.

Thorson, E., & Lang, A. (1992). The effects of television videographics and lecture familiarity on adult cardiac orienting responses and memory. *Communication Research, 19,* 346–369.

Winegarden, A., Fuss-Reineck, M., & Charron, L. (1993). Using *Star Trek: The Next Generation* to teach concepts in persuasion, family communication, and ethics. *Communication Education, 42,* 179–188.

ACTIVITIES

1. Perform your own qualitative study of the relationship between academic achievement and television. Contact the administration of a middle or junior high school in your community. Seek permission to enter the school and to ask teachers about the topic of television and academic achievement. Find out where and when teachers can be contacted, such as in their homerooms after school, the teacher's lounge, and so on. Be sure to introduce yourself and explain the general purpose

of your visit. Ask if they have any comments on the relationship between academic achievement and television. Be sure to follow up with any questions having to do with concepts or key phrases used by teachers when answering your general questions. Also be sure to ask them if their responses would apply to the case of their own children or grandchildren. Summarize your findings and compare them with others performing the same task.

2. Interview informed experts in your community about television's potential as a tool for classroom instruction. These experts could be professors in education, communication, or library science. Or they might be educational technology specialists in public or private school systems. Still others could be professionals in the business of providing educational technology solutions to clients in the public or private sectors. Explore with these experts the range of television's possible applications in the classroom. What do they think has been the most fruitful among these applications? What in their opinion has been the least fruitful? What do these experts see as the future of television in the classroom?

3. Television in the United States is largely an entertainment medium. As such, generations of audiences tend to approach the experience of television as a time for relaxation and escape, one characterized by so-called "lean back" behaviors compared to "lean in" behaviors more typical of people using computers. You are the consultant hired by a very large public school system charged with developing a video curriculum designed to bolster basic math skills on the part of elementary school students. Write a one-page proposal addressing such issues as content, production elements, and instructional settings geared toward combating television's typical "lean back" characteristics.

QUESTIONS

1. Do you think television remains an effective tool for classroom instruction or have such things as computers and the Internet made television obsolete? If yes, why? If no, why not? Be sure to demonstrate your knowledge of some research in this area of inquiry as part of your response.

2. Some of the research reviewed in this chapter argued that a better predictor variable of television and academic achievement would be a measure of the *kind* of television programming viewed by children and adolescents, compared to straightforward measures of *amounts* of television viewed. Assume for a moment that you are the researcher who has been given a large federal grant to study the question. What kinds of television programs would you hypothesize are associated with higher levels of academic achievement? What kinds of programs are associated with lower levels? Does it make sense to assume that he type of television programs we view are somehow linked to how well we perform in terms of academic grades and standardized tests of comprehension and aptitude? Why or why not? Are there other questions you should be asking as the researcher?

3. One study reported in this chapter argued that popular television programming fare could be used to teach any number of communication principles. Find out what were last week's top-ten television programs for the prime-time national audience. Typically these lists can be found in entertainment sections of newspapers, websites, or industry trade magazines. List the top program for the previous

week. Perhaps you have viewed this program. What, if any, educational concepts, principles, or even theories might be taught or reinforced by viewing this program? You can probably answer this question even if you haven't watched the program. Most television programs belong to a larger group or genre of television programming, such news, drama, sports, comedies, reality, and so on. If you can place the program in its larger group, chances are you can surmise any concepts, principles, and so on for a particular program. Perform this exercise for each of the top ten programs in last week's lineup. What, across all programs and program categories, can you surmise about television's capacity to teach?

ADDITIONAL READINGS

Bowman, J., & Plaisir, J. (1996). Technology approaches to teaching ESL students. *Media & Methods, 32*(3), 26–27.

Gaddy, G. (1986). Television's impact on high school achievement. *Public Opinion Quarterly, 50,* 340–359.

Mielke, K. (1994). On the relationship between television viewing and academic achievement. *Journal of Broadcasting and Electronic Media, 38,* 361–366.

Smith, T. (1990). Time and academic achievement. *Journal of Youth and Adolescence, 19,* 539–558.

Williams, P., Haertel, E., Haertel, G., & Walberg, H. (1982). The impact of leisure time television on school learning. *American Educational Research Journal, 19,* 19–50.

CHAPTER EIGHT

RACE AND ETHNIC STEREOTYPING

This chapter examines recent research on race, ethnicity, and media. Chances are you have completed a survey including a question about race. For example, the U.S. government collects race data as part of census information and typically the answer categories from which to choose include African American, Asian Pacific Islander, Caucasian, Hispanic/Latino, and Native American. Hopefully, you will soon see that these simple categories, while perhaps serving the purpose of classification, do not really help us understand media, audiences, and effects. With this in mind, we need to spend a moment reviewing some basic terms and concepts important for such understanding. Specifically, we need to define what is meant by race, ethnicity, and stereotyping. We also need to understand some of the fundamental concerns on the part of those researchers who study race, ethnicity, and the media.

Researchers across a number of academic disciplines have long debated both the use and misuse of the concept we know as race (Kuper & Kuper, 1996, p. 711). Introductory textbooks in physical anthropology include discussions about the increasingly problematic nature of the term. Much of this debate is in reaction to changing perceptions about what constitutes race in society (p. 711). At the present time, most researchers define race as "a broad range of issues regarding the construction and perception of racial categories; the consequences of racial stratification . . . and the means of bringing equality of opportunity and other forms of social justice across racial lines" (Calhoun, 2002, p. 397). To summarize, race has come to represent more than a means of classifying people based on their physiology. The construct also includes an awareness of how people come to see differences between each other and how those perceptions can impede or enhance social and economic equality.

What about ethnicity? The term is equally complex. Most researchers now recognize the power of ethnicity as a research construct, because it takes into account "common historical origins and which may include shared culture, religion or language" (Kuper & Kuper, pp. 260–261). For some, ethnicity is often seen as a larger, umbrella-like term of which race is a part. For our purposes, **ethnicity** is "A highly elastic concept applied to groups who say they share or are perceived to share some combination of cultural, historical, racial, religious, or linguistic features . . . and some modern notions of race" (Calhoun, 2002, p. 148).

A key term used in this and the following chapter is **stereotype.** Stereotyping is an important human process. You have no doubt encountered one or more theories about human cognition. These theories are called by many names, but most have in common the recognition that humans organize their perceptions about the world in patterned and predictable ways. Perception is a progression of directed effort, starting with choosing to attend to, or ignore external stimuli. If we choose to perceive, cognitive theory and research show us that we engage the world with a preexisting set of filters. Stereotyping is one such filter. Previous experiences, including mass media experiences, help frame our interpretation of new information. We do this in order to help sort our ongoing world of experience. One can only imagine what the world would be like if we had to start over every time we encountered a new piece of information in the external world. So, stereotyping in and of itself is not a bad thing, because it actually helps us to be more efficient social actors.

Of course, there are positive and negative stereotypes, and a good deal of research summarized in this and other chapters attempts to document whether things heard or seen in the mass media represent positive or negative messages. A number of suggested readings at the back of this chapter pursue this issue in greater detail. For example, Graves (1999) provided an excellent summary of television's contribution in providing "vicarious" learning opportunities for reinforcing both negative and positive stereotypes. At the core of research in this chapter is concern about mass media depictions about race and ethnicity. Recall if you will the definition of race found at the beginning of this section. Researchers who focus on race as a keystone variable in their work are usually concerned with how media depictions of race may serve to reinforce social or economic inequities between groups of people. This focus serves as the core for much of the content analysis reported in this chapter examining negative race or ethnic media stereotypes. Other media effects researchers are also interested in the potential for such media content to help frame or reinforce these negative stereotypes and use the tools of experimentation, surveys, or qualitative methods to study these processes.

With this background in mind, you might be considering a number of questions about your own experiences with race, ethnicity, and media. What do you think have been some of the prevailing images of race and ethnicity in the media in general and in such things as news, advertising, and television programs in specific? Does exposure to race and ethnicity portrayals in the mass media create negative or positive stereotypes on the part of audiences? Does this kind of exposure simply trigger existing stereotypes? Does this kind of exposure influence future race and ethnic-based experiences? Do personal experiences with different race and ethnic groups offset any exposure to negative media images? These are among the questions examined by researchers whose work is summarized in this chapter. This work includes content analyses, experiments, surveys, and qualitative studies. You should note that this chapter works in combination with the following chapter on sex and gender.

CONTENT ANALYSES

As you are probably already aware, the U.S. Latino population is the fastest-growing ethnic group in the country. Have advertisers in this country responded to this growth by increasing representations of Latinos in major mass media advertising? Taylor and Bang (1997) examined this issue in their content analysis of magazine advertisements. Of particular interest was documenting whether any portrayals of Latinos were stereotypic (p. 286). Their approach was anchored in **expectancy theory,** wherein the mass media are seen as significant disseminators of cultural transmission. "For example, since Latinos have often been stereotyped as being uneducated, Latino children may feel more inclined to drop out of school earlier than the average American" (p. 286). Major general circulation magazines ranging from *Time* to *Popular Mechanics* were sampled for 12 months between 1992 and 1993. All magazines included "substantial Latino readership" (p. 290). All full-page or larger advertisements were included in the sample, resulting in a total of 1,616 advertisements (p. 290). Results showed only 4.7 percent of advertisements portrayed Latinos, compared to 10.5 percent represented in the U.S. population. When Latinos were present, they occupied major roles 47.4 percent of all advertisements (p. 294). The researchers expressed concern about the underrepresentation of Latinos in magazine advertising.

Few studies have examined portrayals of Asian Americans. Taylor and Stern (1997) reviewed population trends and demographic characteristics perceived as contributors to "positive stereotyping of Asian-Americans as intellectually gifted, mathematically skilled, technically competent, hard working, serious, and well assimilated" (p. 48). One week of prime-time television programming from summer 1994 was recorded for the four major broadcast networks (ABC, CBS, Fox, and NBC; p. 51). Results showed that "Male and female Asian-Americans were represented in 8.4% of the advertisements . . . which is more than double their proportion in the overall population (3.6%)" (p. 52). Asian models in television advertisements occupied major roles in nearly half of all commercials in which they appeared, but females lagged behind males in such representations. Asian American portrayals were most often found with products or services associated with affluence or work settings (pp. 53, 55). The authors concluded that, while Asian Americans were clearly "overrepresented" in television commercials, there are concerns about token portrayals and the inequity between females and males within such representations (p. 57).

Gunter (1998) examined 1,161 British television dramas on 10 different channels and content-analyzed the race of aggressors and victims in violent depictions (p. 685). Results showed that almost 80 percent of aggressors and 77 percent of victims were Caucasian, with slightly over 5 percent of aggressors and 4 percent of victims African American (p. 688). The researcher argued that such findings reinforce those from previous studies and suggested that "frequency of involvement in violence on the part of different ethnic groups is only one indicator of power relations between different sectors of the population" (p. 700).

Larson and Bailey (1998) examined five years of "Person of the Week" segments featured as part of the ABC television network's nightly newscast. The researchers predicted "Person of the Week" segments would embrace American values such as "individualism, unselfishness, patriotism, inventiveness, capitalism, populism, competition, and meritocracy" (p. 489). A total of 230 segments were analyzed, spanning 1989 to fall 1994. Results showed that of those people featured, "63% were white, 13% black, and only 4% were Hispanic or Asian" (p. 491). An additional 14 percent were coded "unknown." In addition, "Blacks were far more likely than whites to be singled out for having succeeded despite a humble background . . . [and] were more likely devoted to social issues compared to . . . whites" (pp. 494–495).

Do images in television advertising reinforce race prejudice? Coltrane and Messineo (2000) analyzed television advertisements aired during highly rated programs in the mid-1990s targeting popular marketing segments (e.g., households, young viewers, women) (p. 371). Results showed that Caucasians were portrayed more often than other groups and more often exercised positions of authority. Caucasians occupied more parental and spousal roles (p. 375). "Taken as a group, non-Whites continue to be relatively absent from these advertisements. . . . Though African American characters are more prominent than other minorities, and . . . more common than they once were, we find evidence that pejorative stereotypes of Blacks are still common" (p. 382).

What characterizes race portrayals in magazines targeting different race and ethnic groups? Thomas and Trieber (2000) examined this issue in their study of *Life*, *Cosmopolitan*, *Ebony*, and *Essence* magazines over a two-year period, to study trends in race stereotyping. Results showed "racial differences became apparent only in the context of race-gender groups" (p. 364), with African American women models appearing more often in everyday contextual settings. Moreover, "it is only by comparing *Life* with *Ebony*, for example, that we discovered the disproportionate selling of sex-romance to Blacks and subtle overuse of affluent images for whites" (p. 370).

Vargas (2000) examined one major daily newspaper's coverage of Latino affairs in the southern United States. Results showed that "media portrayals of Latinos tend to reproduce negative stereotypes. And . . . the coverage often represents Latinos as objects of the news rather than as authoritative subjects with valuable perspectives" (p. 285).

What of racial portrayals in recent prime-time television? Mastro and Greenberg (2000) collected a one-week sample of broadcast network prime-time programming. Results showed that 80 percent of all characters were Caucasians, 16 percent were African American, 3 percent were Latino, and 1 percent Asian (p. 695). The researchers argued that results demonstrated, consistent with findings from previous research, a "pattern of inclusions of African Americans and the near exclusion

■ ■ ■ ■ ■ ▬▬▬▬▬▬▬▬▬▬▬▬▬▬▬▬▬▬▬▬▬▬▬▬▬▬▬▬▬▬▬▬▬▬

BOX 8.1
NAACP TV DIVERSITY STUDY

The National Association for the Advancement of Colored People, established in 1909, is the oldest civil rights organization. The NAACP periodically measures the U.S. television industry's efforts to reflect racial and ethnic diversity in programming and employment opportunities. The most recent report covered a period from 2000 to 2003. Overall, results indicated "small gains in on-air roles, [but] practically no representation of people of color in the top echelon of production, which is the nucleus of the industry" (NAACP.ORG, 2003). The analysis included breakouts for the four major broadcast networks in terms of portrayals of "minorities in a regular or recurring role." For a recent television season, Fox had 121 such roles, compared to CBS with 99, NBC with 81, and ABC with 74. All networks showed increases in such roles compared to previous television seasons. However, NCAAP leadership was quick to emphasize, "This is not just about numbers, it's about content and stereotypes as well." Behind-the-scenes trends painted a much different picture. "In the area of writing, producing, and directing, the problem of not including people of color is widespread and pervasive" (NAACP.ORG, 2003).

of all other ethnic minorities" (p. 695). Notable was the absence of Latinos "on an absolute and comparative basis" (p. 699) (see Box 8.1).

EXPERIMENTS

Do predetermined racial attitudes filter audience perceptions of television news? Peffley, Shields, and Williams (1996) argued that television news portrayals would trigger negative racial stereotypes on the part of Caucasian audiences when exposed to images of African American criminal suspects. A total of 95 Caucasian university students participated in the study. Results showed "the brief visual image of the race of the suspect in the news story did appear to trigger powerful racial stereotypes, which biased judgments of the presumed guilt of the suspect" (p. 315). The independent variables tested in this study helped to predict 19 to 36 percent of racial stereotyping. In related research, Power, Murphy, and Coover (1996) examined how media messages containing stereotypes influenced later judgments about race. A total of 110 Caucasian students from a university in the western United States were studied. Results showed a relationship between the type of stereotype and later perceptions of prominent African Americans. Students who were exposed to negative stereotypes also perceived prominent African Americans negatively, compared to those who received "counter-stereotypic portrayals" and then displayed non-stereotypic perceptions. In a related study, Valentino (1999) examined how crime reporting influences racial attitudes and how such views influence perceptions of presidential candidates (p. 295). The researcher used the 1996 presidential race between Clinton and Dole for study. Participants were 298 adults representing a cross-section of the Los Angeles population. Results showed that "coverage of minority suspects benefits Dole most. Conversely, Clinton suffers most when minorities are featured as suspects" (p. 306).

Do where you live and local television news help to frame your perceptions about race and crime? Gilliam, Valentino, and Beckmann (2002) studied how direct and indirect experiences help frame racial attitudes. They hypothesized that individuals from racially mixed neighborhoods would "be more likely to possess nonviolent crime schemas for blacks," and would be less susceptible to news stereotypes (p. 759). Their sample consisted of 390 Caucasian adults representing a cross-section of the Los Angeles population. Results showed that "Those from more racially homogeneous neighborhoods . . . are more likely to endorse negative stereotypes after such exposure" (p. 766).

SURVEYS

How do media images exported to other countries influence foreign perceptions of Americans? Willnat, He, and Ziaoming (1997) predicted that greater exposure to American media would result in more "positive stereotypical perceptions of Americans" (p. 741) on the part of three distinct Chinese audiences. They also hypothesized that these perceptions may be contingent on the type of mass media used (pp. 741–742). Their sample consisted of 625 undergraduates enrolled at separate universities in Hong Kong, Shenzhen, and Singapore. Results showed "the relationship between media exposure and stereotypical perceptions of Americans is not evident among all of our subjects and is not necessarily characterized by a positive correlation between more exposure and higher levels of positive stereotypes" (p. 748). Overall, the authors indicate that findings suggested Western media was a significant but not the "best" predictor of perceptions of Americans.

Does membership in a particular "ethnic subgroup" influence use of mass media in order to maintain one's culture? Rios and Gaines (1997) studied individuals identified as predominant in Mexican heritage, those who were bicultural, and those low in identifying with their Mexican heritage. A total of 269 Hispanics of Mexican heritage residing in or around Austin, Texas, were surveyed. Results showed distinct patterns of media use contingent on ethnic subgroup membership. "Those participants from the high Mexican heritage cluster and the bicultural cluster appear to be keeping closer ties to their ethnic heritage group. They find utility in Spanish-language media for serving Mexican heritage cultural functions because they have interest, motivation, and Spanish-language skills" (p. 212).

Tan, Fujioka, and Lucht (1997) surveyed Caucasian college students to assess stereotyping of Native Americans. The researchers offered a number of predictions based on the belief that increased contact with Native Americans would result in positive stereotypes whether by direct contact or exposure to television portrayals (p. 271). A total of 191 Caucasian undergraduate students at two northwestern U.S. universities completed surveys. Results showed that "direct contact [with Native

Americans] is related to positive evaluations of contact, which leads to positive stereotyping" (p. 276). Direct contact contributed 23 percent to positive stereotyping. The results for media experiences were more complex. "TV attributes predict stereotyping only for traits more easily depicted in television, such as violence and affluence" (p. 279), with the television variable contributing only 5 percent to stereotyping.

Davis and Gandy (1999) examined African-American perceptions of mass media representations of males and domestic violence, specifically portrayals of African-American males (p. 385). They hypothesized that those audience members with stronger racial group identity would be more critical of television's portrayals of domestic violence (p. 385). Telephone surveys were administered to 405 African Americans in three U.S. states. Results showed that "Criticism of the media varied significantly by state, with Californians emerging as the most critical. . . . Those who were more strongly identified tend to be more critical of the media" (p. 387). Ethnic identity contributed 10 percent to the perception that television's portrayals of African American men were negative.

Tan, Fujioka, and Tan (2000) studied how positive and negative perceptions of African Americans lead to corresponding positive or negative stereotypes of African Americans, which in turn leads to favorable or unfavorable attitudes toward affirmative action policies (p. 365). A total of 166 university students identifying themselves as "white" participated in the study. Results showed that "Perceptions of negative TV portrayals significantly predicted some negative stereotypes, which in turn significantly predicted opposition to affirmative action policies" (pp. 369–370).

A major school of thought in mass communication theory and research suggests that individuals who are heavy consumers of a particular form of media, or a particular form of content in such media, will by nature come to adopt the dominant perspectives reflected in prevalent content. This **cultivation theory** was the basis of work by Vergeer, Lubbers, and Scheepers (2000), who studied relationships between newspaper content emphasizing crime and negative audience perceptions toward certain "ethnic minorities" (p. 127). They hypothesized that exposure to three separate Nederland newspapers, characterized by differing degrees of coverage about ethnic-related crime, would result in separate perceptions of ethnic groups (p. 131). Surveys were administered over five years in communities served by the three different papers. A total of 2,661 respondents were interviewed. Results showed that exposure to the two newspapers reporting less ethnic-related crime "leads people to perceive ethnic minorities as less threatening than exposure to the [third newspaper] does" (p. 136). The content of these two newspapers helped explain 16.4 percent of the perception that ethnic minorities were less threatening.

QUALITATIVE RESEARCH

Ross (1997) studied "black" audience perceptions of British television. Focus groups consisting of 353 individuals in 35 groups were used to collect questionnaire, personal diary, and audiotape data. Of these groups, "slightly more than half the sample [came] from Indian, Pakistani, or Bangladeshi communities and slightly less than half [claimed] African, African Caribbean or other 'black' identities" (p. 238). Results suggested that "Black minorities are visible in television spaces in two discrete ways, first in mainstream programmes where stereotyping and charicature are the main criticism, and secondly in multicultural programming strands, where they are effectively denied access to the public mainstream space" (p. 244).

Mayeda (1999) performed a content analysis and critical reading of two Japanese baseball pitchers playing in U.S. major-league baseball, Hideo Nomo and Hideki Irabu. Mayeda reviewed the stereotypes of Asian American "model minority" and Japanese national "economic threat" as potential roadblocks to true understanding between United States and Asian cultures. The researcher argued that a useful crossroads for examining these phenomena could be found in the study of Japanese baseball players working for U.S. professional teams. He sampled articles from the sports sections of the *Los Angeles Times* and *New York Times* for a 12-month period in 1996 and 1997. Articles in the magazine *Sports Illustrated* were also analyzed. Results showed that "Nomo was . . . presented as a very typical model minority. Hard working, self-sacrificing, and quiet" (p. 211). For Irabu, "the American media had already conditioned its readers to view Japan and Japanese nationals as economic threats" (p. 213). The author concluded that unchecked, such misrepresentations of sports figures will continue to feed negative stereotypes of individuals from diverse races, ethnic groups, and cultures.

Tovares (2000) utilized interviews with community members to examine influences behind the construction of television news stories about youth gangs. A total of 27 field interviews were conducted with law enforcement, journalists, community leaders and young people between 1993 and 1995 in Austin, Texas. Results showed a common theme in news reporting to be parental apathy, a theme generated primarily from near exclusive reliance on law enforcement personnel as journalistic sources. The author concluded that reporting about gangs stems from very few reporters who rarely venture beyond typical sources and perspectives.

Fuller (2001) examined audience perceptions of recent television advertising portrayals related to historical and negative stereotypes. She explored audience interpretations of an African American model in a Pinesol commercial to historical portrayals of Aunt Jemima for a major brand of pancake syrup. A convenience sample of 34 African American college students was shown a videotaped version of the Pinesol commercial. Part of this presentation included "comparison of the text of the commercial and the text of an actual advertisement for Aunt Jemima Pancakes . . . a comparison of the features of the Pinesol model with the descriptives of Aunt Jemima and mammy" (p. 124). Students were then interviewed utilizing a semi-structured interview technique designed to solicit individual perceptions and opinions. Results indicated that students used terms and descriptions traditional to historical stereotypes when describing the actress in the Pinesol advertisement. The researcher argued, "The social consequences of the resurgence of the mammy or Aunt Jemima are serious not only because of the social messages they disseminate but . . . because of the impact on the self-concept and self-esteem of Black females" (p. 130).

SUMMARY

What can we summarize from this previous research?

- Whites, or Caucasians, still predominate in the mass media landscape. African Americans and Latinos are often underrepresented, and Asian Americans are somewhat overrepresented.
- When non-Caucasian portrayals are at the forefront, they often reinforce stereotypic ideals of long-standing race and ethnic power hierarchies.
- Results from surveys and experiments suggest that ethnic and race prejudice is alive and well, but the mass media's role in creating or reinforcing such views is statistically quite small.
- Consistent across many studies is the finding that personal contact and experiences with difference races and ethnic groups encourages cross-cultural understanding and reduces the tendency toward negative stereotyping.

A question typical in content analytic work is, "How do my findings in terms of percentage of character or role representations stack up in terms of important societal trends?" One assumes that content analyses like the ones reported in this chapter will compare media trends with census or related statistics. For example, implicit in research examining race portrayals on prime-time televisions is concern about whether such images are an under- or overrepresentation of actual population trends. Unfortunately, too few of these studies do this kind of comparing as a first step in analyses. Even when such analyses are performed, it is important to keep in mind that additional analyses are important. For example, you might find in your own research that a particular television program matches up pretty well in terms of racial representations when compared to national population statistics. However, researchers would be quick to point out that you should also examine the relative power reflected in the roles portrayed by different characters in your television program. Who plays major roles? Who is on screen most of the time? How do these factors influence the conclusions you can draw about any one program's treatment of race and ethnicity? We also need to keep in mind that content analyses are only systematic accounts of media messages. You may recall from Chapter 2 that content analyses alone do not tell us what audiences are reading, viewing, or the attitudinal or behavioral effects of such exposure. Those questions are best answered by audience studies, and the ones summarized in this chapter only tell us that media messages may contribute to negative race and ethnic stereotypes on the part of audiences.

Such findings force us to confront an old conundrum once again. Do individuals predisposed toward negative race or ethnic stereotypes seek out similar fare in the media in order to reinforce existing beliefs? Do media compel or encourage individuals to exercise bias against certain ethnic groups or practice racist tendencies? Or, as some of the previously reviewed research suggests, do media images regarding race or ethnicity actually help to educate and close the gap of misunderstanding between people of different backgrounds? Many of the scholars whose work is reported in this chapter call for additional research. Such research, they argued, must be attentive to the increasing flow of media channels available to audiences. For example, multichannel television can provide uniquely different programming experiences for audience members, including audience members characterized by similarities in terms of race, ethnicity, class, and culture. Future research would do well to examine constructs including ethnicity and trends in program viewing within this larger video landscape. If we agree that ethnicity is "the living practice of social actions on the part of individuals who share a common historical origin, who maintain through social interaction a dynamic system of beliefs founded in formal and informal rituals that may include the use of special languages" (Traudt, 1990, p. 246), then how the mass media become part of those actions and help inform social life remains largely elusive at this point in time.

REFERENCES

Calhoun, C. (Ed.). (2002). *Dictionary of the Social Sciences*. New York: Oxford University Press.

Coltrane, S., & Messineo, M. (2000). The perpetuation of subtle prejudice: Race and gender imagery in 1990's television advertising. *Sex Roles, 42*, 363–389.

Davis, J., & Gandy, O. (1999). Racial identity and media orientation: Exploring the nature of constraint. *Journal of Black Studies, 29*, 367–397.

Fuller, L. (2001). Are we seeing things? The Pinesol lady and the ghost of Aunt Jemima. *Journal of Black Studies, 32*, 120–131.

Gilliam, F., Valentino, N., & Beckman, M. (2002). Where you live and what you watch: The impact of racial proximity and local television news on attitudes about race and crime. *Political Research Quarterly, 55*, 755–780.

Graves, S. (1999). Television and prejudice reduction: When does television as a vicarious experience make a difference? *Journal of Social Issues, 55*, 707–725.

Gunter, B. (1998). Ethnicity and involvement in violence on television: Nature and context of on-screen portrayals. *Journal of Black Studies, 28*, 683–703.

Kuper, A., & Kuper, J. (Eds.). (1996). *The Social Science Encyclopedia* (2nd ed.). London: Routledge.

Larson, S., & Bailey, M. (1998). ABC's "Person of the Week": American values in television news. *Journalism and Mass Communication Quarterly, 75*, 485–499.

Mastro, D., & Greenberg, B. (2000). The portrayal of racial minorities on prime time television. *Journal of Broadcasting and Electronic Media, 44*, 690–703.

Mayeda, D. (1999). From model minority to economic threat: Media portrayals of major league baseball pitchers Hideo Nomo and Hideki Irabu. *Journal of Sport and Social Issues, 23*, 203–217.

NAACP.ORG. (2003, October 28). *NAACP TV diversity report yields mixed results on networks performance*. Retrieved December 8, 2003, from http://www.naacp.org/news/releases/tvdiversity102803.shtml.

Peffley, M., Shields, T., & Williams, B. (1996). The intersection of race and crime in television news stories: An experimental study. *Political Communication, 13*, 309–327.

Power, J., Murphy, S., & Coover, G. (1996). Priming prejudice: How stereotypes and counter-stereo-types influence attribution of responsibility and credibility among ingroups and outgroups. *Human Communication Research, 23*(1), 36–58.

Rios, D., & Gaines, S. (1997). Impact of gender and ethnic subgroup membership on Mexican Americans' use of mass media for cultural maintenance. *Howard Journal of Communications, 8,* 197–216.

Ross, K. (1997). Viewing pleasure, viewer pain: Black audiences and British television. *Leisure Studies, 16,* 233–248.

Tan, A., Fujioka, Y., & Lucht, N. (1997). Native American stereotypes, TV portrayals, and personal contact. *Journalism and Mass Communication Quarterly, 74,* 265–284.

Tan, A., Fujioka, Y., & Tan, G. (2000). Television use, stereotypes of African Americans and opinions on affirmative action: An affective model of policy reasoning. *Communication Monographs, 67,* 362–371.

Taylor, C., & Bang, H. (1997). Portrayals of Latinos in magazine advertising. *Journalism and Mass Communication Quarterly, 74,* 285–303.

Taylor, C., & Stern, B. (1997). Asian-Americans: Television advertising and the "model minority" stereotype. *Journal of Advertising, 26*(2), 47–61.

Thomas, M., & Treiber, L. (2000). Race, gender, and status: A content analysis of print advertise-ments in four popular magazines. *Sociological Spectrum, 20,* 357–371.

Tovares, R. (2000). Influences on the Mexican American youth gang discourse on local television news. *Howard Journal of Communications, 11,* 229–246.

Traudt, P. (1990). Ethnic diversity and mass-mediated experience. In S. Thomas (Ed.), *Communica-tion and culture: Language, performance, technology, and media* (pp. 244–254). Norwood, NJ: Ablex.

Valentino, N. (1999). Crime news and the priming of racial attitudes during evaluations of the president. *Public Opinion Quarterly, 63,* 293–320.

Vargas, L. (2000). Genderizing Latino news: an of local newspaper's coverage of Latino current affairs. *Critical Studies in Media Communication, 17,* 261–293.

Vergeer, M., Lubbers, M., & Scheepers, P. (2000). Exposure to newspapers and attitudes toward ethnic minorities: A longitudinal analysis. *Howard Journal of Communications, 11,* 127–143.

Willnat, L., He, Z., & Ziaoming, H. (1997). Foreign media exposure and perceptions of Americans in Hong Kong, Shenzhen, and Singapore. *Journalism and Mass Communication Quarterly, 74,* 738–756.

ACTIVITIES

1. Save the issues of a major metropolitan daily newspaper in your region for a one-week period. Ideally, this one-week period should be as "normal" as possible, thus avoiding the potential for interruptions in everyday reporting because of a major story. Typically, such papers have a section devoted to metropolitan or regional news. Carefully read the headlines and corresponding stories in this section for the one-week period. Use a highlighter or similar tool to note those stories and specific passages in reporting making reference to race or ethnic-ity. Having completed this task for each of the seven issues of the paper, go back and clip each story you highlighted. Perform a rudimentary qualitative analysis of these stories, grouping stories with other stories appearing to match in terms of topic, story, or similar coding scheme growing out of your collection of clippings. Then answer the following questions. In what ways does your daily newspaper make reference to race or ethnicity? Are references to race or ethnicity

associated with any recurring themes or types of stories? What do you think these trends say about reporters and their perceptions of race and ethnicity? What do you think these trends say about reporter perceptions of the audience for newspapers?

2. A number of studies predating those reported in this chapter examined the popular prime-time television program *The Cosby Show* concurrent and after its network run beginning in the 1980s. Some scholars criticized the program because they felt it provided an unrealistic portrayal of African American family life in America. Choose a more contemporary television comedy or drama depicting an African American family, one either enjoying first-run status on a broadcast or cable network or one still airing as a syndicated program. Videotape the program or watch a couple of episodes. Then answer the following questions. What is the name of the program? What character roles are portrayed in the program? What is the family setting, if known, in terms of geographic location, social status, economic well being, and so on. Describe a typical episode in terms of plot and problem. Do you think this television representation of an African American family is a realistic or unrealistic depiction? Why or why not?

3. Surf the Internet to explore television-programming schedules in other countries. These schedules may be found in countries where the government owns and controls all programming, or in countries where some networks are government owned and others are independently owned, or in other countries where all television is independently owned. Scan the programming schedule for each day of the week in an attempt to identify U.S. programming airing on the foreign television network. What are the programs? What would you estimate the percentage of U.S. programming to be compared to all other programming? Compare your analysis with others who examined the programming schedules for other countries. What, if any, are the implications of airing U.S. programming in these other countries?

QUESTIONS

1. Research shows that U.S. television underrepresents African American and Latino cultures. Television industry spokespersons often defend this practice by arguing that television is primarily targeted to Caucasian females aged 18–45, who wield a majority of the economic power in this country. Where do you stand on this issue? Do you agree that the commercial system of television in this country legitimately serves an economic majority in terms of viewers and consumers? Or do you believe that this industry should pay attention to factors beyond economics?

2. Imagine that you were living in a foreign country and had no direct contact with Americans. Your only indirect contact was exposure to a regular stream of imported prime-time television programming with audio translation to your native tongue. What do you think your collective perception of Americans might be based on a steady diet of American comedies, dramas, and so-called reality programs?

3. Based on the chapter and other readings, do you believe that race and ethnicity are important factors when examining media effects? If so, why? If not, why not?

ADDITIONAL READINGS

Bird, S. (1999). Gendered construction of the American Indian in popular media. *Journal of Communication, 49*(3), 61–83.

Frey, D. (2002). Aristocrats, gypsies, and cowboys all: Film stereotypes and Hungarian national identity in the 1930s. *Nationalities Papers, 30,* 383–401.

Greenberg, B., & Brand, J. (1994). Minorities and the mass media: 1970s to 1990s. In J. Bryant & D. Zillman (Eds.), *Media Effects: Advances in theory and research* (pp. 273–314). Hillsdale, NJ: Erlbaum.

Lester, P., & Smith, R. (1990). African-American photo coverage in *Life, Newsweek* and *Time,* 1937–1988. *Journalism Quarterly, 67,* 128–136.

Pickering, M. (1995). The politics and psychology of stereotyping. *Media Culture and Society, 17,* 691–700.

Rodriguez, A. (1996). Objectivity and ethnicity in the production of *Noticiero Univision. Critical Studies in Mass Communication, 13,* 58–81.

Shim, D. (1998). From yellow peril through model minority to renewed yellow peril. *Journal of Communication Inquiry, 22,* 385–409.

Tait, A., & Perry, R. (1994). African Americans in television: An afrocentric analysis. *Western Journal of Black Studies, 18,* 195–200.

CHAPTER NINE

SEX AND GENDER STEREOTYPING

This chapter examines media portrayals of sex and gender roles and audience effects. Sex and gender role research has traditionally been conducted in academic disciplines such as anthropology, communication, sociology, psychology, and women's studies. The study of how mass media portray human female and male roles and how audiences may perceive and act upon such information has long been an area of mass communication theory and research. Signorielli (1990) provides a review of major literature dealing with gender socialization and television predating 1990.

Earlier in the previous century, most research in this area was known as "sex-role research," as differences between females and males were largely seen in biological terms. More contemporary thinking recognizes that one's sex and one's thinking about being female or male can be two very different things. Gender is now seen as the "culturally constructed forms of behavior that roughly correlate with sexual difference. . . . Modern social science . . . has become careful to distinguish between *gender* and *sex* [emphasis in original]; it has generally laid the burden of explaining behavior, practices, roles and social organization on the former" (Calhoun, 2002, p. 187). In other words, sex may remain, for most of us, biologically determined, but more important is how one comes to view one's gender as a function of socializing factors such as family, institutions, and mass media. This perspective is what direct most research activity within the area now called **gender studies,** which is "concerned with the cultural construction of embodied human beings, women and men . . . the differences and similarities as experienced and interpreted in various contexts . . . all relationships whether they involve subjects of the same or different genders" (Kuper & Kuper, 1996, p. 327). Current gender studies in mass communication theory and research examine "differences and similarities" of female and male stereotypes in media messages and potential audience effects. Often, researchers working in this area are concerned with how such images inform audience perceptions of power and equity as they relate to gendered relationships. Perhaps you can begin to see how many of the issues raised in the introductory comments in the previous chapter on race and ethnicity have close bearing on research conducted by scholars in the area of sex, gender, and media.

What do you think? Do you think that media images of gender have changed over time? Do gender images in television differ across genres such as soap operas, advertisements, animated cartoons, sports, and other forms? Do these images differ across networks or across different systems of television in different countries? What are some of these gendered characteristics? What is the effect of viewing gendered roles on television? When do children begin to exhibit gender roles? How do these roles influence what they perceive in media content? Does using a product influence perceptions of advertising for such products and is that perception influenced by gender? These are but some of the questions posed by researchers whose research is included in this chapter. Recent content analyses are summarized, as are experiments, surveys, and qualitative studies. You may note that a portion of the experiments include research with children. Cognitive developmental theory suggests that children come to acquire an increasingly hard and fast sense of their own gender sometime later in the second stage of development, 2 to 5 years of age. Consequently, experiments reported in this chapter often test children during this critical time in development. Readers are also encouraged to consult related chapters where gender is often included as a key variable in the generation of research questions or hypotheses. These include Chapter 8, "Race and Ethnic Stereotyping"; Chapter 10, "Sex, Sexuality, and Pornography"; Chapter 11, "Children, Television, and Violence"; and Chapter 12, "Music Videos."

CONTENT ANALYSES

Television programmers have long known that audiences differing by ages and genders watch different television programs. They also often watch these programs at different times of the day. Do gender stereotypes in television advertisements change during these day parts as well? Craig (1992a) examined portrayals of both women and men on U.S. network television for weekday afternoon soap operas, weekday prime-time programming, and weekend afternoon sports. Results showed that "television commercials targeted to one sex tend to portray gender differently than ads targeted to the other sex" (p. 207). More specifically, "Daytime ads, generally aimed at women homemakers, focus on the traditional stereotypical images associated with the American housewife . . . cooking, cleaning, child care, or maintaining an attractive physical appearance" (p. 208). In a related study, the same researcher (Craig, 1992b) found traditional female gender stereotypes for women as "caregivers and nurturers" for over-the-counter drugs during U.S. prime-time television.

One of the concerns about the ways women are portrayed in mass media has to do with the ways their bodies are objectified—how they are made to appear as things rather than human beings. One technique for such objectification is the use of body shots, versus full-torso or head-only shots in portrayals of women. Hall and Crum (1994) analyzed the use of such techniques in television advertisements. The researchers examined television beer advertising because of the potential links between beer and spirits advertising, gender and sex stereotyping, alcohol consumption, and violence toward women. Seventy hours of weekend sports programming were videotaped during 1991 and 1992, resulting in 59 unique television advertisements for 23 brands of beer. Results indicated more men than women were portrayed in these advertisements, but the images of women were more often objectified. "Results showed an average of 1.15 male body shots per ad, compared to an average of 2.18 female body shots per ad" (p. 335).

Thompson and Zerbinos (1995) conducted a 20-year follow-up study of animated cartoons. Their goal was to compare current results to a study conducted 20 years earlier when male characters dominated animated cartoons and females, when represented, were stereotypic and reliant on men for romance and rescue. The authors hypothesized that female and male characters would be represented in qualitatively different and "gender-role stereotypic ways" (p. 655). A total of 175 cartoon episodes produced from 1935 to 1992 were analyzed. Results indicated a preponderance of male over female lead characters. Male and female characters also differed significantly in terms of traits and behaviors. Male characters were more "independent, assertive, stereotypical, athletic," compared to females, who were "more emotional, warm, romantic, affectionate" (p. 659). More recent cartoons produced after 1980 "had more male and female leads, male and female minor characters, and more gender-neutral characters" and at times these lead and minor characters exhibited more gender-neutral behaviors (p. 663). The researchers noted some progress in gender-neutral representations since 1980, particularly for adventure series programs.

What characterizes the differences, if any, of stereotypic depictions on the so-called newer television networks compared to traditional over-the-air network broadcasters? Eaton (1997) studied prime-time promotional announcements for ABC, CBS, Fox, NBC, and UPN in fall 1995. The researcher hypothesized more male than female promotional characters overall and more stereotypic females when promoting programming targeting younger males (p. 861). Network promotions were recorded over a two-week period, resulting in 811 promotions including 969 characters. Results showed that males were represented in 96 percent of all voice-overs and 56 percent of all character portrayals. "All . . . networks except FOX portrayed more women in major roles than minor ones. FOX and UPN more frequently portrayed female characters in very provocative dress" (p. 862). There was some support for the argument that women were portrayed more often to promote programming targeting younger males. In conclusion, the researcher argued that results show the "symbolic annihilation of women" continued during the mid- to late 1990s on these U.S. television networks.

Cross-national studies provide the opportunity to compare trends in gender stereotyping for two or more countries. Browne (1998) compared gender stereotypes in television advertisements targeting children between the United States and Australia, two countries perceived to share economic practices, language, and family patterns. Browne predicted an overall reduction in stereotypes compared to previous research, but she also predicted that U.S. television advertisements would contain more gender stereotypes compared to those in Australia. Data were collected in 1995 and the sample included 268 television advertisements almost evenly divided between U.S. and Australian versions (p. 86). Results were "generally similar to those of previous studies and indicate substantial gender stereotyping" (p. 93). Also, "Australian commercials tended to contain more nearly equal male-to-female proportions, more often depicted both boys and girls . . . and less frequently portrayed girls as shy or giggly" (p. 93).

The mid-1990s saw regulatory changes in children's television programming. The FCC required television broadcasters to air three hours of "educational and informational" children's core programming each day. Barner (1999) examined gender content in this programming, in order to determine if positive or negative stereotypes were being reinforced. The sample consisted of three weeks of children's core programming from the five broadcast networks (ABC, CBS, Fox, NBC, and WB). Results showed that "Male characters were significantly more likely to exhibit activity, construction, dominance, aggression, and attention seeking behaviors. Female characters were significantly more likely to exhibit deference, dependence, and nurturance" (p. 559). The researcher author concluded that results indicated that federally mandated programming portrays traditional sex-role stereotypes with the potential to reinforce a child's expectations about roles in society.

Have changes in gender and race characteristics of sports announcers resulted in a reduction of negative stereotypes in sports coverage? Eastman and Billings (2001) examined televised college basketball to answer this question. The researchers advanced a number of hypotheses, including proposed differences in "descriptive commentary" between men's and women's basketball coverage and gendered stereotyping of "team" attributions for women's versus "individual" characteristics of men's basketball (p. 188). Televised college games were videotaped during spring 1999 on major over-the-air as well as cable sports networks. Results showed that announcers did not " 'talk less' about women players than they do about men players" (p. 191). "When the comments were analyzed separately for men's games and women's games . . . women's games contained 13 comments about player's backgrounds—their fathers, coaches, and families" (p. 195). As part of their conclusions, the authors noted that, on par, announcers treated female basketball players the same as their male counterparts even if such treatment was often stereotypic, particularly when race enters into the equation.

Moon and Chan (2002) examined television advertisements in Hong Kong and Korea in order to perform a cross-cultural comparison of gender stereotypes. The authors cited census data and cultural indicators to demonstrate cultural differences between Hong Kong and Korea. They predicted more feminine portrayals in Korean television advertisements, more depictions of work situations in Hong Kong advertisements, and greater sex-role differences in Hong Kong compared to Korea (p. 106). The sample included 147 Hong Kong and 198 Korean television advertisements. Results showed predominant use of male voiceovers in production, but significantly more female voiceovers for Korean advertisements (p. 111). There were no significant differences in terms of sex of central characters (p. 112). However, "Korean male characters were more likely to be inactive" (p. 114). The authors concluded that results were in contrast to expectations. Hong Kong television advertising, anticipated to reflect more masculine traits, "did not exhibit less rela-

■ ■ ■ ■ ■

BOX 9.1

NOW 2002 FEMINIST PRIMETIME REPORT

The National Organization for Women started their *Watch Out, Listen Up!* content analyses of prime-time portrayals on ABC, CBS, Fox, NBC, UPN, and WB in 1999. Results from their third and most recent study showed the six broadcast networks portrayed 134 more men than women in primary television roles, with twice as many programs representing a male-centric view of the world compared to those from a female-centric perspective. Compared to previous years' studies, the current analysis discovered a widening gap between "shows that portray female characters with dignity and respect . . . and programs that sexually exploit women." Situation comedies were the biggest culprits, often depicting women who were "beautiful, thin and younger than their male counterparts . . . and willing to use their sexuality for laughs and titillation." The report criticized television's preoccupation with younger adult viewers aged 18 to 34 and programming emphasizing a perspective "lost in an adolescent boy's fantasyland" (National Organization for Women Foundation, 2003).

tionship roles and more sex-role differences between male and female characters" (p. 114). Box 9.1 summarizes a report provided by the National Organization for Women about portrayal of women in prime-time television.

EXPERIMENTS

Gender constancy is an important part of a child's development—the process of acquiring hard and fast concepts about who they are in terms of gender. Once developed, gender constancy helps frame information about gender and gender-based behaviors. Luecke-Aleska, Anderson, Collins, and Schmitt (1995) also argued that gender constancy influences what children remember from watching television. This study utilized two experiments. The first examined differences between gender-constant and pregender-constant children, hypothesizing that the former would attend more to same-sex characters. A total of 99 5-year-old children were studied. Results indicated support for the hypothesis for boys but not for girls. Boys attended to "adult human characters," "child human characters," and "adult non-human characters" (p. 776). The second study "tested the hypothesis that, compared with gender preconstant children, gender constant children view programs that are more oriented to adult audiences" (p. 777). This time, 313 5-year-old children were studied. Results indicated the hypothesis "that gender constant children would shift their viewing to adult programming was . . . supported only for boys" (p. 778), in part explained by increased viewing of sports. The researchers concluded that results suggest some support for the relationship between gender constancy and television-viewing behaviors.

Collins-Standley, Gan, Yu, and Zillman (1996) cited the abundance of research literature on childhood gender socialization, including research on the interplay between parental influences, marketing influences, and children's toys. They focused on the role children's books play in such gender socialization and hypothesized, based on cognitive stage theories, that younger children (2 years old) would not exhibit "gender-specific preferences" compared to older children. They studied 72 preschool children. Results showed that 2-year-olds did not choose books as a function of gender, but "for the 3- and 4-year olds, gender was significantly differentiated" (p. 291). The authors concluded that findings were more or less as expected, with female children showing increasing interest in romance themes and declining interest in violence, and with boys exhibiting the opposite traits.

How does gender role socialization help filter cognitive perceptions of negative female stereotypes? Lafky, Duffy, Steinmaus, and Berkowitz (1996) tested high school student perceptions of magazine advertisements to answer this question. They hypothesized that short-term exposure to stereotyped messages could affect perceptions of sex and gender roles. They also argued that gender would inform different cognitive processing of advertised depictions of roles (p. 382). The study's participants were 125 high school students in a Midwest community. Results indicated that those students exposed to stereotypic images "tended to agree somewhat more with the stereotypical statements in reference to the woman" (p. 383). The researchers argued that results showed "there are some conditions in which exposure to stereotypical images leads to the reinforcement of gender role stereotypes for both males and females, and other conditions in which the effects are gender specific" (p. 385).

Slater, Rouiner, Domenech-Rodriguez, & Beauvais, et al. (1997) argued that little research has examined the relationships between adolescent gender differences and perceptions of television beer advertisements placed in sports and entertainment programming. The researchers based their approach on **persuasion theory,** suggesting that advertising messages have less effect in conditions where audiences use counter arguments to filter or negative message impact. They hypothesized that female adolescents, by virtue of drinking fewer alcohol-related products, would be less responsive to beer advertisements compared to their male counterparts. They also hypothesized that adolescent males would be more responsive to advertisements placed in sports programming compared to females. Participants were 244 junior and senior high students from a western U.S. city. Partial support was found for the hypothesis that female adolescents would respond less positively to beer advertising. In addition, "Males responded more positively than did females to the beer ads with sports content" (p. 114) and "Female adolescents responded more negatively to ads during sports" (p. 114).

How do audiences respond to and enjoy gendered television portrayals? Oliver and Green (2001) "examined gender differences in reactions to media associated with gender stereotyped emotional responses" and "how gender differences in enjoyment of media entertainment may reflect perceptions of media offerings as more or less appealing to one gender" (p. 71). A total of 176 children aged 3 to 9 years were tested. Results showed for scenes depicting sad themes that females did not report greater enjoyment than males. Age was not a predictor of gender differences (p. 76). However, more female children reported feeling sadness, an experience increasing with age (p. 77). Males did not report greater enjoyment than females when watching action adventure segments as predicted, nor did they report greater feelings of fear. The researchers noted that differences revealed do not speak to why such perceptions exist on the part of female and male children.

The construct of **stereotype threat** is when "the risk of being personally reduced to a negative stereotype can elicit a disruptive state among stigmatized individuals that undermines performance and aspirations" (Davies, Spencer, Quinn, & Gerdhardstein, 2002, p. 1616). The researchers used this construct in a series of experiences designed to expose audiences to stereotypic messages. A total of 83 Canadian undergraduates participated in the study. The researchers hypothesized that exposure to stereotypic television advertisements would prime stereotypes in males and females. Further, female test subjects were expected to perform more poorly on math tests consequent to viewing stereotypic advertisements. Results showed that "women and men performed equally well . . . on the difficult math test following exposure to the counterstereotypic ads. . . . Further simple-effect tests confirmed that women in the stereotypic condition underperformed on the math test" (p. 1620). The authors concluded that stereotype threat occurs when women engage "situational predicaments" where such stereotypes are elicited (p. 1626).

SURVEYS

Conventional logic dictates that advertisers would use characters and models that resonated with target audience values. Ford, LaTour, and Lundstrom (1991) examined women's perceptions of advertising portrayals. Respondents were 296 "upscale" women. Results showed women perceived advertisements portrayed women as dependent on men, as sex objects, and belonging in the home. Respondents also indicated more increasing sensitivity to negative stereotypes they find offensive. These factors contributed from 2 to 12 percent to perceptions about negative female stereotypes. Ford and LaTour (1993) argued that broad-based advertising campaigns targeting all women as a homogeneous consumer market run the risk of offending groups of women and that they are inefficient marketing. The researchers hypothesized that women who were members of different political groups would have different perceptions of roles portrayed in advertising (p. 45). The sample included 94 surveys from members of the League of Women Voters (LWV), and 130 from National Association of Women (NOW). Women from a large "midatlantic" metropolitan area completed an additional 150 surveys. Results showed that members of LWV and NOW were "significantly more critical of the way women are characterized in ads than the general area sample respondents" (p. 49). Members of NOW were more inclined to believe negative stereotype advertising practices were a reflection of a company's perceptions of the role of women in society compared to the other two groups. Finally, LWV and NOW members were less inclined to purchase products promoted by advertising they found offensive. The researchers concluded that different groups of women engage the advertising experience differently, suggesting that advertisers should be careful to more carefully match persuasive messages with different women's values.

What are the relationships between audience perceptions of sex-role stereotypes and media behaviors? Fung and Ma (2000) measured "gender or sex-role" stereotypes in Hong Kong, audience perceptions of gender roles on television, and the relationship between these two measures (p. 62). Sampling generated 2,020 subjects 16 years of age or older. Results showed that "Hong Kong Chinese were gender stereotypic in terms of masculine characteristics and values" (p. 67). Neither females nor males "possessed any degree of counter stereotypic tendency" (p. 67). The researchers also found "the Hong Kong public was quite weak in their awareness of the media stereotype" (p. 70).

QUALITATIVE RESEARCH

Jewkes (2002) combined **uses and gratifications theory** with sociological perspectives to show how "the mass media provide a key source of empowerment for the confined" (p. 205) in her study of media use in men's prisons. Uses and gratifications theory gained wide support as a theory of media effects beginning in the 1970s. The theory suggests that individuals have needs and wants, that they are capable of expressing what these needs are, and that media can gratify some of those needs. Jewkes examined how media are incorporated into everyday prison life as means for projecting amplified male personas (p. 208). Utilizing qualitative methods including observation in public spaces, participation in debating clubs and various group discussions, classes, researcher focus groups, and in-depth interviews with 62 prisoners, the researcher collected data from four different prisons in England (pp. 209–210). Prison administrators were also interviewed and surveys were distributed to high-level government prison officials. Results showed "patterns of family viewing are frequently replicated, whereby the content, manner and viewing context of television consumption is commonly determined by the biggest, strongest, loudest or most intimidating members of the group. . . . Media—especially personal media—are highly effective devices of social and behavioral control" (p. 222).

Goodman, Duke, and Sutherland (2002) analyzed television advertisements aired during the 2000 summer Olympics. A sample of 15 days of Olympics coverage was generated from which 31 advertisements containing Olympic athletes were analyzed. Analysis revealed, "Although most of the primary female characters were depicted as strong, skillful Warriors, one-third of the commercials sexualized the female athlete" (p. 381). While males were more often portrayed as "conquering heroes," females were "more likely to be celebrated for their athletic skills and achievements" (p. 387).

SUMMARY

Here are some of the things we can summarize from this research on sex and gender stereotyping in the media.

- Results from the majority of content analyses reported here are consistent with findings from previous decades—negative gender stereotypes, particularly for women, continue to proliferate in the mass media, particularly U.S. television and magazines.
- Similar analyses in foreign media would suggest some progress in terms of depicting gender in equitable or counter-stereotypic ways, though too few studies are included in this chapter to draw hard and fast conclusions regarding the international media scene. However, since the United States is a major exporter of media worldwide, one can infer that many of those print and electronic images reinforcing objectified and stereotypic images of women are enjoying global dissemination.
- Researchers who conduct content analyses typically stop short of suggesting that negative media stereotypes of women result in corresponding audience perceptions and behaviors. These same researchers often call for additional research to assess short- or long-term audience effects from exposure to such content.
- Results from some experiments demonstrate that social constructions of gender begin to take shape in children as young as 3 years of age and are probably well formed by the time they are 6 years old.
- Results from experiments also show that self-constructions of gender on the part of the developing child are helping to frame media experiences in terms of preferences for and selection of certain kinds of visual content.
- Survey-based studies are relatively few and typically employ samples much smaller than those used in health or related areas.
- The body of qualitative fieldwork examining gender and media is relatively new, but the studies reported here document, in depth, examples of how gender-based analysis can provide fruitful and informing insights into general media content and audiences.

Now might be a good time to provide some additional commentary about some of the methods used by researchers studying this and related topics. One problem with content analyses is the fundamental flaw in the way we often think about sampling media. Traditionally, researchers have sampled composite weeks or months of television or print media. Many of the studies reported in this chapter sampled prime-time television programming, or advertisements airing during that popular audience viewing period. Other studies have systematically sampled a genre or type of magazine, such as women's fashion magazines. A potential problem with this approach is that most audiences do not view all prime-time television programming fare, or do not read every print vehicle within the category called women's fashion magazines. Rather, we know inherently, a fact supported by research, that most people navigate television experiences as a combination of preplanned or habitual television viewing as well as those times when television programming is less important than the simple act of turning on the television receiver to pass the time or because "there is nothing else to do." Either way, there is a method to our madness in the pursuit of television content. In short, we watch certain kinds of programming on certain television channels with a rhythmic predictability. Further, because television's content is relatively limited, despite increasing numbers of channels, there is predictability in the type of **content threads** we pursue. Finally, these content threads may be predictable as a function of psychological and social variables, including gender. Marketers have long known and utilized research services that segment the U.S. consumer public into twenty or so different groups, all differentiated in terms of contextual, economic, and gendered factors. Advertising is placed on major media this way, so it only stands to reason that we should consider pursuing future content analytic studies of television and other media this way too. My personal television experience is a composite of morning, late afternoon, occasional weekday evening, and weekend programming, including news, comedies, dramas, and sports. Those are my content threads, and chances are that they are threads common to others in the television audience who match up in terms of where I live, how I live, and how I think about gender. Those programming threads should be the kinds of things we study in the future for gender images, as such information would tell us a lot about the consistent images projected to certain groups within television's larger domain. We can do the same for magazines and other media as well.

REFERENCES

Barner, M. (1999). Sex-role stereotyping in FCC-mandated children's educational television. *Journal of Broadcasting and Electronic Media, 43,* 551–564.

Browne, B. (1998). Gender stereotypes in advertising on children's television in the 1990s: A cross-national analysis. *Journal of Advertising, 27*(1), 83–96.

Calhoun, C. (Ed.). (2002). *Dictionary of the Social Sciences.* New York: Oxford University Press.

Collins-Standley, T., Gan, S., Yu, H., & Zillman, D. (1996). Choice of romantic, violent, and scary fairy-tale books by preschool girls and boys. *Child Study, 26,* 279–302.

Craig, R. (1992a). The effect of television day part on gender portrayals in television commercials: A content analysis. *Sex Roles, 26,* 197–212.

Craig, R. (1992b). Women as home caregivers: Gender portrayals in OTC drug commercials. *Journal of Drug Education, 22,* 303–312.

Davies, P., Spencer, S., Quinn, D., & Gerdhardstein, R. (2002). Consuming images: How television commercials that elicit stereotype threat can restrain women academically and professionally. *Personality and Social Psychology Bulletin, 28,* 1615–1628.

Eastman, S., & Billings, A. (2001). Biased voices of sports: Racial and gender stereotyping in college basketball announcing. *Howard Journal of Communications, 12*(4), 183–201.

Eaton, B. (1997). Prime-time stereotyping on the new television networks. *Journalism and Mass Communication Quarterly, 74,* 859–872.

Ford, J., & LaTour, M. (1993). Differing reactions to female role portrayals in advertising. *Journal of Advertising Research, 33*(5), 43–52.

Ford, J., LaTour, M., & Lundstrom, W. (1991). Contemporary women's evaluation of female role portrayals in advertising. *Journal of Consumer Marketing, 8*(1), 15–28.

Fung, A., & Ma, E. (2000). Formal vs. informal use of television and sex-role stereotyping in Hong Kong. *Sex Roles, 42,* 57–81.

Goodman, J., Duke, L., & Sutherland, J. (2002). Olympic athletes and heroism in advertising: Gendered concepts of valor? *Journalism and Mass Communication Quarterly, 79,* 374–393.

Hall, C., & Crum, M. (1994). Women and "body-sisms" in television beer commercials. *Sex Roles,31,* 329–337.

Jewkes, Y. (2002). The use of media in constructing identities in the masculine environment of men's prisons. *European Journal of Communication, 17,* 205–225.

Kuper, A., & Kuper, J. (Eds.). (1996). *The Social Science Encyclopedia* (2nd ed.). London: Routledge.

Lafky, S., Duffy, M., Steinmaus, M., & Berkowitz, D. (1996). Looking through gendered lenses: Female stereotyping in advertisements and gender role expectations. *Journalism and Mass Communication Quarterly, 73,* 379–388.

Luecke-Aleska, D., Anderson, D., Collins, P., & Schmitt, K. (1995). Gender constancy and television viewing. *Developmental Psychology, 31,* 773–780.

Moon, Y., & Chan, K. (2002). Gender portrayal in Hong Kong and Korean children's TV commercials: A cross-cultural comparison. *Asian Journal of Communication, 12*(2), 100–119.

National Organization for Women Foundation (2003). *Watch out, listen up! 2002 feminist primetime report.* Retrieved December 8, 2003, from http://www.nowfoundation.org/issues/communications/watchout3/index.html.

Oliver, M., & Green, S. (2001). Development of gender differences in children's responses to animated entertainment. *Sex Roles, 45,* 67–88.

Signorielli, N. (1990). Children, television, and gender roles. *Journal of Adolescent Health Care, 11,* 50–58.

Slater, M., Rouner, D., Domenech-Rodriguez, M., Beauvais, F., Murphy, K., & Van Leuven, J. (1997). Adolescent responses to TV beer ads and sports content/context: Gender and ethnic differences. *Journalism and Mass Communication Quarterly, 74,* 108–122.

Thompson, T., & Zerbinos, E. (1995). Gender roles in animated cartoons: Has the picture changed in 20 years? *Sex Roles, 32,* 651–673.

ACTIVITIES

1. Secure permissions to observe preschool children at a daycare or other childcare facility. Your purpose in doing this research is to observe and record children at play, in an attempt to observe gender-related behaviors and any links to media exposure. Upon gaining permissions and access, try to position yourself close enough to see and hear child behaviors but situated so as to be an unobtrusive observer. Be sure to bring a pad or notebook with you, because capturing verbatim child utterances as well as jotting down any descriptions of physical behavior is your goal. Observe groups of children at play. Be patient, since sometimes you will have to make repeated visits to one or more childcare facilities in order to see relevant behaviors. After a period of time you should have notes containing verbal utterances as well as recorded nonverbal and physical behaviors. Consult with one or more of the childcare providers to ask them questions about the behaviors you observed. These "experts" can often be very helpful in explaining and fleshing out things you have observed. Then organize all of your notes in order to answer the following questions. To what extent, if any, did you observe gender or sex-role behaviors on the part of children? Were any of these behaviors linked to the child's media experience (e.g., did the child mimic the behavior of favorite television

characters, or did children use lines of dialogue from animated cartoons as part of everyday interactions). What do your observations tell you about children, gender, and mass media?

2. Much of the research reviewed in this chapter is concerned with major mass media such as television and magazines. Notably missing from this current body of research are studies of children's or young adult interactive video games. Perhaps you have played these games or own some of these games. Or perhaps you know someone who regularly plays these interactive video games. Either way, your task is to perform a rudimentary content analysis on one of these interactive games. If you're skilled at such gaming, you can conduct the research on your own. If you have little or no experience, then you will need to acquire an "expert" who can sit with you as you explore the game's content. Your task is to analyze the interactive video game for its treatment of gender issues. Specifically, you want to compare the number of times that female and male characters are portrayed, the roles they occupy in such portrayals, and the presence of traditional or counter-stereotypic depictions. Choose different games when more than one of you is doing this research. Compare your results. What can you infer, given your basic research, about gender portrayals in interactive video games?

3. Visit a fairly extensive magazine rack at your local bookstore, grocery store, or related place of business. For this activity, you want to have access to a large assortment of magazines catering to different groups and lifestyles. Note how many different groups of magazines there are. For example, you should see men's fashions, computers, women's sports, brides, cycling, and so on. List every different magazine group, then perform analysis on each and every group. Does the group of magazines exhibit gender-specific or gender-neutral tendencies? For example, the group of magazines you might call "women's fashions" would be coded gender-specific. A group such as "computers and computing" would probably be coded as gender-neutral. Finally, for each group you coded as gender-specific, try to determine if the magazines in that group reinforce negative gender or sex-role stereotypes. Finally, answer the following questions. How many different magazine groups did you classify? How many of these groups were gender-specific versus gender-neutral? Were there any obvious trends for gender-specific magazine groups or for gender-neutral groups? Of those groups you coded gender-specific, how many reinforced negative gender or sex-role stereotypes? How many reinforced counter-stereotypic values? What do these results tell you about the role magazines may play in promoting values relative to sex roles or gender?

QUESTIONS

1. Content analyses of U.S. television show that women are often negatively portrayed in terms of sex-role or gender stereotypes. Despite increasing channel technologies and programming diversity, the primary target audience for television remains females 18–49 years of age. In light of such demographics, why do you think the televising industry continues to portray women as they do?

2. To what extent do you think that your own views toward women and men have been shaped in some way by your experiences with the mass media? To what

extent do you think that the views of others concerning sex-role and gender stereotypes have been shaped by the mass media?

3. Research reviewed in this chapter shows that mass media images continue to emphasize negative female stereotypes, including themes emphasizing physical beauty and women as sex objects. Do you think that these images cause negative stereotypes on the part of audiences? Why? Or, do you think that the mass media simply reflect negative sex-role stereotypes in society? Why?

ADDITIONAL READINGS

Artz, N., Munger, J., & Purdy, W. (1999). Gender issues in advertising language. *Women and Language, 22*(2), 20–26.

Furnham, A., & Farragher, E. (2000). A cross-cultural content analysis of sex-role stereotyping in television advertisements: A comparison between Great Britain and New Zealand. *Journal of Broadcasting and Electronic Media, 44,* 415–436.

Pickering, M. (1995). The politics and psychology of stereotyping. *Media Culture and Society, 17,* 691–700.

Johnson, F., & Young, K. (2002). Gendered voices in children's television advertising. *Critical Studies in Media Communication, 19,* 461–480.

Lauzen, M., & Dozier, D. (2002). Equal time in prime time? Scheduling favoritism and gender on the broadcast networks. *Journal of Broadcasting and Electronic Media, 46,* 137–153.

CHAPTER TEN

TELEVISION SEX/SEXUALITY AND PORNOGRAPHY

This chapter explores two related topics: television sex/sexuality and pornography. The first section reviews recent literature examining television portrayals of sex and sexuality as well as studies examining audience perceptions of and reactions to such portrayals. The second part of this chapter focuses on pornography.

Sexuality is "The patterning of human sexual responses . . . learnt through symbolically mediated experience in particular groups" (Gould & Kolb, 1964, p. 637). In many cultures, the mass media come to represent a potential source of models for such patterns of human response and, as you will soon find, some researchers argue a powerful influence on human sexuality. Much of the research summarized in this chapter examines television content, children and adolescents, and relationships between exposure to such content and sex and gender socialization. Chapin (2000) provides a useful review of cognitive developmental approaches to the study of mass media and sexuality, and Brown (2000) discusses the relationship between adolescents and sexual development.

Those few among you old enough to remember television's first 25 years recall a sexually sanitized landscape where only subtle innuendos cleared broadcast network censors. In the late 1970s, in part as a response to concerns about portrayals depicting gratuitous violence, the broadcast television networks at the time (ABC, CBS, and NBC) embarked on a strategy of titillation with programming promoting physically prominent and scantily clad female stereotypes. More of you are very familiar with television's more recent landscape. The advent of alternative delivery systems for video delivery into homes, including videocassette recorder/players, cable television, and then satellite systems of video transmission provided competitive and expanded programming venues we now enjoy, or endure. These now well-established systems of video delivery forever established U.S. television as a prominent source for the depiction of sex themes and sexual behaviors. Even the traditionally conservative broadcast network channels air regular dramatic and comedic series promoting a range of sexual preferences and behaviors.

What were these images of sex and sexuality on television in previous decades? What are some of those images in more recent television? Does the television industry use sex and sexuality as a way to promote audience viewing? If so, how and when do they do this? Does television contribute to sex socialization on the part of younger audiences and if so how? These are among the questions directing recent research in this area. Those among you who may be interested in studies beyond television should consult Garner, Sterk, and Adams (1998). Chapter 9, "Sex and Gender Stereotyping," is a useful companion to the research presented here. A substantial area of research in this area focuses on music videos. Those studies warrant their own chapter and will be systematically reviewed and summarized in Chapter 12, "Music Videos." What follows are content analyses, experiments, surveys, and qualitative studies examining television sex and sexuality.

TELEVISION SEX AND SEXUALITY

Content Analyses

What characterized sex portrayals on prime-time television between the late 1970s and late 1980s? Sapolsky and Tabarlet (1991) compared prime-time network television portrayals over a ten-year span. Results showed that "the frequencies of noncriminal sex acts, sexual language, and verbal innuendo remained unchanged" (p. 509). Criminal sex acts and suggestive displays declined, but sexual touching increased (p. 509). The researchers argued that television networks offered a steady diet of sex-related behaviors and innuendo without corresponding messages regarding the "consequences of sexual behavior" (p. 513). In related work, Lowry and Shidler (1993) tested the widely held belief that mainstream U.S. television had increased sex-related portrayals during late 1980s and early 1990s. One composite week of programming drawn from a four-week period in fall 1991 was collected from ABC, CBS, Fox, and NBC television networks, resulting a total of 76 hours (pp. 630–631). Results showed "the overall amount of sex on prime time network TV programs decreased somewhat from fall 1987 to fall 1991" (p. 634). Within overall findings, the amount of "physical suggestiveness" had declined while the amount of "intercourse-related behaviors" had increased (p. 634). Additional analyses suggested that networks seldom addressed "the consequences of sexual behavior" including sexually transmitted diseases and "that intercourse is primarily for unmarried partners" (p. 635).

The television networks are often accused of "hypoing the ratings" during sweeps weeks, the time when Nielsen ratings are generated based on how many viewers tune into a particular program. One way that the networks are accused of attempting to inflate the number of television viewers is through their use of increased levels of sex-related programming themes during sweeps weeks. Shidler and Lowry (1995) videotaped a composite week of U.S. television network programming during February 1992 sweeps for ABC, Fox, and NBC. CBS was airing Olympic coverage during this time, so part of the study examined counter-programming strategies on the part of the other three networks in response to CBS sporting venues. Results showed no "significant . . . overall change in the hourly rate of sexual behaviors during the sweeps period" (p. 151). Hourly rates actually dropped by half for ABC compared to nonsweeps periods, while Fox depictions nearly doubled for the same time. No relationships were found between each network's amount of sexual portrayals and earned audience ratings (p. 152–153).

Davie and Lee (1995) examined the extent to which competing local television stations duplicate or differ in terms of sex-related news stories. The researchers sampled 1 medium, large, and top-ten television market in Texas (p. 130). Two weeks of late evening news broadcasts from nine different network affiliate stations were videotaped during fall and winter 1988. Results indicated that "the ratio of duplicated to unique stories was highest in the categories of fires-accidents-disasters, government-politics, crimes-courts, and education." (p. 135). Sex "coverage was duplicated [the same story by different stations] 70% of the time, suggesting that TV editors tend to select the same sensational stories" (p. 135).

Is sex a prevalent theme in daytime television talk shows as critics claim? Greenberg, Sherry, Busselle, Hnilo and Smith (1997) noted the importance of this topic given research demonstrating that children are a common part of audiences for such programming. Random samples of talk shows were videotaped during summer 1995 resulting in ten hours of programming for each of 11 shows (p. 414). Results showed that female guests outnumber male guests two to one, and guests aged 20 to 29 years of age outnumbered all other age groups. Fifty-one percent of all guests were in "family networks" (p. 416). Family issues were the dominant topic in 48 percent of talk shows analyzed, marriage and dating 37 percent, and sexual activity 36 percent of all shows analyzed (p. 418). In terms of how topics are treated, the authors noted that audiences encounter "interpersonal and dating problems and often with sex as a component of those problems. At the same time, relational partners were not very open in expressing their feelings toward each other" (p. 423).

Experiments and Surveys

To what extent does television help inform adolescent perceptions about sex? Ward (2002) studied television's role in sex socialization with an experiment. Participants were 269 U.S. undergraduate students. Visual stimuli included 18 two- to five-minute segments of *Friends, Seinfeld,* and *Ally McBeal.* Results showed college-aged women who viewed more hours of prime-time and music video programming and who identified with popular female television characters were more likely to believe that "females are sex objects, males are sex-driven, and dating is a game" (p. 8). The factors contributed between 2.5 and 10 percent to those beliefs. For college-aged men, "the more hours of music videos men watched, the more strongly they endorsed each of the gender and sexual stereotypes" (p. 9). Music videos contributed between 5 and 14 percent to those stereotypic beliefs.

To what extent does prior beliefs about sexuality influence interest in decisions to pursue sexually oriented media content? Bogaert (2001) used survey methods in an attempt to measure relationships between sexual preferences and interests in certain "*types* of sexual media" (p. 30). Respondents were 160 Canadian male undergraduate students (p. 33). Results showed a male with "a high self-report arousal to [sexually violent] . . . films, is higher in antisocial tendencies . . . is lower in IQ . . . and has a high interest in sexual variation" (p. 48). These factors contributed 50 percent to attraction to sexually violent content.

Qualitative Research

What message about "nonconforming genders and sexualities" does one gain from viewing a steady diet of daytime talk shows? Gamson (1998) examined this question through a combination of interviews with talk show producers and guests, content analyses of talk show transcripts and videos, and focus group interviews with heterosexual talk show viewers. Data in the form of interview transcripts were used to support three central findings. The first was that talk show portrayals contribute to a "class division" between nonconforming sexual groups, amplifying existing social tensions between the effort to maintain unique identities and conformance to dominant sexual patterns. The second finding was that game shows producers feature guests who display "rowdy outrageousness" which only serve to increase "animosities" within nonconforming populations. Finally, the researcher argued that prominence of sexually lesbian, gay, bisexual, and transgender guests on talk shows heightens social tension with heterosexuals (pp. 13–14).

Durham (1999) examined how adolescent girls negotiate sexuality within peer groups, and how gender identity influences mass media use. In addition to peer groups, the researcher examined the roles played by race and class. Methods of data collection included participant observation and in-depth interviewing. Results showed "peer context was one in which emergent gender identity was consolidated via constant reference to acceptable sociocultural standards of femininity and sexuality" (p. 210). Moreover, the researcher found "race and class were differentiators of girls' socialization and concomitant media use" (p. 211). She also found Caucasian upper-middle-class females in the rural-suburban setting more responsive to messages in "advertising-driven media" (p. 211).

Summary

What can we summarize from this recent literature?

- Content analyses support the contention that sex and sexuality continue to be prominent themes in the television landscape and often emphasize youthful partners, sex outside of the traditional institution of marriage, and an apparent disregard for responsible sex relations in an era of health-related concerns regarding sexually transmitted diseases.
- The majority of content analyses reported in this chapter examined an aspect of prime-time television fare, at a time when multichannel opportunities, remote control technologies, and digital programming guides provide more and more opportunities for personal navigation of television programming.
- The one experiment reported in this chapter demonstrated short-term effects between higher levels of exposure to prominent sexual themes in television

■ ■ ■ ■ ■

BOX 10.1

SEXUALLY ORIENTED TELEVISION MAY BE COUNTERPRODUCTIVE

The Parents Television Council (PTC) is a nonpartisan group established in 1995 whose mission is to promote responsible television. Their website (www.parentstv.org) provides a storehouse of information about the group's activities, news about television policies and regulations, and educational resources for parents and others. The PTC cited two recent studies suggesting that sexually oriented content in television programming may be having an effect other than that intended. In the first study, they reported how a poll of British citizens showed that 85 percent did not feel that "raunchy content" would make them watch more television. In the same study, 90 percent of all women polled stated that sexual content "did not attract them to a program." In the second study, the PTC cited a journal article from the field of psychology showing a negative relationship between exposure to sexual content and the ability for television viewers to remember advertising content. The PTC summarized these studies as pointing to the potential for sexually oriented television content to be "counterproductive for the network and advertiser alike" (Parents Television Council, 2002).

and a tendency to adopt television's values regarding sexual relations as one's own. The amount such exposure contributes to these values is very low.

■ There is an apparent and consistent pattern of documenting television's contribution to sex socialization, though this influence is small and based on small research samples.

Future research in this area would do well to begin documenting the next step based on preliminary findings. If, as present research suggests, there is a small but significant relationship between exposure to sexually oriented television programming and one's own sexual values, then future research should begin to examine *how* such processes happen. Research summarized in this section of the chapter begins to shed some light on this process, and perhaps yet unexplored factors may be useful predictors of how and why some audiences engage television sex and sexuality and not others. Social alienation, race, ethnicity, and class would all appear to play important roles in determining the extent to which individuals take up and engage television's sexual imagery and should be systematically studied in future research (see Box 10.1).

PORNOGRAPHY

This section of the chapter reports recent research on sexually explicit or pornographic media content. Historically, even the U.S. Supreme Court has deferred attempts to operationally define what is meant by **pornography.** Leong (1991) provided a useful discussion on the topic, and generated a working definition useful for our purposes here. "Pornography is first and foremost mass-produced representations of sexuality which consumers use as fantasy material for sexual arousal. It is not sex, but a medium that may assume various forms: words, still photographs, motion pictures or sound" (p. 94). Mass communication theory and research examining sexually explicit media and potential audience effects is a long-established venue for study. Readers are encouraged to read some of the earlier and important research conducted in this area, including Zillmann and Bryant's (1982) study of pornography and audience desensitization. Donnerstein, Linz, and Penrod (1987) summarize previous research and discuss policy implications. This section does not include reviews of literature examining Internet pornography, though a growing body of literature exists for interested readers.

What are the prevailing subjects and themes in sexually explicit videos and films? How are women portrayed in these media? Are sex and violence thematically linked in such media? Are audience attitudes toward self and others affected after exposure to such media? Do males and females use sexually explicit media in different ways? If so, how do they use these media? Do audiences who watch sexually explicit media have different opinions regarding rape? Do they have different opinions about women's rights? Does using sexually explicit media result in higher levels of sexual permissiveness? These are among the many questions asked by researchers whose work is reported and summarized in this section of the chapter. We begin by reviewing recent content analyses, experiments, and survey studies.

Content Analyses

Yang and Linz (1990) pointed to the increased availability of premium cable channels and video playback technologies resulting in increased availability of both R- and X-rated films. The purpose of their content analysis was to assess "sexual, violent, and sexually violent behaviors in R-, X-, and XXX-rated videotapes" to see if those videos with more "restrictive" ratings contained more violence (p. 31). Their sample population included 1,635 video listings from two rental guides, from which they randomly selected 30 videos each from R, X, and XXX categories. Results showed sexual behaviors were found in equal proportions across X- and XXX-rated videos. Violence was "most prevalent" in R-rated videos. Sexually violent behavior was "infrequent in all categories" (p. 34).

What were the roles portrayed by women and men in "sexually explicit" German films during the late 1970s through the late 1980s? Brosius, Weaver, and Staab (1993) asked this and other questions in their content analysis of fifty randomly chosen pornographic videos of which 65 percent were estimated to have originated from the United States (p. 163). Results showed an average of 2.04 "individual women" appeared in each film compared to 1.76 males. A majority of actors were Caucasian (94 percent) with some indication that more African American and Asian actors appeared in latter years of the sample. Female actors spoke almost twice as often as males. More than one-half of all scenes depicted heterosexual couples. More than one-third of all sexual scenes depicted casual acquaintances or working colleagues and nearly one-third of all scenes depicted sex acts between strangers (p. 165). "[P]leasure emerged as the predominant reason for sexual behavior in more than 77% of the sexual scenes" (p. 166). The researchers found that coitus was depicted in 81 percent of all scenes including one female and male. In addition "fellatio (54%), cunnilingus (40%), fondling of female genitalia . . . (40%), and fondling of male genitalia . . . (22%) were also commonly portrayed sexual behaviors" (p. 167). The researchers concluded that women "were, as a group, portrayed as promiscuous sexual creatures who were subordinate and subservient to men" (p. 168).

Monk-Turner and Purcell (1999) examined the extent to which "extreme violence" is common fare in "videocassette pornography" (pp. 59–60). They predicted most "vignettes" would contain "sexual violence or degrading/dehumanizing theme material" (pp. 60–61). The researchers sampled 40 videos from a pool of over 3,000 X- or XXX-rated videos. Results showed violent themes occurred in 17 percent of all "vignettes," hereafter referred to as scenes. Intimacy themes were evident in 29 percent of all scenes, and "casual sex between partners" predominated in 92 percent of all scenes. Race of characters appeared to be a potential predictor of violence in scenes, since "black women were the more likely targets of violent acts from both white and black men than were white women" (p. 66).

Experiments

Does exposure to sexually explicit content, particularly scenes depicting the degradation of females, result in male attitude changes toward women? Jansma, Linz, Mulac, and Imrich (1997) based their approach on **priming theory.** Research has shown that exposure to certain kinds of messages can stimulate and influence, or prime, future experiences. Most of the research in this area uses experimental methods and has typically demonstrated short-term effects. The researchers argued that "women should detect differences in their male partners' sexual interest or dominance and, depending on their partners' film exposure and sex-role orientation, feel degraded during subsequent interaction" (p. 6). A total of 142 U.S. male and female undergraduate students participated in the study. Results showed that "men who viewed the sexual films perceived their female partners to be less sexually interested in them than . . . men who viewed a non-sexual film" (p. 13). However, the researchers concluded that results did not support the argument that male exposure to sexually explicit or sexually explicit and degrading filmic content contributed to negative perceptions of female intellectual ability or sexuality.

The **elaboration likelihood model** of perception suggests that there are both direct and peripheral routes to cognitive processing of messages, including messages designed to persuade. Direct routes are those where you and I attend fully to the incoming message and draw from previous experiences to embrace or reject the persuasion. Peripheral routes are those where you and I pay less attention to the message, resulting in less elaboration and counter-argument. Some researchers have examined how audiences attend to different types of media via direct or peripheral routes. Bauserman (1998) argued: (1) sexist and sexually aggressive scenes would "increase attitudes and beliefs accepting of inequality and male dominance"; (2) "only . . . sexually aggressive scenes would increase attitudes and beliefs accepting of rape myths"; and (3) subjects would favor egalitarian sexual portrayals (p. 245). Participants in the study included 122 U.S. undergraduate male students. Results showed that "there was minimal evidence for different attitudinal effects," (perceived as soliciting direct or peripheral routes to attitude change; p. 250).

Surveys

Perse (1994) explored two schools of thought regarding sexually explicit materials. One school maintains that erotica and pornography provide sex education, enhance sexual experiences, and evidence that such material does harm has yet to be conclusively demonstrated via research evidence. A second school of thought anchored in **feminist theory** advances the notion that sexually explicit media portray women as sex objects and in demeaning roles—themes consequently embraced by consumers of such media. Perse generated a series of research questions and one hypothesis designed to assess audience motives for using sexually explicit media and any relationships between exposure and negative perceptions of women, including acceptance of rape myths (pp. 491–494). Participants were 569 U.S. undergraduate students at a "midsized eastern university" (pp. 495–498). Results showed "males were more likely to report using erotica for Sexual Release" and "Substitution . . . than females" (pp. 499–500). Gender, age, and feelings of hostility toward women helped to predict 49.1 percent of erotic media use. These same factors helped contribute 37.8 percent to the acceptance of rape myths. The researcher concluded results supported both perspectives concerning sexually explicit media content.

The **third-person effect** is when audiences believe that mass media have greater effect on others than themselves. How does the third-person effect factor into perceptions of and censorship of pornography? Gunther (1995) used survey methods to assess audience perceptions of pornography and to see if those perceptions were related to "support for pornography restrictions" (p. 30). Participants were 648 U.S. citizens aged 18 years or older who participated in telephone surveys (p. 31). Results showed that 61 percent of all respondents believed "others to be more negatively influenced by X-rated material than themselves" (p. 33). The more one believed in third-person effects, the more one also believed in pornography censorship.

Davies (1997) examined statistical relationships between males' viewing of sexually explicit videos and "attitudes toward feminism and rape." Unique in the researcher's approach was study of men "who rented . . . videos of their own choosing" (p. 131). Participants were 202 males who had rented videos during a three-week period in 1989. Results showed that "men who . . . viewed one, two, or three or more X-rated videos are not significantly different from one another in their support or opposition for the ERA" (p. 136). Further, "only 53% of those who had rented one explicit video favored a marital rape law, whereas at least 70% of those who had seen two, three, or more X-rated videos did so" (p. 135).

What, if any, are the relationships between exposure to sexually explicit media content and sexually permissive behaviors in adolescents? Lo, Neilan, Sun, and Chian (1999) studied this question using Taiwanese tenth, eleventh, and twelfth graders sampled from Taipei, Taiwan, high schools in 1996. Respondents were 1,858 students who completed a self-administered survey (p. 58). Results showed 90.9 percent of all students indicated some exposure to "pornographic media with males reporting significantly higher frequencies" (p. 63). Exposure to both print and electronic versions of pornography were positively related to sexually permissive attitudes and behaviors. These exposure variables contributed from 3.2 to 8.4 percent to such attitudes and behaviors (p. 65). Finally, males "exhibited a significantly higher level of sexually permissive attitudes than did females. . . . Grade average was also a significant predictor" (pp. 66–67). These factors contributed from 10 to 16 percent to male attitudes.

What is the relationship, if any, between sexual violence and pornography? Bergen and Bogle (2000) examined "women's experiences of sexual violence and their abusers' use of pornography" (p. 227). Rape crisis center employees administered a survey to 100 women who had contacted the center after experiencing abuse or violence (p. 230). Results showed that 28 percent of women interviewed indicated, "their abusers used pornography" (p. 230). "Approximately 40% said . . . pornography was part of the abusive incident" (p. 230). Finally, of "those whose abusers used pornography, 43% of survivors believed . . . pornography affected the nature of the abuse" (p. 231).

Still another study examined the third-person effect on Taiwanese teens, a population gaining more and more access to sexually explicit materials as a function of advances in technology and relaxing governmental policies. Lo and Paddon (2001) assessed teenager perceptions of "perceived effects on self and perceived effect on others as predictors of support for restriction of pornography" (p. 121). Respondents were 1,854 tenth through twelfth graders randomly drawn from 15 high schools in Taipei, Taiwan. Results showed both female and male students perceived sexually explicit materials to have a greater effect on others than on themselves (p. 133). Males had significantly higher levels of exposure to sexually explicit content in both electronic and print media (p. 134). In addition, those who were exposed to higher levels of both print and electronic materials perceived "less negative effects of pornography on themselves" (p. 136). Results also showed those perceiving sexually explicit media's harm to both self and others were more supportive of governmental policies and restrictions.

Sharp and Joslyn (2001) examined the extent to which people believe that pornography causes rape. They based their approach in **attribution theory,** arguing that the reasons individuals provide for why rape occurs are central to the "politics of pornography regulation" (p. 501). Results indicated that "those who had seen an

X-rated movie are significantly less likely to attribute rape effects to pornography" (p. 511). Results also indicated no change in this demonstrated relationship during the time span tested, a time of considerable social discourse regarding relationships between pornography and rape.

Summary

What can we summarize from this literature on pornographic content and audience effects?

- The target audience for such content would appear to be heterosexual males who find appeal in narrative themes reinforcing myths of casual sex and women as wanton and subservient sexual beings.
- The studies reported here are inconsistent in how they define content variables such as sex, sexual behavior, and violent sex.
- Results from experiments suggest, consistent with findings from previous studies, that exposure to sexually explicit media content desensitizes male attitudes toward females, if even on a short-term basis and perhaps via direct routes to cognitive attitude change.
- Results from survey studies represent a mixed bag. Some studies suggest little or no differences between audiences who engage or choose not to engage sexually explicit media content in terms of a range of resulting attitudes and perceptions, including perceptions of criminal acts toward women and policy restrictions on pornography. Other studies reported in the same section demonstrate linkages between consumption of such content and negative attitudes toward females, some demonstrating statistical power approaching compelling levels.

Allen, Emmers, Gebhardt, and Giery (1995) conducted a meta-analysis of 24 studies, mostly experiments, assessing relationships between exposure to pornography and "acceptance of a rape myth" (p. 18). The authors reported an "average positive correlation" but the statistical power of these relationships were very small. Allen, D'Allessio, and Brezgel (1995) conducted a similar meta-analysis of 33 experimental assessing relationships between pornography and aggressive behavior. Once again, results indicated an average positive correlation, one somewhat larger than those analyzed by Allen, Emmers, Gebhardt, and Giery (1995), but nonetheless still small. Another approach to the study of pornography and rape is to compare crime statistics relative to changes in policies and laws. Kutchinsky (1991) provided such an analysis for Denmark, Sweden, and then West Germany where pornography was legalized and readily available. The comparative study included U.S. crime statistics. Crime data were analyzed over a 20-year period between 1964 and 1984 (p. 51). Results indicated the United States was the only country where reported incidents of rape increased during the study period and may have been a function of increased levels of reporting and documenting these violent crimes (p. 51). In no cases did "rape increase more than nonsexual violent crimes" (p. 61).

Clearly, documenting relationships between exposures to sexually explicit media content and audience remains an important area for future inquiry. You no doubt recognize the myriad of problems inherent in such study. Experimental approaches using students on university campuses generate results from a volunteer pool whose motives for serving as subjects are rarely explored. Laboratory or survey situations create their own realities. Exposing subjects to sexually explicit media content under controlled conditions may or may not remove potential social stigmas associated with more personal and private consumption of such materials. Survey methods may or may not produce greater validity in responses, given the often-sensitive nature of self-administered instruments designed to assess sexual attitudes and behaviors. Ongoing efforts to overcome these methodological shortcomings and advance our understanding in this area may now be impeded. The current political reality on U.S. university and college campuses, where ethical bodies provide oversight to research on human subjects, has resulted in increasingly restrictive practices when engaging human subjects for social science research. Well-intending researchers engaging sophisticated and reliable methods have to overcome more and more bureaucratic obstacles in order to gain access to people for study. The long-term effects of such institutional policies informed by U.S. federal guidelines may well stifle efforts to increase our knowledge about the relationships between sexually explicit media content and human behavior. At the current time, our knowledge about such behavior remains inconclusive. Time may well tell whether those adopting so-called liberal perspectives wins the day, arguing that sexually explicit media serve important educational and therapeutic functions for personal and consensual sexual behavior in contrast to many embracing feminist ideologies suggesting that such depictions contribute to ongoing efforts to control, through the power of media, an objectified and subservient role for women.

REFERENCES

Allen, M., D'Alessio, D., & Brezgel, K. (1995). A meta-analysis summarizing the effects of pornography II: Aggression after exposure. *Human Communication Research, 22(2),* 258–283.

Allen, M., Emmers, T., Gebhardt, L., & Giery, M. (1995). Exposure to pornography and acceptance of rape myths. *Journal of Communication, 45(1),* 5–26.

Bauserman, R. (1998). Egalitarian, sexist, and aggressive sexual materials: Attitude effects and viewer responses. *Journal of Sex Research, 35,* 244–253.

Bergen, R., & Bogle, K. (2000). Exploring the connection between pornography and sexual violence. *Violence and Victims, 15,* 227–234.

Bogaert, A. (2001). Personality, individual differences, and preferences for the sexual media. *Archives of Sexual Behavior, 30,* 29–53.

Brosius, H., Weaver, J., & Staab, J. (1993). Exploring the social and sexual "reality" of contemporary pornography. *Journal of Sex Research, 30,* 161–170.

Brown, J. (2000). Adolescents' sexual media diets. *Journal of Adolescent Health, 27*(Suppl.), 35–40.

Chapin, J. (2000). Adolescent sex and mass media: A developmental approach. *Adolescence, 35,* 799–811.

Davie, W., & Lee, J. (1995). Sex, violence, and consonance/differentiation: An analysis of local TV news values. *Journalism and Mass Communication Quarterly, 72,* 128–138.

Davies, K. (1997). Voluntary exposure to pornography and men's attitudes toward feminism and rape. *Journal of Sex Research, 34,* 131–137.

Donnerstein, E., Linz, D., & Penrod, S. (1987). *The question of pornography: Research findings and policy implications.* New York: Macmillan.

Durham, M. (1999). Girls, media, and the negotiation of sexuality: A study of race, class and gender in adolescent peer groups. *Journalism and Mass Communication Quarterly, 76,* 193–216.

Gamson, J. (1998). Publicity traps: Television talk shows and lesbian, gay, bisexual, and transgender visibility. *Sexualities, 1,* 11–41.

Garner, A., Sterk, H., & Adams, S. (1998). Narrative analysis of sexual etiquette in teenage magazines. *Journal of Communication, 48*(4), 59–78.

Gould, J., & Kolb, W. (Eds.). (1964). *A dictionary of the social sciences.* New York: Free Press.

Greenberg, B., Sherry, J., Busselle, R., Hnilo, L., & Smith, S. (1997). Daytime television talk shows: Guests, content and interactions. *Journal of Broadcasting and Electronic Media, 41,* 412–426.

Gunther, A. (1995). Overrating the X-rating: The third-person perception and support for censorship of pornography. *Journal of Communication, 45*(1), 27–38.

Jansma, L., Linz, D., Mulac, A., & Imrich, D. (1997). Men's interactions with women after viewing sexually explicit films: Does degradation make a difference? *Communication Monographs, 64,* 1–24.

Kutchinsky, B. (1991). Pornography and rape: Theory and practice? *International Journal of Law and Psychiatry, 14,* 47–64.

Leong, W. (1991). The pornography "problem": disciplining women and young girls. *Media, Culture and Society, 13,* 91–117.

Lo, V., & Paddon, A. (2001). Third-person effect, gender differences, pornography exposure and support for restriction of pornography. *Asian Journal of Communication, 11,* 120–142.

Lo, V., Neilan, E., Sun, M., Chiang, S. (1999). Exposure of Taiwanese adolescents to pornographic media and its impact on sexual attitudes and behaviour. *Asian Journal of Communication, 9,* 50–71.

Lowry, D., & Shidler, J. (1993). Prime time TV portrayals of sex, "safe sex" and AIDS: A longitudinal analysis. *Journalism Quarterly, 70,* 628–637.

Monk-Turner, E., & Purcell, H. (1999). Sexual violence in pornography: How prevalent is it? *Gender Issues, 17*(2), 58–67.

Parents Television Council. (2002, August 12). *1. Maybe sex doesn't sell after all.* Retrieved December 8, 2003, from http://www.parentstv.org/PTC/publications/ealerts/2002/ealert081202.asp#1.

Perse, E. (1994). Uses of erotica and acceptance of rape myths. *Communication Research, 21,* 488–515.

Sapolsky, B., & Tabarlet, J. (1991). Sex in primetime television: 1979 versus 1989. *Journal of Broadcasting and Electronic Media, 35,* 505–516.

Sharp, E., & Joslyn, M. (2001). Individual and contextual effects on attributions about pornography. *Journal of Politics, 63,* 501–519.

Shidler, J., & Lowry, D. (1995). Network TV sex as a counterprogramming strategy during a sweeps period: An analysis of content and ratings. *Journalism and Mass Communication Quarterly, 72,* 147–157.

Ward, L. (2002). Does television exposure affect emerging adults' attitudes and assumptions about sexual relationships? Correlational and experimental confirmation. *Journal of Youth and Adolescence, 31,* 1–15.

Yang, N., & Linz, D. (1990). Movie ratings and the content of adult videos: The sex-violence ratio. *Journal of Commuication, 40*(2), 28–42.

Zillmann, D., & Bryant, J. (1982). Pornography, sexual callousness, and the trivialization of rape. *Journal of Communication, 32*(4), 10–21.

ACTIVITIES

1. The past decade has seen an increase in U.S. prime-time television depictions of gays and lesbians. Choose one or more of these programs to analyze. Programs no longer part of first-run network lineups may be accessible via off-network syndication on one or more cable network channels. Perform a sociocultural role analysis of the central gay or lesbian characters in one of these programs. Screen enough episodes so as to be able to answer the following questions. What is the name of the series? Describe a typical plot or situations in which central characters engage. What role(s) is/are played by central gay or lesbian characters (e.g., secretary, son, doctor, friend, no discernable role)? To what extent do you think this character's role is realistic—an accurate depiction of gays or lesbians in society? To what extent do you think the role is a negative or positive stereotype of gays or lesbians? Compare your findings to others who analyzed the same or different programs. What, collectively, do the findings suggest about television's portrayal of gays and lesbians?

2. Watch a U.S. daytime soap opera for one complete week. Note, during each episode, the number of times one or more actors refer implicitly or explicitly to sex or sexual behaviors. You may want to further break out your analysis to differentiate between verbal utterances and/or visual depictions of sex or sexual behaviors. Also note whether such references involve heterosexual or nonheterosexual behaviors with married or unmarried partners. Calculate averages for your observations at the end of one week, by dividing the total number of observations for each category by the number of episodes analyzed. What was the average number of implicit or explicit references to sex or sexual behaviors per episode? Were these verbal utterances or visual depictions? Were interactions heterosexual or nonheterosexual in nature? Compare your results to peers who might have analyzed the same or different programs. What do overall results tell you about the nature of sex as depicted in daytime soaps?

3. Content analytic findings suggest that sexually explicit videos tend to depict female sexual actors twice as often as their male counterparts and in subservient or degrading roles. Review the research literature in this chapter and in other readings and create your own operational definition for such terms as "subservient" and "degrading." Armed with these definitions, compare content analytic findings from previous analyses to the range of sexually explicit videos now in the marketplace. There is a range of methods one could use in order to conduct a sample of content for this activity. For example, you could interview employees or owners of businesses renting or selling sexually explicit videos. Or you could access one or more online Internet sites featuring such videos for sale and analyze the promotional content for a sample of videos. Video critics abound online for both general audience as well as X- or XXX-rated videos. Such critics might provide information in their reviews suitable for analyzing video content. Regardless of approach, analyze enough videos so as to be able to generalize your findings in

order to answer the following question. What characterizes the portrayal of female actors in sexually explicit videos in recent years? Do these portrayals differ in terms of depictions of subservient or degrading roles relative to findings in earlier content analyses?

QUESTIONS

1. This chapter reports recent efforts to content-analyze sex and sexuality on television. What can you summarize from these and/or other studies? To what extent do you think your summary of media content parallels contemporary society's views on sex and sexuality? To what extent does television's picture of sex and sexuality differ from your perceptions of society's sexual mores?

2. Much of the research attempting to demonstrate linkages between exposure to sexually explicit media and negative attitudes or behaviors toward members of the opposite sex accounts for very little, if any, of the variance explained between these two phenomena. Should sexually explicit materials be regulated in light of such findings? If so, how? If not, why not?

3. Where do you stand on the issue of sexually explicit media content? Do you endorse what some researchers refer to as the "liberal" view, proposing that such material actually helps to promote the public good by providing educational examples of sexual behavior or enhances sexual pleasure? Or do you adopt more of the feminist model, arguing that sexually explicit materials objectify and demean women? Your views should be supported by research literatures reported in this chapter and elsewhere.

ADDITIONAL READINGS

Allen, M., D'Allessio, D., & Emmers-Sommer, T. (1999). Reactions of criminal sexual offenders to pornography: A meta-analytic summary. In M. Roloff (Ed.), *Communication Yearbook 22* (pp. 139–169). Thousand Oaks, CA: Sage.

Battles, K., & Hilton-Morrow, W. (2002). Gay characters in conventional spaces: *Will and Grace* in the situation comedy genre. *Critical Studies in Media Communication, 19*, 87–105.

Brown, J., & Cantor, J. (2000). An agenda for research on youth and the media. *Journal of Adolescent Health, 27*(Suppl.), 2–7.

Ciasullo, A. (2001). Making her (in)visible: Cultural representations of lesbianism and lesbian body in the 1990s. *Feminist Studies, 27*, 577–608.

Davies, J. (1993). The impact of mass media upon the health of early adolescents. *Journal of Health Education, 24*(Suppl.), S28–S35.

Harris, R. (1994). The impact of sexually explicit media. In J. Bryant & D. Zillmann (Eds.), *Media effects: Advances in theory and research* (pp. 247–272). Hillsdale, NJ: Erlbaum.

Malamuth, N. (1996). Sexually explicit media, gender differences, and evolutionary theory. *Journal of Communication, 46*(3), 8–31.

CHAPTER ELEVEN

CHILDREN, TELEVISION, AND VIOLENCE

Almost everyone has an opinion about children and television violence, and most of us encounter televised depictions of some form of violence on a daily basis—whether in the form of conflict between talk show guests, an action drama, our favorite grid-iron team at play, or children's cartoons. Estimates suggest that you have seen over 200,000 acts of televised violence, including 40,000 murders, by the time you are 18 years of age. Over 1,000 studies have examined the relationship between media violence and children's aggressive behavior (National Institute on Media and the Family, 2002). Results from this research are mixed, but many studies suggest that some relationship exists between exposure to television violence and antisocial behaviors on the part of children.

What are the predominant themes and images about violence in recent television programming? Do these depictions vary across different networks and countries? Is there a difference in the way violence is portrayed in children's versus programming targeting older audiences? Do children behave differently after being exposed to television violence under experimental conditions and, if so, how and in what ways? Can children be taught to filter antisocial messages in television programming? Does where a child lives influence how they perceive violence on television? Do other factors such as gender influence such perceptions? These and related research questions are those advanced by researchers whose work is summarized in this chapter.

You may recall from introductory chapters the discussion about Professor Albert Bandura's influential "Bobo Doll" studies with children. Now may be a good time for you to review how these experiments demonstrated that children can learn and model violent behaviors (Bandura, 1965). You may also want to review the work by Professor George Gerbner and colleagues, who have studied television portrayals of violence and audience perceptions for many years (Gerbner, Gross, Morgan, & Signorielli, 1980) and have content-analyzed prime-time and Saturday morning television programs. They have also conducted large-sample surveys in order to measure relationships between this content and those among us who watch considerable amounts of television (Gerbner, Gross, Morgan, Signorielli, & Shanahan, 2002).

The National Cable Television Association (NCTA) funded the largest U.S. study of television ever in the mid-1990s. Researchers at four major U.S. universities took part in the National Television Violence Study (NTVS), results of which were published in three volumes (*National Television Violence Study*, Volume 1, 1997; *National Violence Study* 2, 1998; *National Violence Study* 3, 1998). Thousands of television programs were content-analyzed. Violence was defined as "any overt depiction of a credible threat of physical force or the actual use of such force intended to physically harm an animate being or group of beings. Violence also includes certain depictions of physically harmful consequences against an animate being or group that occurs as a result of unseen violent means" (*National Television Violence Study*, Volume 1, 1997, p. 41). Violence on television, therefore, could be one of three types: "credible threats, behavioral acts and harmful consequences" (p. 41). This definition has become the new standard for many studies of television violence completed since the 1990s, including many reported in this chapter.

You will also note that a number of studies compare children of various age levels, in keeping with our growing understanding about the qualitatively different levels of developing cognitive ability. Finally, please keep in mind that similar approaches can be found in Chapter 6, "Children and Advertising"; Chapter 7, "Television and Education"; Chapter 10, "Television Sex and Sexuality, Pornography"; and Chapter 13, "Video Games." Predictably, content analyses, experiments, and surveys have a presence in this chapter too, but qualitative work is also included. A summary of this research conducted since 1990 takes stock of what we do and do not know given this very active area of inquiry.

CONTENT ANALYSES

Eaton and Dominick (1991) studied levels of violence in "toy-linked cartoons" to those not featuring children's toys. Their sample consisted of 16 programs. Results showed that toy-linked programs "had 20% more overall antisocial acts" than non-toy-linked cartoons but the latter "were more likely to use verbal aggression" (p. 73). And what of British television? Gunter and Harrison (1997) examined children's television programming in Great Britain, part of a research study funded by the British Broadcasting Corporation (BBC) and Independent Television Commission. The sample was drawn from nine different networks or channels, and included BBC channels, other British independent and movie channels, as well as the Movie Channel (p. 145). A total of 943 children's television programs were coded over a four-week period. Results showed that 39 percent of all programs contained "at least some violence" (p. 146). Over 50 percent of all violent acts appeared in what the researcher identified as "general children's drama" and 43 percent appeared in cartoons (p. 147). Shooting, pushing, tripping, and hitting with objects accounted for slightly more than 45 percent of all types of violence portrayed, with fists, hands, and laser devices accounting for almost 30 percent of types of weapons used (p. 148). Most violent acts were bloodless (82.7 percent), and most aggressors and victims were young, white, male adults (p. 150).

Do television programs aimed at children differ in terms of types and extent of violent portrayals? Wilson, Smith, et al. (2002) used NTVS data to answer this question. Their approach was based in the rationale that younger children are a very unique television audience because of their inability to distinguish fantasy from reality. Results indicated that only 33 percent of those committing violent acts in children's programs were human, 52 percent were "anthropomorphized," and "the vast majority" were males (p. 21). Lethal violence accounted for 53 percent of children's shows (p. 21). Violent acts were highly prominent in "slapstick" and in "superhero" type programs and very prominent in "adventure/mystery" programs (p. 23). Violence constituted "nearly 30% of program time" for slapstick and super-hero venues (p. 25). The researchers found such patterns compelling in light of the younger child's inability to distinguish fantasy from reality.

Do child, teen, and adult perpetrators in television differ in terms of amount and type of violence inflicted? Wilson, Colvin, and Smith (2002) used NTVS data to study the question. Their approach was informed by theory suggesting that children may identify more closely with some television characters compared to others, particularly those characters perceived to be similar to the child in terms of motives, gender, and age. The sample consisted of a composite week of television programming featuring morning through late-night programming drawn from 23 different broadcast and cable television networks. Results indicated that 89 percent of perpetrators were adults, 7 percent were teens, and 4 percent were children. Child perpetrators committed a violent act "approximately once every 1.5 hours" (p. 45). Four out of every five perpetrators were male, and there were no differences in this ratio between children, teens, or adult depictions (p. 46). Children and teen perpetrators, compared to adult portrayals, possessed "good qualities" (p. 46). Children and teens "were significantly more likely to engage in . . . overt [violent] acts" compared to adults (p. 47). The researchers concluded that "younger perpetrators are more likely to be portrayed as attractive, are punished less often, and engage in violence that results in fewer negative consequences" (p. 53).

EXPERIMENTS

One children's television program receiving considerable attention in the 1990s was *The Mighty Morphin Power Rangers*, hereafter referred to as *TMMPR*. Boyatzis, Matillo, and Nesbitt (1995) studied the relationship between children's exposure to this program and consequent aggressive behaviors. The researchers argued that the program's "popularity and visibility" made it a particularly compelling source of behavior modeling on the part of children (p. 47). Participants were 52 5- to 11-year-old girls and boys. Results showed those children who saw *TMMPR* programming "committed significantly more aggressive actions per 2-minute interval . . . than did children in the control group" (p. 49). Boys who viewed the episode also committed significantly more acts than any other group.

Do family communication patterns filter children's interpretations of violent television programming? Krcmar (1998) studied this issue by anchoring method and approach in **individual differences theory,** where factors such as gender and age were seen to play roles in how children engage and filter television content. Family communication style was also seen to be an important filter. Results showed that gender was not a factor in determining whether children perceived portrayals of violence as justified. In contrast, "older children did perceive . . . violence as more justified" (p. 258). In addition, "Children whose families rated higher on the communication dimension perceived motivated violence as being more justified" (p. 259). This factor contributed 4 percent to the perception that violence was justified.

Does empathy toward a television cartoon character influence a child's tendencies to behave violently after being exposed to antisocial television content? Nathanson and Cantor (2000) argued that children could be taught counter-attitudinal strategies in order to block television's potential for harm. A total of 351 second through sixth graders from six Midwest schools participated in the study. Results showed that children who were asked to relate to the portrayed cartoon victim "liked the perpetrator significantly less than children in the no-mediation condition" (p. 133). Younger children who were told to relate to the victim "liked the victim significantly better than younger children in the no-mediation condition" (p. 134). Older children, regardless of treatment condition, did not differ on this factor. Results also showed that children who were asked to relate to the victim "perceived the violence inflicted . . . to be significantly less justified" (p. 134). The researchers concluded that program-mediation training works, and should be exercised, particularly for boys.

Additional research has examined the use of alternative mediation strategies designed to help children filter experiences with violent television programming. Nathanson and Yang (2003) examined whether fact-based mediation would have greater effect with younger children, while "social reality-based mediation" (p. 114) would have greater effect with older children. Participants were 103 children in a "large midwestern" U.S. city aged 5 to 12 years, spanning two cognitive developmental stages. Results showed that "Mediation statements were [statistically more] helpful to younger children because they decreased the children's positive orientations toward the program," while "Mediation questions were somewhat helpful to the older children in that they were associated with slightly less favorable orientations" (p. 122).

SURVEYS

Can exposure to television news influence perceptions of violence in one's own neighborhood? Cairns (1990) examined this relationship with children in Northern Ireland. A total of 520 children aged 8 and 11 years drawn from five different "small and rural" Irish towns participated in the study. Two towns were located in areas where political violence was above national averages, two towns were in geographic locales where violence was below average, and one town was far removed from any political violence. Results showed that "the mean level of violence reported by children for their area corresponded . . . to the rank order of the areas in terms of actual levels of violence" (p. 449). Results also showed that "the children who reported the greatest news exposure perceived significantly higher levels of violence" (p. 449). Cairns suggested that for Irish children included in the present study, watching television news "may have heightened the perception of social reality" (p. 450).

Much of the audience research on television violence examines reactions to fictional or entertainment programming. What about programming inherently imbued with violent content, such as news? Cantor and Nathanson (1996) assessed parental perceptions of children's "fright reactions" to television news. They hypothesized older children, who come to view television news as more real, would experience more "fright responses" than younger children. Participants were 285 parents of children in one northern Midwest school district with children in either kindergarten, second, fourth, or sixth grades. Results showed that 43 percent of parents provided an account of a fright response on the part of their child, with 37 percent reporting news as the agent for distress (p. 145). Kindergarten children were significantly more frightened than all other grade groups combined. Results also showed that "the younger children were more likely to have been upset by portrayals of fantastic stimuli than older children" (p. 146). The researchers also examined types of news content and fright response and found that "Violence between strangers was the most frequently cited source of children's fright reaction to news" (p. 147).

The same authors, Cantor and Nathanson (1997), interviewed 285 parents in order to measure a child's interest in violent television programming. The researchers predicted that male children would be more attracted to violent television, that age may play a role, that interest in violent television would be positively related to levels of aggression, that children restricted by parents in viewing violent television programming will show more interest in such programming, and that children who have been frightened by such programming will show greater interest in violent programming and particular narrative devices (pp. 156–158). A total of 285 parents of kindergarten, second, fourth, and sixth grade children from the northern Midwest participated. Results showed that parents of male children perceived their child to be more interested in violent television content compared to parents of females. Interest in cartoons and "live action shows" declined with a child's age, but interest in "reality shows" increased with age (p. 161). Results did not find that children from more television-restrictive households were more attracted to violent television programming. "Children's fright reactions" (p. 161) were positively related to most television programming analyzed and "children who were upset by television were more interested than other youngsters in violent shows that typically feature justice-restoration" (p. 162). The researchers concluded that the type of violence portrayal is an important factor when considering relationships between children and televised violence.

Groebel (1998) reported summary findings from a UNESCO worldwide study on media violence and children conducted between 1996 and 1997. Subjects were 12-year-old children from 23 countries who completed the same survey translated into numerous languages. Overall results included 97 percent of all children receiving "at least one TV broadcast channel" with the average somewhere between four and nine channels (p. 222). One-third of all children resided in "a high aggression environment or problematic neighborhood" and almost the same percentage believe that "most people in the world are evil" (p. 224). Where the child resided was perceived to influence perceptions of media reality and fiction. "In all cases, the high-aggression-area group [of children] reported a stronger overlap between reality and fiction than the low-aggression-area group" (p. 225). The author concluded that children, globally, are exposed to high levels of media content depicting violence as a solution for many problems.

Krcmar and Valkenburg (1999) argued that an important component in the measurement of relationships between children, television, and violence is underexplored—moral development. They tested 189 children aged 6 through 12 years of age. Results showed that "children judged justified violence as less wrong than unjustified violence," with boys finding violence more justified than girls (p. 622). The researchers also found that children judged violence in "violent fantasy programs" more justified than when depicted in "violent realistic programs" (p. 623). These two types of television programming accounted for 15 percent and 31 percent of the perception that violence was justified.

Do children from different countries differ in terms of television program preferences? Valkenburg and Janssen (1999) compared Dutch and U.S. children in order to assess the role played by cultural differences in countries with different television landscapes. Dutch television prior to 1989 was government controlled, and only since then have "commercial broadcasters" entered into the scene. Dutch television features a great deal of imported U.S. programming, including popular children's programs containing violence and sexual themes. Participants were 100 Dutch and 100 U.S. school children ages 6 to 11. Results showed that "The most important program characteristics for the entire sample were comprehensibility and action, closely followed by humor, interestingness, and innocuousness. The least weight was given to realism, violence, and romance" (p. 13). Generally, Dutch and U.S. children found these program characteristics "equally important," though U.S. children were a bit more interested in "realism" (pp. 13–14). Both Dutch and U.S. boys preferred action and violence compared to girls, who "value the comprehensibility and innocuousness of a program" (p. 15).

Increasingly rare is the opportunity to study communities before and after television becomes a household entity. Gunter, Charlton, Coles, and Panting (2000) were given such an opportunity in their two-wave study of a British colony of 6,000 persons located on an island in the South Atlantic Ocean. The purpose of their study was to assess individual television viewing habits on the part of children who experienced television for the first time. Data were collected in two stages. Stage one included teacher assessments of 47 preschool children $3\frac{1}{2}$ years of age in 1993, one and one-half years prior to the arrival of television. The second stage of data collection, completed five years later, included each child's (now 8 years old) completion of a three-day television-viewing diary. Results showed that just over half of all children in the study watched television during the second stage of study, with those watching averaging slightly over three hours of time spent with television during the three-day period of data collection. Half of such viewing time was spent watching "cartoons" (p. 75). Results also indicated that only children with preexisting antisocial tendencies were rated similarly during the second stage of assessment. Strong family and community ties among these islanders were identified as potentially key factors in social and behavioral traits among children studied.

Is television viewing as a child a later predictor of aggressive behavior as an adolescent? Anderson, Huston, Schmitt, Linebarger, and Wright (2001) reported findings from a longitudinal study using data collected in two phases from two U.S. locales. The first wave of data was collected in the 1980s when children were preschoolers. Of all original study participants, 570 agreed to telephone interviews in 1994 (pp. 11–12). Results showed female adolescents on the East Coast who viewed violent television content "had relatively high levels of aggression" (p. 85). Television violence accounted for 14.4 percent contribution to level of aggression. In addition, "for children in the top two thirds of the distribution on a measure of talking about television and using television themes in play, those who watched more violence in preschool were more aggressive as teenagers" (p. 86). These factors contributed 8.8 to 11.1 percent to level of aggression (see Box 11.1).

■ ■ ■ ■ ■

BOX 11.1

AMERICAN MEDICAL ASSOCIATION TAKES STAND ON MEDIA VIOLENCE

The American Medical Association (AMA) is the national organization for physicians in the United States (www.ama-assn.org). Their mission has been to help physicians improve the nation's health for over 150 years. Consistent with this mission, the AMA has taken an active role in educating the public about health risks in society. For example, the AMA's Commission for the Prevention of Youth Violence published *Youth and Violence* in 2000 and identified six key risk factors: alcohol and other drugs, child maltreatment, gangs, guns, violence among intimates and peers, and media. In terms of media, the report noted the average child is exposed to 25 acts of televised violence daily and over 200,000 by the age of 18. The report cited research conducted by media researchers. One study found that teenagers do not believe violence in television *causes* actual violence in real life, but these same teenagers agreed that such depictions could *promote* violence. The report summarizes additional research, noting that television violence can make audiences less sensitive to violence, can create the impression that violence can be a tool for solving problems, and that violence can be modeled. Finally, the report summarized 30 years of previous research, noting, "viewing entertainment violence can lead to increased aggressive attitudes, values, and behavior, particularly in children" (Commission for the Prevention of Youth Violence, 2000). Based on your reading thus far in this chapter, do you think that the AMA's position on children, television, and violence is consistent with what you have come to learn about what the research in this area tells us?

QUALITATIVE RESEARCH

The development of emotion is seen as an indicator of a child's developmental stage. Allerton (1995) examined the relationship between children's emotions and television. Specifically, the author sought to explore the questions "how does what children feel relate to what they see?" and "what do children *do* [emphasis in original] when they are upset by what they see on television?" (pp. 1–2). A total of 72 children from four different areas of London, England, spanning the ages of 6 to 16 years of age, participated. Open-ended-type questions were used to ask children about television programming. Results suggested that children understand the differences between various types of television, such as fictional or nonfictional forms. Results also indicated that children understood that "news reports about famine and war are more complex than a sad film and demand different methods of coping" (p. 14). Finally, the researcher found that "Appraising the same film as scary, sad or pleasurable may depend on differences in previous experiences, both with media . . . and with other life events" (p. 21).

SUMMARY

What can be distilled from this summary of recent research?

- The three-year NTVS project conducted in the mid-1990s is of great benefit for a number of reasons. For example, the NTVS definition of violent television content has found widespread adoption, thus providing increasing standardization in content analyses resulting in useful comparisons across studies.
- Among the appealing aspects of the NTVS definition is the understanding that not all verbal or physical acts between television characters are intended as "credible threats" or are designed to "physically harm" another. Prominent definitions of television violence predating the NTVS version often counted verbal or physical humor as violent incidents.
- Viewed as a whole, the content analyses presented in this chapter are consistent with findings from previous decades. Violence is a prominent feature of the television narratives in venues such as dramas, action-adventures, and cartoons.
- The predominance of violent television programming is compelling in light of our understanding that younger children aged 2 to 6 do not always possess meta-cognitive abilities when compared to older children. They do not tell time, they have shorter attention spans, they think only in real time and not in terms of past or future, and they do not distinguish between real and make believe. When one matches such cognitive ability with predominant television fare, violent act after violent act, there is potential for harm.
- Younger children with comparatively fewer cognitive filters do not always see the larger story in a cartoon or television series. Their experiences are a host

of individual actions or scenes. Therefore, when the larger story in a program is "crime doesn't pay," younger children may not understand this larger message and attend more to the outcomes of individual actions or scenes.

■ The NTVS project went a long way in documenting violent depictions, but this work reflects television programming in the mid-1990s. The television landscape has changed considerably since that time, and includes a shift on the part of the traditional broadcast networks toward lower-priced productions such as reality programming and its many derivatives. Children, along with parents or guardians, watch such programming in increasing numbers. The implied or overt violence in such programming remains woefully underexplored and represents a prime candidate for systematic content analysis.

Wood, Wong, and Chachere (1991) conducted a meta-analysis of violence studies using experimental methods and where the dependent variable was aggression "as it occurred in the free-play behavior of children or in unconstrained social interaction among adults" (p. 373). The researchers included 23 studies conducted between 1971 and 1988. Results showed that "For 16 of the study outcomes, greater aggression was apparent in the experimental (vs. control) group, whereas for 7 . . . greater aggression was obtained in the control group" (p. 374). The researchers argued that findings support the argument that "exposure to media violence increase[es] viewers' aggression" (p. 378), with "the mean effect of exposure to violent media on unconstrained aggression . . . in the small to moderate range" (p. 378). What about the experiments summarized in this chapter?

■ More recent findings from experiments reported in this chapter represent something of a similar mixed bag. Some find little or no difference between treatment and control groups when assessing either the effect of violent television content or efforts to influence the children's interpretation of antisocial programming.

We would do well to revisit briefly some of the concerns known to researchers who employ experimental methods. Can experiments do more than measure the capacity for children (as well as adults) to perform as well as they can in artificially contrived situations, no matter how solid or well reasoned the approach? Do experiments document the cognitive mechanisms for short-term effects, but fail to broach actual effects in the "real world" of everyday mass mediation? Put another way, do children attempt to understand the purpose behind most experimental designs and try as hard as they can to perform in ways they think will help the researcher? Even more specific, do most children understand that violence hurts and that kick boxing in a socially sanctioned experimental setting is okay, but behaving the same way in public is inappropriate behavior? Finally, one should remember that even well-designed experiments such as many of those reported here are only able to demonstrate short-term effects in carefully controlled settings.

- Male children appear to sanction and enjoy violent television programming more than females.
- A child's geographic locale appears to inform the context for interpreting television messages, including programming deemed violent.
- Most children seem to understand that violence is wrong, and engage programming they both understand and find entertaining.
- Most statistical analyses used in survey-type studies do not claim to document the direction of causality between these statistically significant relationships. Therefore, one is again saddled with the problem of trying to figure out if television violence results in aggressive behaviors, or if children already predisposed to violence are simply attracted to such programming.
- The statistical relationships demonstrated in survey research on children and violence in television are characteristically small, and typically account for only a small percentage of audience perceptions.

A potentially valuable course of action stems from those studies where children are trained in ways to recognize and filter antisocial or violent programming content. This approach is often referred to as **critical television viewing** and has included efforts over the decades to integrate television-viewing training in school curricula spanning K–12. Unfortunately, efforts to mediate television's prevailing themes through counter-attitudinal training have always met with failure because of one simple reason. A majority of families simply do not exercise or reinforce critical mediation strategies in the home setting. Results from current research examining television viewing contexts and family communication patterns are inconclusive, and may be susceptible to the same cultural dilemma. In short, children may learn ways to demystify television's cultural landscape, but parents generally are poor role models for critical television viewing in the home.

Does television violence inform and persuade children to think and behave in violent ways? Or are children predisposed toward violence as a function of gender, geographic location, or unidentified factors drawn to television's more violent programming fare? Many researchers whose work is summarized in this chapter call for more longitudinal and in-depth qualitative studies. This represents a potentially rewarding venue for future research in light of our emerging understanding of the complex interplay between television violence and the child's understanding and use of such content as a positive or negative tool in everyday life.

REFERENCES

Anderson, D., Huston, A., Schmitt, K., Linebarger, D., & Wright, J. (2001). Early childhood television viewing and adolescent behavior. *Monographs of the Society for Research in Child Development*, *66*(1), 1–158.

Allerton, M. (1995). Emotions and coping: Children's talk about negative emotional responses to television. *Early Child Development and Care, 109*, 1–22.

Bandura, A. (1965). Influence of model's reinforcement contingencies on the acquisition of imitative responses. *Journal of Personality and Social Psychology, 1*, 589–595.

Bandura, A. (2002). Social cognitive theory of mass communication. In J. Bryant & D. Zillmann (Eds.), *Media effects: Advances in theory and research* (2nd ed.) (pp. 121–153). Mahwah, NJ: Erlbaum.

Boyatzis, C., Matillo, G., & Nesbitt, K. (1995). Effects of "The Mighty Morphin Power Rangers" on children's aggression with peers. *Child Study Journal, 25*, 45–55.

Cairns, E. (1990). Impact of television news exposure on children's perceptions of violence in Northern Ireland. *Journal of Social Psychology, 130*, 447–452.

Cantor, J., & Nathanson, A. (1996). Children's fright reactions to television news. *Journal of Communication, 46*(4), 139–152.

Cantor, J., & Nathanson, A. (1997). Predictors of children's interest in violent television programs. *Journal of Broadcasting and Electronic Media, 41*, 155–167.

Commission for the Prevention of Youth Violence. (2000, December). *Youth and violence. Medicine, nursing, and public health: Connecting the dots to prevent violence.* Retrieved December 9, 2003, from http://www.ama-assn.org/ama/upload/mm/386/fullreport.pdf.

Eaton, C., & Dominick, J. (1991). Product-related programming and children's TV: A content analysis. *Journalism Quarterly, 68*, 67–75.

Gerbner, G., Gross, L., Morgan, M., & Signorielli, N. (1980). The 'mainstreaming" of America: Violence Profile no. 11. *Journal of Communication, 30*(3), 10–29.

Gerbner, G., Gross, L., Morgan, M., Signorielli, N., & Shanahan, J. (2002). Growing up with television: Cultivation processes. In J. Bryant & D. Zillmann (Eds.), *Media effects: Advances in theory and research* (2nd ed.) (pp. 43–67). Mahwah, NJ: Erlbaum.

Grimes, T., & Bergen, L. (2001). The notion of convergence as an epistemological base for evaluating the effect of violent TV programming on psychologically normal children. *Mass Media and Society, 4*, 183–198.

Groebel, J. (1998). Media violence and children. *Educational Media International, 35*, 216–227.

Gunter, B., & Harrison, J. (1997). Violence in children's programmes on British television. *Children and Society, 11*, 143–156.

Gunter, B., Charlton, T., Coles, D., & Panting, C. (2000). The impact of television on children's antisocial behavior in a novice television community. *Child Study Journal, 30*, 65–90.

Krcmar, M. (1998). The contribution of family communication patterns to children's interpretations of television violence. *Journal of Broadcasting and Electronic Media, 42*, 250–264.

Krcmar, M., & Valkenburg, P. (1999). A scale to assess children's moral interpretations of justified and unjustified violence and its relationship to television viewing. *Communication Research, 26*, 608–634.

Nathanson, A., & Cantor, J. (2000). Reducing the aggression-promoting effect of violent cartoons by increasing children's fictional involvement with the victim: A study of active mediation. *Journal of Broadcasting and Electronic Media, 44*, 128–142.

Nathanson, A., & Yang, M. (2003). The effects of mediation content and form on children's responses to violent television. *Human Communication Research, 29*, 111–134.

National Institute on Media and the Family. (2002, February 27). *Fact Sheet: Children and Media Violence.* Retrieved November 24, 2003, from http://www.mediafamily.org/facts/_vlent.shtml.

National Television Violence Study, Volume 1. (1997). Newberry Park: CA: Sage.

National Television Violence Study, Volume 2. (1998). Thousand Oaks, CA: Sage.

National Television Violence Study, Volume 3. (1998). Thousand Oaks, CA: Sage.

Valkenburg, P., & Janssen, S. (1999). What do children value in entertainment programs? A cross-cultural investigation. *Journal of Communication, 49*(3), 3–21.

Wilson, B., Colvin, C., & Smith, S. (2002). Engaging in violence on American television: A comparison of child, teen, and adult perpetrators. *Journal of Communication, 52*, 36–60.

Wilson, B., Smith, S., Potter, W., Kunkel, D., Linz, D., Colvin, C., & Donnerstein, E. (2002). Violence in children's television programming: Assessing the risks. *Journal of Communication, 52*, 5–35.

Wood, W., Wong, F., & Chachere, J. (1991). Effects of media violence on viewers' aggression in unconstrained social interaction. *Psychological Bulletin, 109,* 371–383.

ACTIVITIES

1. Secure the proper permissions to gain access to a preschool or day-care facility. Ideally, you want to conduct a series of observations of children at play. The purpose of your study will be to observe children's play to assess the nature of and degree to which exposure to violent media content may factor into everyday social interactions. Try to find a physical location near children's play areas, but not so close as to become an obtrusive observer. Determine which are the best times to observe, based on the advice from expert informants such as supervisors or facility administrators. Your goal is to record child conversations and behaviors. Pay particular attention to what is said and behaviors during free-play periods. Be patient; you may have to spend a few sessions observing and listening. Then review your field notes and answer the following questions. What was the general setting and individual or group child play that you observed? How many times did you visit the play setting? How many total hours did you spend observing? What, if any, behavioral episodes did you observe where you believed children's play reflected experiences with violent media content? Why do you believe these behaviors are linked to media experiences? Do you think that the child or children understood the difference between actual play and real violence? If so, why? If not, why not? What do you think your research tells you in terms of the relationship between exposure to such media as television and violence in the real world? Share your perceptions with peers who conducted research at the same or similar settings.

2. Interview at least five family members or friends about television and violence. Use an open-ended interview format. Begin the interview by telling family members or friends that you are conducting a study as part of a larger project on television and human behavior. Assure family or friends that you will not refer to individuals by name or family role, only by gender and age. Begin each case study by asking the participant the following question: "Was there ever a time when you saw something on television that you considered to be violent?" Please try to refrain from telling participants, if they ask, what you mean by "violent." The goal in this exercise is to discern what respondents may consider violent television programming. If the respondent says yes, proceed to your initial query, then ask, "Okay, could you tell me what you saw?" Be sure to take notes or record the conversation. Also be sure to prompt the participant for additional information, such as "Can you think of any other time?" or "Anything else?" Your goal, in this effort, is to generate as many television program content examples of what other people think constitutes violence on television. Once you have completed your five interviews, look over your information and see if there are any patterns to responses from different participants. Are there any common themes or types of programming mentioned by participants? Try to generate a larger definition of what your small sample considered to be violent television program content. Share your definition with peers who conducted the same study with other participants. Can all of you generate a larger definition of what television audiences consider

violent television program content? How does this definition match up with definitions used by researchers summarized in this chapter and in other research?

3. Research summarized in this chapter and elsewhere makes the case that children's television programming contains more violent acts than programming targeting adults. This activity requires at least a group of ten individuals in order adequately cover the task. Your goal is to use the NTVS definition of violence as provided in the introduction to this chapter and apply it to two different types of television programming: children's Saturday morning programming and prime-time weekday entertainment programming. As a group, assign individuals to one hour of television programming for analysis. Five group members should each be assigned to one of five different hours of Saturday morning children's programming (including one or more programs), either on the same or different television channels/networks. The other five group members should each be assigned to one of five different hours of prime time weekday television programming (including two half-hour or one one-hour program). Choose the dates for content analysis and have each member count the number of violent acts during her or his assigned hour. Combine group results, keeping track of the number of violent acts per particular program, and combined number of violent acts for each of the two groups of programming. Do your results concur with general research findings that children's television programming contains more violent acts than programming targeted at adults? What, if any, do you think were the limitations of this study? What additional procedures would you include in a second effort?

QUESTIONS

1. Much of the research reported in this chapter and elsewhere suggests that violence is a prominent feature of children's television programming. Why, despite expressed concerns regarding the potential harm in such practices, do you think the industry continues to emphasize violence in children's programming? Would you force the television industry to cease such programming? How would you do that in light of the First Amendment and censorship restrictions regarding free speech? Would you urge parental intervention? If so, be sure to read some of the research literature regarding parents and "critical television viewing" practices. Be sure, whatever tact you suggest, to anchor your response in informed argument based on hard evidence and research.

2. Where do you stand on the debate concerning children and television violence? Do you think such portrayals are harmful and lead to increased aggressiveness on the part of children? Or do you think that children comprehend that violence on television is not real? Perhaps you fall into an area of middle ground, where you think some violence on television may be harmful to some children some of the time. Justify your response based on your understanding of research findings.

3. The introduction to this chapter included mention of a large content analysis conducted in the 1990s called the National Television Violence Study (NTVS). Participants in that three-year effort used an operational definition of violence to conduct research. Review that definition at the beginning of this chapter. Think about your own accumulated experiences with portrayals of television violence. Does the NTVS definition match your own perceptions of what constitutes vio-

lence on television? Is it too specific? Is it too broad? Be sure to cite specific examples of television programming in order to justify your response.

ADDITIONAL READINGS

Barker, M., & Petley, J. (Eds.). (2001). *Ill effects: The media/violence debate* (2nd ed.). New York: Routledge.

Cesarone, B. (1998). Television violence and children. *Childhood Education, 75,* 56–58.

Dudley, W. (Ed). (1999). *Media violence: Opposing viewpoints.* San Diego: Greenhaven Press.

Krcmar, M., & Cooke, M. (2001). Children's moral reasoning and their perceptions of television violence. *Journal of Communication, 51,* 300–316.

Krcmar, M., & Valkenberg, P. (1999). A scale to assess children's moral interpretations of justified and unjustified violence and its relationship to television viewing. *Communication Research, 26,* 608–634.

Kunkel, D., Farinola, W., Farrar, K., Donnerstein, E., Biely, E., & Zwarun, L. (2002). Deciphering the V-chip: An examination of the television industry's program rating judgments. *Journal of Communication, 52,* 112–138.

Peters, K., & Blumberg, F. (2002). Cartoon violence: Is it as detrimental to preschoolers as we think? *Early Childhood Education Journal, 29*(3), 143–148.

Potter, J., & Smith, S. (1999). Consistency of contextual cues about violence across narrative levels. *Journal of Communication, 49*(4), 121–133.

Signorielli, N., & Gerbner, G. (1988). *Violence and terror in the mass media: An annotated bibliography.* Westport, CT: Greenwood Press.

The national television violence study: Key findings and recommendations. (1996). *Young Children, 51*(3), 54–55.

Timmer, J. (2002). When a commercial is not a commercial: Advertising of violent entertainment and the First Amendment. *Communication Law and Policy, 7,* 157–186.

Tulloch, M. (1995). Evaluating aggression: School students' responses to television portrayals of institutionalized violence. *Journal of Youth and Adolescence, 24,* 95–115.

CHAPTER TWELVE

MUSIC VIDEOS

The MTV music video network first aired in 1981. Since that time at least two generations have supplemented or replaced radio listening with music videos. Mid-1990s estimates summarized by Seidman (1999) suggested that adolescents under 18 years of age use music video network programming a minimum of 25 minutes and as much as two hours per day. MTV is the preferred cable network music channel, reaching an estimated 350 million households worldwide (National Institute on Media and the Family, 2001). Music videos have become a central, driving force in the marketing of music, goods, and services to younger generations.

What do you think characterizes the content in these videos? How are artists and characters portrayed? How does exposure to music videos stimulate other feelings and actions on the part of viewers under controlled experimental conditions? What factors work as filters in terms of the kinds of impressions audiences take away from the music video experience? What do music video audiences tell us in terms of the kinds of things they find appealing, and the kinds of things they feel as a function of including this type of television in their everyday lives? These and other questions have propelled the study of music videos since their inception in the early 1980s. Those of you interested in more background might turn to Villani (2001), who provided a brief summary of ten years of research in this area. The research on music videos overlaps with that found in related chapters. Specifically, you are encouraged to compare findings in this chapter to those in Chapter 8, "Race and Ethnic Stereotyping"; Chapter 9, "Sex and Gender Stereotyping"; Chapter 10, "Television Sex and Sexuality, Pornography"; Chapter 10, "Children, Television, and Violence"; and Chapter 13, "Video Games." Typical of research examining a particular type of television programming, this chapter includes a good number of content analyses, some experiments, but fewer survey and qualitative audience analyses. These findings are then summarized.

CONTENT ANALYSES

How are occupations depicted in music videos, and to what extent do they portray sex-role stereotypes? Seidman (1992) recorded 60 hours of MTV in February 1987 and analyzed 182 nonperformance music videos. A total of 1,942 characters were analyzed, with males outnumbering females almost two to one. Males were often depicted as laborers, doctors, and in service roles such as mechanics and firefighters. Females were often depicted as secretaries, telephone operators, and cheerleaders (p. 211). In addition, "98% of the soldiers, 94% of the security and police personnel . . . 90% of the athletes, and all scientists, politicians, and business executives and managers were males" (p. 212). The researcher concluded that results coincided with earlier examinations of MTV content and served to reinforce traditional stereotypes and negative feelings of self-worth on the part of female and male adolescents. Seidman (1999) replicated his study and reexamined occupational roles and behaviors of primary characters in MTV music videos to assess differences, if any, over a five-year span. A total of 60 hours of MTV music videos were compiled during early 1993. Results showed male characters still outnumbered females two to one. There was a 26 percent increase in the portrayal of "nonwhites" compared to the previous study. "More than 9 out of 10 of the occupational roles classified as stereotypically male . . . were played by male actors. . . . All of the occupational roles thought of as stereotypically female . . . were portrayed by females" (p. 14). The researcher's previous study showed females employed in "blue-collar" roles, in contrast to this second study showing women evenly distributed between blue- and white-collar occupations (p. 14). Male characters "were more adventuresome and violent," while females were "more affectionate and nurturing" (p. 14). The researcher concluded that MTV videos remained largely sex-role stereotypic.

Do trends in gender portrayals found in other forms of television also prevail in music videos? Sommers-Flanagan, Sommers-Flanagan, and Davis (1993) content-analyzed MTV programming for representations of "sexual, dominant/submissive, and violent gender role behaviors" (p. 746). Results showed males outnumbered females almost two to one. "[M]ales exhibited significantly more dominant [13.7 versus 6.1 percent] and implicitly aggressive behavior [11.3 versus 4.9 percent] than females. In contrast, females were significantly more likely to engage in implicitly sexual [45.1 versus 33.6 percent] and subservient behavior" (p. 750).

Tapper, Thorson, and Black (1994) challenged the perception that music videos are mostly the same in "structure and content" (p. 103). The researchers explored the argument that music videos differ across and within network channels. Four networks were chosen for analysis (BET, TNN, MTV, and VH-1). A total of 16 hours of randomly selected music video programming was sampled from each of the four networks, yielding a final total of 161 videos. Results indicated that rap, heavy metal, pop, and alternative rock were the primary domain of MTV and pop dominated all other genres on VH-1. Country was the exclusive feature on TNN and rap and soul dominated all other genres on BET (p. 110). Results also showed that the greatest diversity in lead performer race and gender was in the pop music genre, though male lead performers dominated all genres (p. 108). Overall incidents of violence were "low" and "showed no statistically significant differences between musical genres" (p. 109). "Minorities appeared in about half of all videos" (p. 109) with fewest representations in the rock genre and most in rap and soul music videos. The researchers concluded that not all music videos are the same, nor are they the same on all music video networks.

What about those advertisements appearing on the MTV network? Signorielli, McLeod, and Healy (1994) cited earlier research suggesting that most television advertising both underrepresents and negatively stereotypes women (p. 91). The researchers hypothesized that females in advertisements appearing on MTV would appear less frequently, and when portrayed the emphasis would be on their physical attributes. They recorded 30 hours of MTV programming during the fourth quarter of 1991, resulting in 550 commercials (p. 93). Results showed males appeared in 54.4 percent of all commercials, compared to females at 45.6 percent. "Women were more likely than men to be portrayed as having very fit or beautiful bodies" (p. 95). "Females were rated as more attractive than males" (p. 96), and "Female characters were more likely than male characters to be portrayed wearing skimpy or sexy clothing" (p. 96). Finally, depictions of females appearing in major roles occurred only for personal product advertisements (p. 98). Results, the researchers argued, showed that advertising on MTV embraced traditional stereotypes of males and females.

In the late 1980s, the music video industry implemented guidelines for the portrayal of gender, in part as a response to concerns expressed by special interest groups and researchers who had demonstrated the ongoing misrepresentation of gender roles in such television. Gow (1996) examined MTV programming from the early 1990s in an effort to assess changes, if any, in the frequency of and types of female and male portrayals in popular music videos. The sample consisted of 100 videos aired by MTV as part of the *Top 100 of the 90s, So Far* program, airing in 1992. Results showed men outnumbered women in all 100 videos nearly five to one. "[W]omen most often appeared as Posers and Dancers" (p. 158), compared to men, who most often appeared as artists and posers but in other lead roles as well. The researcher noted that MTV's most popular videos in the early 1990s "suggested that for women to star . . . they had to affect an attitude or demonstrate physical talents, rather than exhibit the musical skills typically displayed by the men who appeared in lead roles" (p. 159).

McKee and Pardun (1996) compared religious and sexual imagery on MTV, TNN, and Z Music Television in 1995. Ten hours of music video programming was recorded for each network, resulting in 207 music videos. Results showed that sexual images appeared in 47.8 percent and religious images in 29.9 percent of all videos in the sample. Sexual and religious images, combined, appeared in 18.8 percent of all videos. In addition, "religious imagery is more likely to appear in combination with sexual imagery than to appear alone" (p. 167), with significantly more instances appearing in MTV videos compared to the other two networks. Finally, fewer sexual images appeared on Z Music Television compared to MTV and TNN.

Most of the research summarized in this chapter deals with the rock music video genre, but you are probably aware that other genres have evolved over time. Andsager and Roe (1999) examined portrayals of women in country music videos. Motivated by parallel findings in rock music videos, the researchers were intent on determining if the country music videos "symbolically annihilate women" (p. 71). Random sampling was used to videotape 283 weekday music videos on the CMT network in late 1997. Results showed that 71 percent of videos in the sample featured male artists, while slightly over 28 percent featured female artists. "Females in female artists' videos were much more likely to be portrayed as *fully equal* than characters in male artists' videos. The women and girls in male artists' videos were most likely to be placed in the *condescending* or the *keep her place* categories" (emphases in original; p. 76). The researchers concluded that trends in country music videos parallel those in other music video genres where female musical artists are "underrepresented" compared to male counterparts, are often younger than males depicted, and wear more revealing clothing.

The music video network industry enjoys a certain level of maturity after two decades or more of growth. What now characterizes the portrayal of aggression in music videos, and do these portrayals differ in frequency as a function of different network channels and genres? Smith and Boyson (2002) revisited the concerns expressed by researchers, public interest groups, and government officials in their content analysis of music video programming on BET, MTV, and VH-1. The researchers utilized National Television Violence Study (NTVS) data collected during 1996 and 1997. You may remember that details concerning the NTVS study are discussed in the introduction to Chapter 11: "Children, Television, and Violence." The researchers studied differences in violent portrayals across music video networks and types of music. Results showed a difference between the three music video channels and number of violent portrayals. MTV and BET programmed more videos with violence than VH-1. Saturation of violent acts was substantial, with at least one violent act (as defined by NTVS guidelines) appearing in all music videos analyzed, with no differences across the three channels. Type of violence differed across the three channels, with "Violent interactions on BET (82%) and VH-1 (86%) . . . more likely to feature behavioral violence than . . . those on MTV (67%)" (p. 70). Differences were also found in the number of violent portrayals across music genres. "Rap videos (29%) were significantly more likely to feature violence than were videos from rock (12%), R&B (9%), adult contemporary (7%), or other (9%) genres" (p. 73). The researchers also noted that overall depictions of violence accounted for only 15 percent of all music videos analyzed.

EXPERIMENTS

Hansen and Hansen (1990) examined the roles played by sex and violence portrayals in the overall appeal of music videos. They advanced a number of hypotheses. Central among these was the proposition that increased levels of "sexual" and "violent imagery" in "rock music videos" would enhance both visual and musical appeal. Results showed "that the visual content of high-sex videos was rated more appealing . . . than the visual content of either moderate- or low-sex videos" (p. 219). Similar results were found in terms of music appeal as "high-sex videos produced a stronger blend of positive emotions, including sexual feelings, than did moderate- or low-sex videos" (p. 221). This outcome was the same for females and males who participated in the study.

What demographic factors influence audience perceptions of music videos? Greeson (1991) assessed how "gender, sociological background, MTV viewing habits, and religion" (p. 1910) contributed to interpretations of a random sample of music videos. Results showed that to varying degree, high school, college, and adult subjects were capable of discerning themes in various types of music videos. Females and older subjects found "explicit" videos less appealing compared to "younger and/or male counterparts" and those who watched MTV "regularly" and attended church "seldom," who reported greater "liking" of music videos (p. 1917).

As you well know, the music video production style has found its way into other television programming. Hitchon, Duckler, and Thorson (1994) examined consumer responses to different types of television advertisements incorporating music video styles. They hypothesized that music video advertisements with higher levels of visual complexity would generate lower levels of favorable consumer attitudes toward both the video and the brand. Participants were 102 undergraduates from a northern Midwest university who viewed, in small groups, a 30-minute documentary containing commercial breaks featuring various styles of television advertising (p. 297). Results showed that visual complexity had no bearing on favorable perceptions of the music video advertisement or corresponding brand. In contrast, respondents more favorably perceived advertisements lower in ambiguity, as they did corresponding brands (pp. 298–299). The researchers concluded that results reinforced an old saying in the advertising business warning against being too clever with advertising so as to confuse the target consumer.

Toney and Weaver (1994) examined how gender influences young adult responses to music videos, part of a growing body isolating the role gender and self-perceptions of gender play in the larger television experience. The researchers hypothesized that males would express greater enjoyment in "hard-rock music videos" while females would do the same for "soft-rock music videos" (p. 570). Participants were 175 female and male undergraduate students at a southeastern U.S. university. Results, as predicted, showed males most enjoyed hard-rock videos and least enjoyed soft-rock videos. Conversely, females most enjoyed soft-rock videos and least enjoyed hard-rock videos. In addition, "Male subjects overestimated the Enjoyment and Disturbance [capitals in original] experienced by female peers across all three music video types. Female subjects, on the other hand, underestimated male peers' Enjoyment of the soft-rock music videos and Disturbance with all three music video types" (pp. 580–581). The researchers concluded that gender is of "critical importance" when examining "affective reactions to popular music" (p. 580).

Kalof (1999) examined how gender and exposure to different types of gender stereotypes in music videos influenced sexual attitudes. Participants were 44 undergraduate students at a northeastern U.S. college who were randomly assigned to one of two treatment groups. The first group viewed the Michael Jackson video *The Way You Make Me Feel*, determined by the researcher to depict gender and sexual stereotypes. The second group viewed REM's *The Stand*, featuring a concert performance by the band. Results showed that those who were exposed to the Michael Jackson video containing traditional gender and sexual stereotypes "scored higher

■ ■ ■ ■ ■

BOX 12.1

NATIONAL INSTITUTE ON MEDIA AND THE FAMILY TARGETS MTV

The National Institute on Media and the Family (NIMF) is a nonprofit clearinghouse for information about media, children, and families (www.mediafamily.org). The organization monitors research on media, audiences, and effects, including studies about music videos. They target MTV music videos as generally glamorizing alcohol and tobacco use, often with links to sexual and violent portrayals. The NIMF cites additional research suggesting links between exposure to music videos and more permissive attitudes toward sex on the part of adolescents. Based on such

findings, the NIMF recommends specific courses of action by parents. These include restricting MTV viewing by younger children; reducing MTV viewing by older teens; talking to teens about MTV content; and making arrangements with your local cable company to block access to all music video channels to your home (National Institute on Media and the Family, 2001). What do you think about these NIMF guidelines? How do the findings from recent research summarized in this chapter factor into your answer?

on the scale [of adversarial sexual beliefs] than the participants who viewed the control video" (p. 382). Viewing *The Way You Make Me Feel* did not result in increased attitudinal scores for "gender role stereotyping, the acceptance of rape myths, or the acceptance of interpersonal violence" (p. 382) (see Box 12.1).

SURVEYS

Brown and Schulze (1990) examined audience perceptions of two of Madonna's music videos, *Papa Don't Preach* and *Open Your Heart*. The researchers predicted that race and gender would influence different interpretations of sexuality portrayed. Respondents were 476 African American and Caucasian students from one northeastern and two southern "schools" (p. 93). Results showed that "almost all of the white females and nearly as many white males said that "Papa Don't Preach" is about teen pregnancy, [while] a large proportion of the black students thought that the 'baby' of which Madonna sings is her boyfriend" (p. 94). Most respondents liked Madonna to "some" degree (p. 95). The second video was more problematic for all respondents, generating a complex array of reactions. Viewed as a whole, the researchers concluded that results pointed to different interpretations on the part of audiences according to race, gender, and "liking of Madonna" (p. 100). In a somewhat related study, Thompson, Pingree, Hawkins, and Draves (1991) used a music video about teenage pregnancy to examine perceptions used by female and male adolescents when watching television. Participants were 186 female and male high school students spanning freshmen through senior years from the Midwest region of the United States. Results showed that females from households emphasizing social harmony paid attention to the video's content and its implications for personal sexual experiences. Results were different for males, who perceived the "video in general as having little application to their lives, and thus a habit of making relevant connections may also lead to avoiding those perceived to be irrelevant" (p. 311). The researchers concluded that family communication patterns proved an important factor in predicting television-viewing motivations. Finally, do psychological factors such as gender and contextual factors such as family "moderate" perceptions of sexual permissiveness in music videos? Strouse, Buerkel-Rothfuss, and Long (1995) used survey methods to interview 214 adolescents to answer that question. Their approach was anchored in findings from previous research suggesting that exposure to music television channels is positively related to higher levels of "premarital sexual permissiveness" (PSP) on the part of adolescents (p. 506). Participants for the study were U.S. female and male high school students from a community in the upper Midwest. Results generally showed that "the percentages of subjects who were permissive and had a high level of exposure to or involvement in music videos were greater for those from low quality family environments" (p. 515).

The impact of American music videos on international audiences is rarely studied. Lloyd and Mendez (2001) examined the adolescent perceptions of U.S. music videos in a region of southern Africa. Of particular interest was the researchers' concern with how media products from a vastly different culture become incorporated as part of everyday social interactions by children from another part of the world. Participants were adolescents in Batswana, where the official language is English in a bilingual environment. Broadcast television includes three or four channels comprised of a mix of local, African, British, and U.S. television programming. The researchers hypothesized that increased adolescent television of televised music videos would result in greater interest in western clothing and U.S. music artists. A total of 191 randomly selected "Black" adolescents from classrooms in five different schools in the nation's capital participated in the study. Results showed that 72 percent of students reported having television receivers in their homes, and averaged five hours of television viewing per week. Music videos were also viewed by two-thirds of all adolescent respondents. "[T]wo thirds of the sample reported that an American music video was their favorite music" compared to only 8 percent indicating a preference for videos of African origin (p. 469). A similar proportion was found for preferences of U.S. over African music artists. Clothing worn by U.S. music video artists was purchased by 70 percent of respondents. Additional findings indicated that Batswana adolescents did not comprehend the language nuances or slang often expressed by U.S. music video artists. The researchers concluded that music videos are regular fare among this population of African adolescents and that few understand "the symbols or language contained within American videos" (p. 471), even though their survey responses indicated that they believed they comprehended such symbols and language.

Historically, most popular songs and consequent music videos are about love. Further, most songs about love fall into one of two camps, being in love or not being but wanting to be in love. Gibson, Aust, and Zillmann (2000) examined how adolescent exhibiting either of these two emotions perceived music videos. Their approach was based on previous work in **mood management theory,** suggesting that audiences pursue certain types of media content consistent with their mood. In the case of love, the authors proposed that "amorously unsuccessful" adolescents would be more attracted to music videos with similar themes, compared to more successful adolescents, who would pursue music video content emphasizing successful-at-love messages. Participants were 135 female and male African American and Caucasian high school students from an unknown location. Results showed that "The more lonely respondents . . . enjoyed positive love music less than their less lonely counterparts . . . and males . . . enjoyed this music less than did females" (p. 46). The authors concluded that adolescents who are "cognizant of their love-related affective state" generally pursue music content consistent with those feelings.

QUALITATIVE RESEARCH

McKee and Pardun (1999) examined religious images in music videos and explored audience perceptions of such imagery. They were intent on discovering if audiences notice religious imagery in "secular" music videos and, if so, how they are perceived and remembered. In addition, they sought to compare interpretations of symbols in religious contexts to the same when portrayed in music videos. The qualitative method incorporated was the focus-group interview. First-year students at both a midwestern and southeastern U.S. university participated. Each focus group appeared to contain approximately eight students who were shown two music videos without sound or music tracks: *Zombies* by the Cranberries, and *Murder Was the Case* by Snoop Doggy Dogg. Both videos were predetermined to contain "manifest and latent religious imagery" (p. 113). Results showed that students "did greatly attend to and recognize . . . religious images" and "interpreted the images as religious in content and context" (pp. 114–115). Additionally, the "presence of the religious images influenced students' interpretation of other visual images" and "some found [such] use offensive . . . [while] others found the religious images evocative and useful" (p. 117). Among conclusions, the researchers argued that visual images in music videos inform interpretations of message meanings and the use of religious symbols helps to frame such meaning.

SUMMARY

You are no doubt becoming familiar with trends in the summaries for these chapters and should see a consistent pattern here as well.

- Regardless of network source or musical genre, gender bias continues to exist in music video content. Male artist or character portrayals in music videos continue to dominate female counterparts, on average, two to one. Some genres, such as country music, appear at face value to be making some strides in terms of so-called "head count" representations, but even more remarkable is the continued misrepresentation of those women who do appear in such videos. Two decades of research show that women continue to be portrayed largely as sex objects who are subservient to men, who often display aggressive forms of social behavior.

- Extensions from NTVS project research (see Chapter 11, "Children, Television, and Violence") suggest that violent depictions play a role in such programming and may be more concentrated in some music channels and musical genres. As the authors of many of these studies make clear, such portrayals may or may not be similar to audience perceptions of females, males, sexuality, or violence.

We have long established in various chapters of this book that content analyses may or may not reflect audience perceptions; however, the case of music may warrant special scrutiny. First, research has long established that music, and now music videos, occupies an important socializing role in child and adolescent development. Think about your own lives and the role music plays in your everyday activities. Music serves many social functions, particularly between early teen and young adult years. Music videos provide a kind of important glue for many young people first experimenting in social relations, including relations with members of the same or the opposite sex. So it only stands to reason that the messages in music videos, both by virtue of the important socializing function played as well as the amount of time spent with such media, have the potential to inform and help frame audience perceptions of such things as gender, sexuality, race, and pro- and antisocial behaviors. When, as the content analyses in this chapter have suggested, such images consistently represent unequal representations of females and males, then there is potential for harm.

If the sample in this chapter is representative, research examining the relationship between exposure to music videos and audience perceptions is dominated by experimental approaches. Readers are reminded that experimental approaches are best when demonstrating cognitive processes consequent to exposure to carefully controlled stimuli. Good experiments can show how some media messages induce short-term attitudinal changes or teach learners to behave in certain ways given appropriate reinforcement cues.

- Compared to many other topics in media research, experimental approaches to the study of music videos have consistently focused on gender as a key, informing variable, when assessing both perception of and cognitive responses to music video content. Results are most clear in this area of inquiry. Gender informs both perception of and reactions to music video content. Results remain somewhat mixed in terms of consistent patterns for how this happens. Males would appear to prefer hard-rock music video genres compared to females, who prefer softer venues.

- Results are more mixed when examining female and male preferences for sexually oriented content in music videos. Some research suggests that both females and males are aroused by music video containing high levels of such content, while results from other studies are less conclusive. Inconsistent results can be explained by differences in the ways researchers defined what was meant by sexually oriented music video content. Regardless, experimental studies in the area of music videos have effectively charted the role gender and other variables such as family socialization and sexual experience play in the process of audience reception.
- Survey methods demonstrate how gender, family-communication styles, and degree of sexual experience play a role in filtering how adolescent and young adult audiences engage and perceive music video images.

Though too soon to tell, some of the survey studies reported in this chapter would appear to have isolated key influences within these sets of variables, as the percentages such variables help explain the presence of one or more dependent variables sometimes exceed those levels typically reported in mass media research. Future research must build on this foundation, and begin to examine *how* such factors as gender, family communication and parenting styles, and relational and sexual experiences inform both attraction to and perceptions of certain kinds of music video content.

REFERENCES

Andsager, J., & Roe, K. (1999). Country music video in country's year of the woman. *Journal of Communication, 49*(1), 69–82.

Brown, J., & Schulze, L. (1990). The effects of race, gender, and fandom on audience interpretations of Madonna's music videos. *Journal of Communication, 40*(2), 88–102.

Gibson, R., Aust, C., & Zillmann, D. (2000). Loneliness of adolescents and their choice and enjoyment of love-celebrating versus love-lamenting popular music. *Empirical Studies of the Arts, 18*(1), 43–48.

Gow, J. (1996). Reconsidering gender roles on MTV: Depictions in the most popular music videos of the early 1990s. *Communication Reports, 9,* 151–162.

Greeson, L. (1991). Recognition and ratings of television music videos: Age, gender and sociocultural effects. *Journal of Applied Social Psychology, 21,* 1908–1920.

Hansen, C., & Hansen, R. (1990). The influence of sex and violence on the appeal of rock music videos. *Communication Research, 17,* 212–234.

Hitchon, J., Duckler, P., & Thorson, E. (1994). Effects of ambiguity and complexity on consumer response to music video commercials. *Journal of Broadcasting and Electronic Media, 38,* 289–306.

Kalof, L. (1999). The effects of gender and music video imagery on sexual attitudes. *Journal of Social Psychology, 139,* 378–385.

Lloyd, B., & Mendez, J. (2001). Batswana adolescents' interpretation of American Music videos: So that's what that means! *Journal of Black Psychology, 27,* 464–476.

McKee, K., & Pardun, C. (1996). Mixed messages: The relationship between sexual and religious imagery in rock, country, and Christian videos. *Communication Reports, 9,* 163–171.

McKee, K., & Pardun, C. (1999). Reading the video: A qualitative study of religious images in music videos. *Journal of Broadcasting and Electronic Media, 43,* 110–122.

National Institute on Media and the Family (2001, August 14). *Fact Sheet: MTV.* Retrieved November 25, 2003, from http://www.mediafamily.org/facts/facts_mtv.shtml.

Seidman, S. (1992). An investigation of sex-role stereotyping in music videos. *Journal of Broadcasting and Electronic Media, 36,* 209–216.

Seidman, S. (1999). Revisiting sex-role stereotyping in MTV videos. *International Journal of Instructional Media, 26,* 11–22.

Signorielli, N., McLeod, D., & Healy, E. (1994). Gender stereotypes in MTV commercials: The beat goes on. *Journal of Broadcasting and Electronic Media, 38,* 91–102.

Smith, S., & Boyson, A. (2002). Violence in music videos: Examining the prevalence and context of physical aggression. *Journal of Communication, 52,* 61–83.

Sommers-Flanagan, R., Sommers-Flanagan, J., & Davis, B. (1993). What's happening on music television? A gender role content analysis. *Sex Roles, 28,* 745–753.

Strouse, J., Buerkel-Rothfuss, N., & Long, E. (1995). Gender and family moderators of the relationship between music video exposure and adolescent sexual permissiveness. *Adolescence, 30,* 505–521.

Tapper, J., Thorson, E., & Black, D. (1994). Variations in music videos as a function of their musical genre. *Journal of Broadcasting and Electronic Media, 38,* 103–113.

Thompson, M., Pingree, S., Hawkins, R., & Draves, C. (1991). Long-term norms and cognitive structures as shapers of television viewer activity. *Journal of Broadcasting and Electronic Media, 35,* 319–334.

Toney, G., & Weaver, J. (1994). Effects of gender and gender role self-perceptions on affective reactions to rock music videos. *Sex Roles, 30,* 567–583.

Villani, S. (2001). Impact of media on children and adolescents: A 10-year review of the research. *Journal of the American Academy of Child and Adolescent Psychiatry, 40,* 392–401.

Walker, G., & Bender, M. (1994). Is it more than rock and roll? Considering music video as argument. *Argumentation and Advocacy, 31,* 64–79.

ACTIVITIES

1. Conduct your own content analysis of the current stream of music videos. Select one channel for analysis. If more than one of you are engaged in this activity, consider assigning different people to different music video channels or different parts of the day for each of those channels. Your unit of analysis is the actual music video. Videotape or watch what you consider to be a representative sample of your network's music video offerings. Note the number of performance versus narrative/story-type videos. Note the gender of the main artist(s) or character(s) in each video. Note any occupational role occupied by males and females playing main character roles (e.g., physical laborer, bar tender, dancer, unknown). Summarize your results in terms of actual percentages for each of these and any other categories you may use for analysis. Compare your results to those generated by peers who may have analyzed the same or different networks or videos. Summarize overall findings. What does your work say about current representations of gender in today's music videos? How do these trends compare to those reported in this chapter?

2. You will need a videotape or digital recording device for this activity. Record an hour or so of music videos from one of the available network channels. Pay careful attention to nonperformance videos for this activity (videos that tell a story, not videos showing an artist or group performing). Screen the videos you recorded and isolate one for further, close-textual analysis of visual settings. You are particularly interested in any video portraying males and females in social roles. Use your play/pause features to stop this video periodically in order to answer the following questions. What roles are depicted by each of the principal characters in this video (e.g., doctor, lawyer, teacher, housewife, son, wife). What larger role in life do these characters play in the video (e.g., maniacal demon, dirty business-man, cheating husband, two-faced daughter)? In other words, what kinds of stereotypes are these characters designed to convey? Finally, what larger lessons in life are given off by individual or combined roles portrayed in this video? One way to think about this last item is to think about what myth or mythology is being reinforced by the depictions found in this video (e.g., Puritan work ethic, the great American dream gone awry, something for nothing). Do you think these larger myths or messages are typical of such music videos? Compare and contrast your findings to those studies conducted by peers. Can you develop a master list of larger messages given off by music videos?

3. Trends in research reported in this chapter suggest that women continue to occupy subservient and sexually oriented roles in music videos. Conduct a content analysis of a representative sample of music videos using some of the techniques reported in studies found in this chapter. Compare your findings to those generated in earlier studies. What does your evidence say about the current role women occupy in music videos? Do these images jive with those realities occupied by women in contemporary society?

QUESTIONS

1. Much of the content analytic work conducted on music videos suggests that women are portrayed in stereotypic and negative ways. Why, in the face of changing roles for women over past decades, do you think music videos continue to project such images?

2. Most who are reading this chapter are experts when it comes to music videos, having acquired years of direct viewing experience. Imagine that you are summoned as a consultant to one of the major music video networks to share your opinions on the following multipart question. Have the videos aired on our network changed over time in terms of their representations of females and males, of sex and sexuality, and of violence? If so, what were those earlier representations and how have they changed? If not, how would you characterize as the consistent message for each of these categories? Please be sure to name particular music videos as part of your answer.

3. Review the NTVS project definition for "violence" found in the introduction of Chapter 11, "Children, Television, and Violence." Keeping that definition in mind, do you think that most, some, or little of the music videos you have viewed over time include violent content? Do you think that the NTVS definition is too broad and sweeping when applied to music video content? Or do you think that

the definition is too limiting? Use examples from actual music videos to support your views.

ADDITIONAL READINGS

Christenson, P., & Roberts, D. (1998). *It's not only rock & roll: Popular music in the lives of adolescents.* Creskill, NJ: Hampton Press.

Emerson, R. (2002). "Where my girls at?" Negotiating Black womanhood in music videos. *Gender and Society, 16,* 115–135.

Gow, J. (1994). Mood and meaning in music video: The dynamics of audio visual synergy. *Southern Communication Journal, 59,* 255-261.

Hansen, C., & Krygowski, W. (1994). Arousal-augmented priming effects: Rock music videos and sex object schemas. *Communication Research, 21,* 24–47.

Smith-Shomade, B. (2002). *Shaded lives: African-American women and television.* New Brunswick, NJ: Rutgers University Press.

Strasburger, V. (1995). Adolescents and the media: Medical and psychological impact. Thousand Oaks, CA: Sage.

CHAPTER THIRTEEN

VIDEO GAMES

As most of you already know, video and computers have married to bring ever more powerful, fast, and realistic gaming technologies to the marketplace. Video games are now a central part of everyday family life. Video game industry sales hit the $20 billion mark in 2000, with most games targeting those under the age of 17 (National Institute on Media and the Family, 2001). An estimated 70 percent of U.S. households have at least one video game console and 33 percent of children in those homes play games in their own bedrooms. Gaming appears to correlate with age, as older children play more frequently and for longer periods each day (Thompson & Haninger, 2001). Villani (2001) reviewed the potential for negative effects of such behaviors, including "cardiovascular implication, video game-induced seizures, 'Nintendinitis,' pathological preoccupation with video games, and aggression and prosocial behavior" (p. 399). Other research has examined academic performance, cognitive development, and gender socialization (Mediascope, 2000). As you will see, most of the research in this area has focused on video game content, particularly on portrayals of gender and aggression. Other research has examined the potential effects of video games on children or adolescents. For example, Dill and Dill (1998) reviewed the nature of violent video game play, and Sherry (2001) provided an overview of theories and methods used to study the relationship between violent video game content and aggressive behavior. Findings from his meta-analysis are summarized at the end of the chapter. Finally, Kirsh (2003) applied the **general aggression model** (GAM) to adolescent development in his review of video game research literature. Many of the issues raised by researchers in this chapter will resonate with themes established in related chapters. Specifically, you are encouraged to consult Chapter 9, "Sex and Gender Stereotyping"; Chapter 10, "Television Sex and Sexuality, Pornography"; and Chapter 11, "Children, Television, and Violence."

What are the predominant character portrayals and themes in video games? Are there physiological, attitudinal, and behavioral consequences from playing video games in general and those with aggressive themes in particular? Are these consequences gender based? Do you think video games are addictive? Is playing a video game similar to watching television? These are among the types of questions posed by researchers whose work is summarized in this chapter. As with any relatively new media, a healthy portion of research activity on this topic has been content-analytic in nature, and continues to be as video games develop in sophistication and complexity. A number of those content analyses are presented. The field of psychology has been very active in investigating message and cognitive variables seen to contribute to various emotional states as a function of video game play. Consequently, a large portion of the research literature, and a corresponding amount summarized in this chapter, are experiments. Some work involving audience surveys has also been included. No qualitative research was found but, as the summary will indicate, there is potential for good work to be done utilizing naturalistic data-gathering techniques.

CONTENT ANALYSES

Symbolic interactionism is a theory purporting that roles are socially defined, including gender roles. Dietz (1998) argued that evolving media technologies play an increasing role in gender socialization. Seventeen Nintendo and 16 Sega Genesis games were included in the analysis. Results showed that 30 percent of all video games analyzed did not portray "the female population at all" and 15 percent of all games analyzed showed women "as heroes or as action characters" (pp. 433–434). However, such portrayals often included stereotypic "female colors and/or clothing" (p. 433). Females were also portrayed as victims in 21 percent of video games analyzed (pp. 434–435). Approximately "one half" of all games analyzed contained violence (p. 437). The researcher concluded that females are portrayed in stereotypic fashion in those rare instances when they are depicted at all in video games.

The Entertainment Software Rating Board (ESRB) rates video games. Their "E" rating is basically the same as the "G" rating given to movies for "General Audiences." Thompson and Haninger (2001) content-analyzed ESRB rated games garnering the "E" rating for violence. A total of 55 games were analyzed. The entire "series" from two of the most popular games in this sample, *The Legend of Zelda* and *Super Mario Bros.*, were also included for additional study. Results showed that sports, racing, and action games accounted for 87 percent of all games (p. 593). The researchers "found 20 games that did not include violent game play, and 35 games (64 percent) that involved intentional violence, with an average of 30.7 percent of the game duration representing violent game play" (p. 594). Each progressive level in *The Legend of Zelda* contained less violence, with less conclusive trends found for *Super Mario Bros.* The researchers noted that games included in their sample did not contain descriptions of violence as part of ratings, comments, or packaging.

As we have seen in previous chapters, gender portrayals in video games have the potential to influence feminine and masculine behaviors on the part of children and adolescents. Beasley and Collins Standley (2002) examined gender and clothing in video games. The researchers anchored their approach in **gender schema theory,** where individuals perceive new information about female or male roles based on previous knowledge, including prior experience derived from video game play. The sample was based on a random sample of all nonadult video games manufactured by Nintendo and PlayStation brands, resulting in a final sample of 47 games. Results

■ ■ ■ ■ ■

BOX 13.1

ENTERTAINMENT SOFTWARE ASSOCIATION

The Entertainment Software Association (ESA) is the U.S. organization representing 90 percent of companies who publish video and computer games. Their website (www.theesa. com) contains useful information about the video and computer gaming industry. The "Media Center" located at their website includes links to summaries and facts about the relationship between playing video games and violence. They also summarize original academic studies by media researchers. Among the key points summarized are the following.

■ The "average" U.S. video game player is 29 years old.
■ Parents "are involved" in the purchasing or renting of video games 83 percent of the time.
■ Many games sold contain violent content, though many sold in foreign markets contain even more violence. However, violence in these foreign markets is lower than that in the U.S. There are other factors in the United States contributing to violence besides video games.

■ Violent crime among the young in the United States has decreased since 1990, even though video game playing has steadily increased.
■ The Entertainment Software Ratings Board (ESRB) rates all video games. People who object to violence in games can use these ratings to screen objectionable content. In 2002, 63 percent of all games sold were rated "E" for everyone (Entertainment Software Association, 2003).

You might want to visit the ESA website and read some of these summaries for yourself. Clearly, the position taken by the ESA is understandably different than some of the findings you are reading about in this chapter. Why do you think this is the case?

showed a total of 597 characters analyzed, with 71.52 percent males and 13.74 percent females. Nintendo games underrepresented females compared to PlayStation games. Most females appeared in one Olympics-sports-themed game, *Sydney 2000*. Females were "shown less clothed" than males, and "Of those characters shown with low necklines, in which cleavage or pecs were visible, 85.7% were women" (p. 287), with "40.85% . . . considered voluptuous" (p. 288). The researchers concluded that females were "vastly underrepresented in video games" and when they do appear, are underdressed compared to males. The researchers found such results compelling in light of the preponderance of such depictions in games rated for younger children (see Box 13.1).

EXPERIMENTS

Irwin and Gross (1995) assessed the influence of violent video games on "impulsive and reflective" children (p. 339). They hypothesized that children who played violent video games would exhibit higher levels of aggressive play, particularly on the part of impulsive children. Participants were 60 males aged 7 to 8 years from two elementary schools at an undisclosed geographic location. A Nintendo-brand player device and two games were stimulus materials. *Double Dragon* was used as the violent video game. *Excitebike* was used as the nonviolent game. Results indicated that children "who played the aggressive video game showed significantly more physical aggression toward objects during free-play than those who played the nonaggressive game" (p. 345), were more verbally aggressive toward toys, more verbally aggressive toward others, and were more physically aggressive (p. 346). There was no difference in heart rate between those subjects playing the violent or the nonviolent video game. The researchers noted that findings do not allow for "strong conclusions" (p. 348) but suggested results may point to the potential harm of violent video game content.

Are there relationships between playing video games and other gaming activities, such as gambling? Gupta and Derevensky (1996) examined such relationships on the part of both children and adolescents. Their approach was anchored in previous research demonstrating parental gambling influences on offspring gambling tendencies, high levels of overall gambling on the part of children and adolescents, and youth interest in video games because of their "dynamic, interactive, and entertaining nature" (p. 378). The researchers hypothesized that children who used video games with "high frequency" would take more risks when playing blackjack and that males would take higher risks than females. Participants were part of a larger sample of "approximately" 500 Canadian students from fourth, sixth, and eighth grades. Results showed "children perceived video-game playing as being more skill driven than luck driven" (p. 383). "High frequency video-game players were significantly more likely to have gambled in general" (p. 384), but females and males did not differ on this finding. High-frequency video game–playing males also wagered more on blackjack compared to all other groups studied. The authors concluded that some of the factors contributing to whether a child or adolescent initiates video game–playing behavior may also help predict whether they choose to engage in gambling behavior.

Kirsh (1998) incorporated a perspective called the **hostile attribution bias** (HAB) in his study of video game play and aggression. HAB suggests that when one is "exposed to a frustrating social stimulus . . . a hostile attribution bias results in cue distortion, which leads aggressive children to interpret the stimulus as an aggressive cue and thus respond aggressively" (p. 178). Kirsh set out to test whether violent video game play could serve as an aggressive cue and hypothesized that children who played a violent video game would "ascribe more hostile intent to the harmdoer," would prescribe more retaliation, and would expect more punishment than children who played a nonviolent video game. Participants were 52 third and fourth graders from the western Midwest. Stimulus materials included a version of *Mortal Kombat*, the violent cue, or *NBA JAM*, the nonviolent cue. Results showed that "children exposed to the very violent video game . . . responded more negatively to the ambiguous provocation stories than children exposed to the relatively nonviolent video game" (p. 181). The researcher concluded that results provided partial support for the HAB perspective. Ballard and Lineberger (1999) also examined relationships between playing violent video games and aggressive behaviors. They manipulated the role of "gender of confederate" to assess outcome effects on aggression. The researchers predicted a relationship between the level of violent game play and the gender of confederate used in the experiment. Specifically, male subjects were predicted to "reward female confederates less and punish them more as the level of video game violence increased" (p. 545). A total of 119 male university students at an undisclosed geographic location participated in the study. Stimulus materials included three levels of *Mortal Kombat,* the violent stimulus, and *NBA Jam T. E.,* the nonviolent stimulus. "[M]ale participants rewarded other males significantly less under the violent game conditions, while females were rewarded similarly across conditions" and "male confederates were not punished differently across varying levels of violence, [while] females were punished most aggressively [when playing] the most violent version of Mortal Kombat" (pp. 553–554). The authors concluded that results suggested the potential for violent video game play to result in decreasing "reward behavior toward others" and increasing "punitive behavior" toward females (p. 554).

Does playing a video game alter a child's mood? Does this mood become aggressive when playing violent video games? Fleming and Rickwood (2001) addressed these and other questions. The researchers noted that video game playing is often very different from that of viewing aggression on television, in that players regularly assume the point of view of the primary aggressor. The researchers hypothesized that experienced video game players, regardless of gender, will be less aroused by violent games compared to their less experienced peers. Participants were 71 females and males from the third through six grades in a Canberra, Australia, school. Parents of subjects provided game-playing experience data. Stimulus materials included a nonviolent video game, *Bouncer II,* and *Herc's Adventures,* the violent video game. Results showed no relationship between subjects' video game experience and arousal measures (p. 2057). There was also "no support for the hypothesis that children will report more aggressive mood after playing violent video games" (pp. 2061–2062), nor for the hypotheses that playing violent or nonviolent video games would result in positive or negative moods based on gender. The researchers concluded that playing video games might have resulted in pleasurable arousal "incompatible with aggressive mood" (p. 2064).

Many of the research findings in other chapters have demonstrated links between exposure to aggression and consequent aggressive behaviors, and many of the researchers demonstrating such linkages argued that future research should begin to explore "why" type questions given such relationships. Bushman and Anderson (2002) used the **general aggression model** and video games to explore this issue. The model purports that "aggression is largely based on the activation and application of aggression-related knowledge structures stored in memory" such as scripts or schema (p. 1680). Playing video games, it was believed, would stimulate such scripts or schema, and both increase and inform consequent aggressive behaviors. Participants were 244 U.S. undergraduate students evenly divided between females and males at an undisclosed geographic region who individually played one of eight video games, four deemed violent (*Carmageddon, Duke Nukem, Mortal Kombat, Future Cop*) and four deemed nonviolent (*Glider Pro, 3D Pinball, Austin Powers, Tetra Madness*). Results showed that "people who played violent video games expected more aggressive responses from the main characters in the stories" (p. 1682). "People who played a violent video game also were more likely to expect the main characters to feel angry and aggressive" (p. 1682). In conclusion, the researchers argued that findings lent support to the general aggression model, and also showed "how people in general would react rather than hypothetical self-explanations" (p. 1683).

Panee and Ballard (2002) also studied video games and their capacity to prime a number of violent game-playing behaviors. The researchers anchored their approach in **social learning theory** and **priming theory.** They argued that "specific effects of violent video games differ depending on gender, measures, context, and game content" (p. 2460) and advanced the hypothesis that "high aggressive priming will result in more frequent violent action during game play and, subsequently, greater cardiovascular activity . . . and higher levels of hostile feelings than will low aggressive priming" (pp. 2462–2463). A total of 36 male undergraduate students from a southeastern U.S. university participated. The stimulus was *Metal Gear Solid.* Results showed those subjects provided with the high aggressive prime "used significantly more violent actions during game play than those in the low aggressive condition" and "reported significantly higher hostility" (p. 2466). There were no appreciable differences in heart rate between high- and low-aggressive treatment groups. The researchers concluded that results demonstrated the capacity to "manipulate the frequency of violent action during game play" (p. 2469). Finally, Bartholow and Anderson (2002) cited a growing body of evidence suggesting linkages to "short-term and long-term increases in aggression-related outcomes for game players" (p. 284) and noted how existing research has yet to generate conclusive evidence relative to gender differences, video game playing, and aggressive tendencies. The researchers hypothesized that violent video game players would exhibit more aggression than subjects playing a nonviolent game. Differences between females and males on such outcomes were a central part of the study. Participants were 43 undergraduates at an undisclosed geographic location. Stimulus materials were *Mortal Kombat* and *PGA Tournament Golf*, the nonviolent simulated golf game. Results showed that subjects who played *Mortal Kombat* "set higher levels of . . . punishment" (p. 287), compared to those who played the golf video game, and males set statistically significantly higher levels [of punishment] and used those levels more often than females. The researchers concluded that results suggest young males "may be more affected by violent video games than are young women" (p. 287).

SURVEYS

Kubey and Larson (1990) studied how children and adolescents use "new video media" including video games. They argued that new media engages audiences in qualitatively different and, therefore, potentially more compelling ways than more traditional media. Surveys were administered to 483 female and male children and younger adolescents from eight different schools in a major metropolitan area in the Midwest. Results indicated that video games accounted for only 3.3 percent of all time spent with media. Overall time spent with media was 17.6 percent of all activities recorded (p. 116). Males accounted for 80 percent of all video game activity (p. 117). In addition, "video-game playing alone increased with age . . . at the expense of a decrease in video-game playing with the family" (p. 120). Cognitive state associated with playing video games was also informed by "social context." "Video game play with siblings was not associated with positive affect, but it was quite arousing. By contrast, video games elicited higher affect when played with parents or with friends" (p. 122). The researchers concluded that results could be explained as a function of gender socialization, the general orientation of new media content (including video game content) targeting males, and potential "innate biological differences" informing media preferences between females and males (p. 125).

What are baseline indicators of both "normal" and "excessive" home video game play on the part of children? Phillips, Rolls, Rouse, and Griffiths (1995) used self-administered surveys with British children in order to answer these questions. A total of 868 11- to 16-year-old students in an unidentified geographic location participated. Results indicated that 77.2 percent of all subjects played video games; 24.2 percent played daily, averaging between 30 minutes and one hour (p. 688). Slightly more than one-third of all respondents indicated they played video games to "pass the time," with this motivation mentioned almost three times as often as any other reason provided. Males spent more time playing video games and were more likely to neglect school homework than females (p. 689). A subsample of survey respondents (7.5 percent) were considered candidates for video game "addiction" as a function of their scores on some survey questions. This smaller group of respondents "felt their parents considered they played video games too much," reported "feeling better after playing video games," and said they "played video games to avoid doing other activities" (p. 689).

Funk and Buchman (1996) explored relationships between violent video game play and adolescent self-concepts. Their study was anchored in the perspective that adolescents display increasing capacities "to judge their overall value as a person" (p. 22). When linked to playing violent video games, the researchers advanced a number of hypotheses linking socially determined levels of competence at video game play, self-concept, and "social support and acceptance" (p. 23). A total of 357 U.S. seventh- and eight-grade students from the Midwest participated. Results indicated that adolescent males spent significantly more time playing video games and indicated a preference for "human violence" games compared to female adolescents, who preferred "fantasy violence" games (p. 25). "[F]or girls, more time spent playing electronic games was associated with lower self-concept scores" (p. 27). These factors contributed from 5 to 9 percent of female perceptions of lower self-concept. Since males play video games more often, the researchers speculated as part of conclusions that only adolescent males "with the most extreme habits" may be affected in terms of self-concept. The researchers concluded that "there is no indication that playing electronic games causes major adjustment problems for most players" (p. 29).

Is video game playing related to aggressive or prosocial behaviors? This was the primary question motivating work by Wiegman and van Schie (1998) when they surveyed seventh and eighth graders in The Nederlands. Their theoretical approach was based in **social learning theory,** where modeling strategies have been shown to induce both aggressive and prosocial modeling. The researchers hypothesized that the "amount" of video game play would be positively related to aggression, negatively related to prosocial behaviors, and subject preference for violent video game play would be positively related to aggression and negatively related to prosocial behaviors (p. 370). A total of 278 school children aged 10 to 14 years from five different schools participated. Support was not found for the relationship between amount of video game play and aggressive behaviors. In contrast, "[h]eavy players showed less prosocial behaviour than the other two groups [light and moderate players]" (p. 373). Subject expressed interest in aggressive video games was significantly related to higher levels of aggression "mainly for boys" and negatively related to prosocial behaviors "only for boys" (p. 374). Finally, results indicated a negative relationship between children's intelligence level and aggressive video games.

Anderson and Dill (2000) applied the **general affective aggression model** to the study of video games. The model "integrates existing theory and data concerning the learning, development, instigation, and expression of human aggression . . . [and] does so by noting that the enactment of aggression is largely based on [cognitive] knowledge structures" (p. 773). The theoretical discussion advanced by the researchers is among the most comprehensive to date. Among hypotheses, the researchers proposed that extended violent video game play would be "positively correlated with aggression in naturalistic settings" (p. 776). A total of 227 female and male undergraduates from a U.S. midwestern university participated. Results showed respondents played video games for an average of 2.14 hours per week, with *Super Mario Bros.* a favorite game among 50 percent of subjects (p. 778). *Tetris* was the second most favorite and *Mortal Kombat* was the third most favorite played by 27 percent of subjects. "Aggressive delinquent behavior was positively related to both trait aggressiveness and exposure to video game violence" (p. 779), with both factors contributing 12.9 percent and 21.1 percent respectively to delinquent behaviors. In addition, "exposure to video game violence was positively related to aggressive personality" (p. 779), accounting for 4.8 percent of this personality trait. Also, "Males felt more safe, played more violent video games, and played more video games in general than did females" (p. 779). The researchers argued that results demonstrated that playing violent video games as well as aggressive personalities contributed "separately and jointly" to aggressive behavior and nonaggressive delinquency, suggesting that ongoing concerns about the harmful effects of such games are warranted.

Are video games addictive? Salguero and Moran (2002) examined this topic using 223 older adolescents aged 13 to 18 years from two secondary schools in southern Spain. The survey was designed to assess numerous measures, including demographics, frequency of video game playing, self-assessment of "problem video game playing" (PVP), and drug dependency (pp. 1602–1603). Results demonstrated that male adolescents played video games significantly more often than females. "Positive relationships were found with frequency of play . . . [average] duration of play . . . and longest time per session" (p. 1604). These three factors contributed 40 percent, 27 percent, and 31.3 percent respectively to video game play. A significant relationship was also found between PVP and drug dependency. The researchers concluded that video game playing is a form of addiction for some adolescents who cannot control the activity, who use it as a form of escape, and who risk impeded social development (p. 1605).

SUMMARY

Research investigating relationships between playing video games and audience effects is relatively new compared to the study of television. The result is fewer studies using similar or common measures, video game stimuli, and subject samples. This is clearly evident in the content analyses summarized in this chapter, particularly those assessing violent content in video games. Operational definitions, when provided in such studies, are unique to each study and lack the increasing level of uniformity now demonstrated in most content analytic work examining television depictions of violence, which increasingly uses the NTVS definition for violence as reported in Chapter 11, "Children, Television, and Violence." Content analyses of video games should be considered a worthy and ongoing enterprise, particularly as video games evolve in speed and complexity as a function of increasingly powerful game consoles and computers. Here is what we can summarize from this existing research:

- In terms of gender portrayals, existing content analyses would appear to support the contention that video game content reinforces a stereotypic male-centric view of the world, where women are missing or underrepresented and when they do appear serve the primary role of sex object. Because the target audience for most video game play, particularly violent video game play, is adolescent males, this outcome is hardly surprising, but nonetheless one warranting guarded concern.

  Future content analyses should continue to assess gender and violence portrayals for the industry's most successful and prevalent video games, particularly when depictions of violence and gender are linked.

- Experiments and some survey-based research have dominated this area's investigation of video games, audiences, and effects, and particularly the most popular games generally associated with violent content.

Bensley and Van Eenwyk (2001) analyzed video game research conducted between 1984 and 2000 by subject age groups. They concluded that "current research . . . is not supportive of a major concern that violent video games lead to real-life violence" (p. 256) and called for further research on adolescents, particularly as game realism evolves. Sherry (2001) conducted a meta-analysis of research and concluded that, when compared to findings relative to television and human aggression, "the existing social science research on the impact of video games is not nearly as compelling" (p. 409). The researcher's conclusion is based on analysis of 25 studies using experimental or survey methods conducted between 1975 and 2000 utilizing violent video game play as the independent variable and a measure of aggression as the dependent variable. Results indicated that "there is a correlation between video game play and aggression, but that relationship is smaller than that found for television" (pp. 423–424).

- Of the experiments and survey studies summarized in this chapter, most discovered insignificant findings or offered cautious statements regarding partial support for claims.
- Notable among the studies included in this chapter is the general lack of unifying theory used to define constructs, operationally define variables, and advance hypotheses or questions.
- Research on the effects of video games remains in its early stages, compared to the greater theoretical sophistication reflected in more mature areas of inquiry such as violence and television.

Gaziano (2001) has suggested the potential value in future research examining relationships between violent video game play and aggression as a function of family childrearing styles, where children from authoritarian households "who feel powerless" may be attracted to violent media content including video games (p. 237).

Some researchers are beginning to suggest that theories and methods used in television research may not be entirely appropriate as models for doing research on video games and audience effects. Many of the articles summarized in this chapter included discussion wherein researchers considered that aggression, per se, may not be an appropriate description for audience experiences. Many of these researchers speculated that the limited conclusions based on current research might have be the result of an inability to recognize and measure the importance of the *arousal* functions apparently evident in much of video game play. Newman (2002) argued, "interactive videogames are not uniquely interactive experiences. Rather, they blend sequences of high-level interaction with segments of almost filmic spectatorship" (p. 418). Newman urged that future study focus on the "importance of the player in the formation and continuation of the videogame experience . . . [who are] highly integrated into and implicated by the system, which does not function without their active input" (p. 418). Many scholars whose work is included in this chapter recognized that video game play differs substantially from traditional television viewing. The activity is more "lean in" than "lean back" in nature—the latter more characteristic of passive television viewing. Many of the most popular video games, including those used as stimulus materials in various studies, force the player to assume the perspective of characters on screen, or assume the player's point of view, as one competes, searches, or hunts for clues or targets to engage. Video game players, as anyone knows who has played even once, are "connected" in cognitive and tactile ways to the often threaded narrative of game content where skill is rewarded by ever-increasingly complex interplay between player and technology, and often other remote players. Success is often contingent on learning and mastering multiple levels of gaming strategy as well as hand-eye coordination. As Newman suggests, video game players can become totally immersed in the experience of video game play, such that the rest of the world drops away. The socio-cognitive world invited by video game play may engage the senses in ways such that content takes a second seat to arousal. Clearly, existing research has demonstrated that gender helps predict both patterns of play and content preferences. Other work by some researchers on the relationships between gambling addiction and video gaming addiction may also prove a worthwhile venue for future study. These promising venues for future research take on increasing importance as today's video game industry continues to push technological frontiers, making today's products even more vivid, interactive, indeed *real* compared to those even a few years ago.

REFERENCES

Anderson, C., & Dill, K. (2000). Video games and aggressive thoughts, feelings, and behavior in the laboratory and in life. *Journal of Personality and Social Psychology, 78,* 772–790.

Ballard, M., & Lineberger, R. (1999). Video game violence and confederate gender: Effects on reward and punishment given by college males. *Sex Roles, 41,* 541–558.

Bartholow, B., & Anderson, C. (2002). Effects of violent video games on aggressive behavior: Potential sex differences. *Journal of Experimental Social Psychology, 38,* 283–290.

Beasley, B., & Collins Standley, T. (2002). Shirts vs. skins: Clothing as an indicator of gender role stereotyping in video games. *Mass Communication and Society, 5,* 279–293.

Bensley, L., & Van Eenwyk, J. (2001). Video games and real-life aggression: Review of the literature. *Journal of Adolescent Health, 29,* 244–257.

Bushman, B., & Anderson, C. (2002). Violent video games and hostile expectations: A test of the general aggression model. *Personality and Social Psychology Bulletin, 28,* 1679–1686.

Dietz, T. (1998). An examination of violence and gender role portrayals in video games: Implications for gender socialization and aggressive behavior. *Sex Roles, 38,* 425–442.

Dill, K., & Dill, J. (1998). Video game violence: A review of the empirical literature. *Aggression and Violent Behavior, 3,* 407–428.

Entertainment Software Association. (2003). *Key facts and research on video games and violence.* Retrieved December 9, 2003, from http://www.theesa.com/pressroom.html.

Fleming, M., & Rickwood, D. (2001). Effects of violent versus nonviolent video games on children's arousal, aggressive mood, and positive mood. *Journal of Applied Social Psychology, 31,* 2047–2071.

Funk, J., & Buchman, D. (1996). Playing violent video and computer games and adolescent self-concept. *Journal of Communication, 46*(2), 19–32.

Gaziano, C. (2001). Toward a broader conceptual framework for research on social stratification, childrearing patterns, and media effects. *Mass Communication and Society, 4,* 219–244.

Gupta, R., & Derevensky, J. (1996). The relationship between gambling and video-game playing behavior in children and adolescents. *Journal of Gambling Studies, 12,* 375–394.

Irwin, A., & Gross, A. (1995). Cognitive tempo, violent video games, and aggressive behavior in young boys. *Journal of Family Violence, 10,* 337–350.

Kirsh, S. (1998). Seeing the world through Mortal Kombat-colored glasses: Violent video games and the development of a short-term hostile attribution bias. *Childhood: A Global Journal of Child Research, 5,* 177–184.

Kirsh, S. (2003). The effects of violent video games on adolescents: The overlooked influence of development. *Aggression and Violent Behavior, 8,* 377–398.

Kubey, R., & Larson, R. (1990). The use and experience of the new video media among children and young adolescents. *Communication Research, 17,* 107–130.

Mediascope. (2000, March 10). *Video games & their effects.* Retrieved November 26, 2003, from http://www.mediascope.org/pubs/ibriefs/vge.htm.

National Institute on Media and the Family. (2001, August 9). *Fact sheet: Effects of video game playing on children.* Retrieved November 26, 2003, from http:///www.mediafamily.org/facts/facts_effects.shtml.

Newman, J. (2002). In search of the videogame player: The lives of Mario. *New Media and Society, 4,* 405–422.

Panee, C., & Ballard, M. (2002). High versus low aggressive priming during video-game training: Effects on violent action during game play, hostility, heart rate, and blood pressure. *Journal of Applied Social Psychology, 32,* 2458–2474.

Phillips, C., Rolls, S., Rouse, A., & Griffiths, M. (1995). Home video game playing in school children: A study of incidence and patterns of play. *Journal of Adolescence, 18,* 687–691.

Salguero, R., & Moran, R. (2002). Measuring problem video game playing in adolescents. *Addiction, 97,* 1601–1606.

Sherry, J. (2001). The effects of violent video games on aggression: A meta-analysis. *Human Communication Research, 27,* 409–431.

Thompson, K., & Haninger, K. (2001). Violence in E-rated video games. *JAMA: Journal of the American Medical Association, 286,* 591–598.

Villani, S. (2001). Impact of media on children and adolescents: A 10-year review of the research. *Journal of the American Academy of Child and Adolescent Psychiatry, 40,* 392–401.

Wiegman, O., & van Schie, E. (1998). Video game playing and its relations with aggressive and prosocial behaviour. *British Journal of Social Psychology, 37,* 367–378.

ACTIVITIES

1. A relatively underexplored area of video game research is the arcade. Locate and visit a video game arcade in your geographic region. This activity does not ask you to conduct research per se, but forces you to think about *how* you might conduct a qualitative study of video game play in an arcade. Assume that relatively little is known about video game play in arcades. Your job is to design a study suitable for answering basic questions about the video arcade scene. Your questions should be preliminary and open-ended, and could include "Who plays?" "When?" "What are the most popular games?" "Who decides what games are installed?" "What factors contribute to that decision?" "What are the most popular games?" "What are the least popular?" "What other activities appear to occur along with video game play?" Obviously, you will want to conduct one or more on-site visits to get a handle on *how you might answer these and other questions.* Review Chapter 3,

"Qualitative Media Effects Research," and decide what approach or approaches you would take to study video game activity at a local arcade. Compare your ideas to peers assigned the same task. What were the overlaps in your field research strategy compared to others?

2. Many researchers who have studied the effects of video game play have suggested that the psychological construct of *arousal* may be a productive approach for future research. Theories of arousal abound, as do many studies stemming from one or more theoretical approaches. Familiarize yourself with one or more theories of arousal, plus actual studies involving audiences. Your goal is to develop a valid measure of arousal for the study of video games. Note how existing theories, and corresponding research studies, have defined and developed measures for assessing arousal. Some of these measures have been used in experimental settings. Others, often in the form of scales, have been used in survey-type approaches. Be prepared to answer the following questions. What theory or theories of arousal did you adopt for the study of video games? What are the component parts of your theory of arousal? What are the typical ways that the component parts of your theory have been measured or assessed by other researchers? What, specifically, would you do either in an experimental, survey, or qualitative study to measure video game arousal? More specifically, what would you measure in an experiment? Or, what questions would you ask as part of a survey? What would be your method for acquiring evidence in a qualitative study? Compare your ideas with others who engaged this activity. Did your ideas overlap with peers? What were the differences? Can you combine different ideas to generate an even more valid measure of video game arousal?

3. Conduct your own content analysis of a popular video game. Choose one or more variables for analysis, such as violence, aggression, or gender stereotyping. Based on your readings in this and other chapters, as well as your own reading of original studies, develop an operational definition for each variable you propose to study. Play the video game or, if you do not feel proficient enough to play the game, find someone who is. Ideally, as is the case with many studies reported in this chapter, you can hook up the output of video game play to a video recording device, thus allowing you to view the content of the game at your own speed with pause and play capabilities. Content analyze at least 20 minutes of the game. What are your results expressed in terms of frequencies and percentages of occurrences? Compare your results with peers who conducted similar studies, for either the same or different games. What, as a group, can you conclude about the content of the video game(s) analyzed?

QUESTIONS

1. Most researchers agree that video game play represents a qualitatively different experience compared to watching television. Logic would dictate that the effects from playing violent video games would be greater, compared to watching violent television, as statistically measured in experiments and surveys. To date, research has shown the effect of violent video game play to be less than that of violent television. Generate three explanations for why you think this is the current state of affairs.

2. Research confirms that males play video games much more often than females. Provide at least three reasons, based on your understanding of research summarized in this chapter, other chapters, or your own readings, for why you think this is the case.

3. One of the criticisms of existing research on video games is that scholars have used many different theories and approaches, thus impeding the development of one unifying theory or approach. What theory or perspective discussed here or in related chapters appears to have the greatest potential in providing a unified approach to the study of video games? Why? Provide at least three points in your rationale.

ADDITIONAL READINGS

Anderson, C., & Morrow, M. (1995). Competitive aggression without interaction: Effects of competitive versus cooperative instructions on aggressive behavior in video games. *Personality and Social Psychology Bulletin, 21,* 1020–1030.

Buchman, D., & Funk, J. (1996). Video and computer games in the '90s: Children's time commitment and game preference. *Children Today, 24*(1), 12–15, 31.

Griffiths, M. (1999). Violent video games and aggression: A review of the literature. *Aggression and Violent Behavior, 4,* 203–212.

CHAPTER FOURTEEN

TELEVISION NEWS

Research has long shown that television news plays an important role in everyday life. One recent study confirmed findings consistent with those in recent decades, that over 80 percent of the U.S. public watch local television affiliate broadcast news "several times a week" and almost half consider this venue their "major source" for information. This same survey of 1,003 respondents also showed more trust in television network and affiliate news than in newspapers. Finally, over 60 percent of respondents from this survey believed that media in general and local television in particular do a "good" or "excellent" job in news coverage (Radio and Television News Directors Foundation, 2003). Clearly, the U.S. public spends a considerable amount of time using television for what it considers to be a credible source of news and information.

A dominant perspective in this area of research is **agenda setting theory** (AST). AST examines how news organizations decide what stories to cover, and how to cover them. Therefore, one component of AST research has been the examination of how news prioritizes topics for people to consider and, in essence, tells news audiences what to think about. More recent decades of AST research have even explored how, under certain conditions, news agenda setters not only tell audiences what topics to think about, but actually what to think about in terms of those topics. Those among you interested in reading more about this subject are encouraged to see some of the original AST work by McCombs and Shaw (1972) or more recent discussion about the evolution of the perspective (McCombs & Reynolds, 2002).

What is the story content in U.S. affiliate-television, traditional broadcast network, or cable news network news? How are certain peoples and groups portrayed? What about trends in news coverage in other countries? What kinds of stories are most attended to and best remembered by audiences? What do audiences think about trends in newscast styles? What are the audience effects, if any, in watching these different news styles? The researchers whose work is summarized in this chapter asked these and related questions. Thousands of news studies have been published over the years by researchers in journalism, mass communication, and related disciplines. As a result, the search for research articles summarized in this chapter included only those published in the past few years from the ComAbstracts database. Content analyses, experiments, and surveys are included and summarized.

CONTENT ANALYSES

How do newscasts differ between traditional U.S. broadcast networks and more recent cable news networks? This was the underlying question motivating asked by Bae (2000), who used economic and market theory to examine "product differentiation" between the major suppliers of network television news in the United States. The researcher predicted basic differences between broadcast and cable networks, differences between the two groups in terms of international news coverage, and differences in the amount of unduplicated news (p. 65). Two weeks of evening newscasts were videotaped during spring 1997 for ABC, CBS, CNN, FNC, MSNBC, and NBC, resulting in 60 newscasts including 1,194 stories. Results demonstrated that "while the cable newscasts covered proportionally more government/politics and human interest/feature news, the broadcast newscasts reported more health/welfare stories" (p. 69). In addition, "the three cable newscasts had more unique stories than the broadcast networks, which is logical since they were longer [in program length]" (p. 71). Both broadcast and cable news networks devoted about 20 percent of coverage to international stories (p. 73).

Television news has been the focus of research examining portrayals of race and ethnicity. Dixon and Linz (2000) examined portrayals of African Americans and Latinos in television news crime stories. The researchers examined how and in what ways some members of the community are associated with crime in society. They hypothesized that African Americans and Latinos would be represented more often as criminals on local-market television news, would appear more often in the role as criminals compared to law enforcement personnel, and would be overrepresented compared to actual crime statistics (p. 137). The newscast sample was randomly drawn over 20 weeks from seven affiliated and independent broadcast stations in the greater Los Angeles and Orange County metropolitan area. A total of 116 newscasts were included in the analysis. Results indicated that African Americans "were almost two and a half times more likely to be portrayed as felons than Whites" and "Latinos were almost twice as likely as Whites to be portrayed as felony perpetrators" (p. 142). In addition, African Americans and Latinos appeared more often as "lawbreakers" compared to appearances as "law defenders" and Caucasians appeared more often as defenders than criminal felons (p. 142). When compared to actual crime statistics, results showed that African Americans were more likely to be portrayed as felons compared to actual arrests, Latinos were less likely compared to actual arrests, and results were inconclusive for Caucasians (pp. 145–146). Results were perceived as part of "unconscious stereotypical assumptions" on the part of news directors and producers. Dixon and Linz (2002) continued their investigation into relationships between television news and depictions of race in their examination of pretrial publicity. The purpose of the study was to content-analyze types and frequency of pretrial publicity as they may relate to the race of defendants. The sample was drawn from the greater Los Angeles and Orange Country metropolitan area. Sample newscasts were videotaped over a 20-week period from affiliated and independent broadcast television stations, resulting in two weeks of newscast programming representing 200 separate programs. Results showed that "19% of the total number of defendants . . . were identified in connection with at least one of the prejudicial statements" (p. 124) including such things as mentioning prior arrests, prior convictions, confessions, or expressed opinions regarding the defendant's guilt. There was a statistically significant difference between portrayals of African American and Latino defendants and associations with prejudicial reporting compared to Caucasian and other race groups.

Much of the research conducted on news occurs in the United States, concerning local affiliate, broadcast network, cable-network practices. What about news in other countries? Cann and Mohr (2001) examined gender roles in newscasts on Australian broadcast networks. The researchers cited literature demonstrating that journalism employment trends in Australia show the profession is no longer male-dominated. However, also consistent with previous research, the researchers sought to assess whether more subtle gender bias prevails in television newscasts. For example, some previous research indicated that on-air personalities are often assigned different types of stories to report as a function of gender. Male anchors are assigned hard-news stories compared to their female counterparts, who are assigned soft-news stories. The sample was drawn from five Australian network channels, resulting in 19.5 hours of programming including 450 individual stories (p. 166). Results indicated that 62.7 percent of all stories were anchored by males, sports were "almost invariably anchored by men" (p. 168), overall anchoring was evenly divided between females and males during weekdays, but males anchored more stories during weekends. Male reporters covered more stories than females at a ratio of over two to one, a finding consistent across all networks analyzed (p. 168). Male sources predominated in sports stories, and "86% of expert sources were male" (p. 169). Finally, "male and female reporters did not differ significantly in their use of male or female sources" (p. 170). The researchers concluded that a gender bias remains in Australian network television news.

First (2002) compared 1988 and 1998 Israeli television news portrayals of Arabs, at two points in time representing key political landmarks: the first Palestinian uprising and five years beyond the peace agreement in Oslo. The study compared two major Israeli television news organizations, Mabat and Chadashot. The 1988 sample was 54 Mabat newscasts. The 1998 newscasts were 20 Mabat and 18 Chadashot programs. Results indicated that Arabs appeared in news stories 15 percent of the time in 1988, and 13 percent of the time in 1998. Arabs appeared first in stories 26 percent of the time in 1988, but increased in first appearances to 46 percent in 1998 (p. 181). Arabs were not identified by name in 75 percent of all cases in 1988, compared to 1998 when 38 percent were identified as Palestinians, 31 percent were identified as enemies, 17 percent were identified as Israeli Palestinians, and 14 percent were identified as Arabs from friendly countries (p. 182). A majority (64 percent) of all Arabs portrayed in 1988 were not identified by profession, compared to 1998 when only 40 percent were similarly not identified (p. 183). Arab homes and neighborhoods were depicted as bare and sparse in 1988, compared to 1998 when more homes were shown with landscaping and well-maintained interiors. Male Arabs were depicted in Western clothes 76 percent of the time in 1988, nearly identical to 79 percent of the time in 1998. The researcher also found some differences in overall percentages of Arab representations between the two networks and concluded "images tend to change according to political necessity, and thus the representation of Arabs in Israeli television news is correspondingly fluid" (p. 182).

Television news-gathering technology has evolved to a point where live reports from the field by a remote reporter are common parts of everyday newscasts. What characterizes the content of such remote feeds? Are journalistic or other purposes served with such practices? Tuggle and Huffman (2001) explored these issues in their examination of newscast content in large, medium, and small U.S. television markets. The researchers reviewed pertinent literature assessing increasing trends toward live reports, perhaps with more interest in station promotion than in relevant news gathering. The sample was generated from live broadcasts during five months between late 1998 and early 1999, from two large, three medium, and three smaller U.S. television markets, consisting of a total of 24 affiliate broadcast television stations and 120 news programs (p. 338). Results indicated that all affiliate broadcast stations "aired more stories containing a live element than standard reporter packages" and "in nearly nine of every ten instances . . . there was no apparent journalistic justification for having the live element as part of the report" (pp. 339–340). The content of live reports was dominated by entertainment, sports, and human interest stories compared to other production styles of reporting where crime, the courts, government, politics as well as sports were predominant (p. 341). The researchers concluded that live reports were of greater potential value as promotional strategies than as a production technique designed to provide access to late-breaking news.

To what extent has conglomerate television ownership influenced news content on the part of broadcast networks, affiliate broadcasters, or cable networks owned by the same companies? McAllister (2002) traced promotional efforts to boost viewer ratings for the last episode of the then popular situation comedy *Seinfeld* in May 1998. The researcher reviewed deregulatory and ownership trends in American media leading to the cross-promotion of programming into areas once considered sacred, particularly television news. A sample of news stories was downloaded from the Lexis/Nexis news database and supplemental information was obtained from a news archive at Vanderbilt University spanning the time from when the NBC network announced the final *Seinfeld* season to the day after the final episode. Results indicated that "NBC had nearly three times as many stories" (p. 389) about *Seinfeld* as CBS. ABC aired only one story during the data collection period. Affiliate broadcast stations in the New York City market were also compared. The NBC affiliate aired ten times as may stories as the ABC affiliate, but the CBS affiliate did air a relatively comparable number of stories. Trends were roughly similar for affiliate stations in Indianapolis (pp. 392–393). The NBC-owned cable news network CNBC aired three times as many stories about the final episode compared to CNN (p. 394). The researcher concluded that results from the study showed how the "current corporate context of news organizations influences the agenda of news" (p. 399), where "journalists [are] being put in the position of

■ ■ ■ ■ ■

BOX 14.1

RADIO-TELEVISION NEWS DIRECTORS ASSOCIATION CODE OF ETHICS

The Radio-Television News Directors Association (RTDNA) is the largest organization for professionals in electronic journalism, including news directors but also for educators and students (www.rtnda.org). The organization includes a voluntary code of ethics in order to guide professionals in the everyday practice of television and radio news. The complete version of the code of ethics can be found at the RTNDA website. Here is a summary of some of the key points in this code of ethics:

- Electronic journalists are trustees of the public and should seek and report the truth accurately, independently, and with integrity.
- Electronic journalists should avoid distortions, disclose sources, and report information provided by other sources.
- Electronic journalists should present significant and relevant news fairly and impartially.

- Electronic journalists should avoid conflicts of interest and respect the intelligence of both those interviewed and audience members.
- Electronic journalists should protect one another when others seek to influence or control news content.
- Electronic journalists should be accountable (Radio-Television News Directors Association & Foundation, 2000).

Think a moment about these voluntary guidelines in light of what you are learning from recent research on television news and from your own experiences with television news. Do you think that most television journalists are following RTNDA guidelines? Provide some recent examples. Or, if you disagree, think about some of the reasons that television journalists might not follow these guidelines.

subordinating news values for a larger entertainment and promotional ethos" (p. 399) (see Box 14.1).

EXPERIMENTS

Does how television news portrays incidents of social protest have an effect on audience interpretations? McLeod and Detenber (1999) used **framing** to inform their approach. Framing is the process by which communication practitioners, including news people, use the particular techniques of storytelling and production to emphasize some parts of a story over others, thus influencing audience interpretations of that story. For example, audiences may perceive a story differently when simply read by a news anchor compared to the same story accompanied by graphics or video footage. A total of 212 U.S. undergraduate students from a "mid-Atlantic" geographic location participated in the study (p. 9). Stimulus materials were three television news stories about "anarchist protests" in a major U.S. northern Midwest city occurring nearly a decade before the current study was conducted. The three stories were rated as low, medium, and high in support of the status quo. Results demonstrated that a news story emphasizing "higher levels of status quo support" resulted in higher levels of criticism of protesters, less identification with protesters, and lowered perceptions of protest effectiveness (pp. 13–15). The researchers concluded that "Although each story was critical of . . . protesters, subtle differences in the level of status quo support in the news stories had a substantial . . . impact" consistent with framing effects.

Does race inform news story memory recall? Oliver (1999) suggested that mental scripts and schema used by audiences filter news accounts in such ways as to reinforce negative stereotypes. She predicted that Caucasian undergraduates scoring high on racial prejudice measures would see news stories about Caucasian versus African American crimes differently than those undergraduates displaying lower levels of prejudice. The researcher tested 60 U.S. undergraduate students at a "mid-Atlantic" university (p. 50). Results indicated that "anti-Black attitudes were positively associated with misidentification scores when the murder suspect was Caucasian . . . but negatively associated with misidentification scores when the murder suspect was African American" (p. 54). These two factors contributed 7.8 and 7.2 percent respectively to racially biased interpretations. The researcher suggested that results lent support to an interaction between negative racial attitudes, existing cognitive schema, and perceptions of news stories related to race.

Do different styles of news reporting, particularly tabloid versus more traditional forms, influence perceptions and evaluations of television news? Grabe, Lang, and Zhao (2003) predicted that tabloid and traditional versions of news containing either compelling or calming stories would result in differences in story recognition and recall (pp. 392–394). The researchers tested 45 male and female adults. Results showed "arousing news content and tabloid packaging both cause increases in arousal and attention" and audiences "recognize the tabloid format . . . and distrust news presented in this sensational style" (p. 407). In addition, subjects in this study "exaggerate the importance of news presented with sensational formal features" (p. 407). The researchers noted the frustrating conclusions drawn from results. Tabloid production techniques may enhance news story recall but border on "journalistic misrepresentation" or worse. In a related study, Grabe, Zhou, Lang, and Bolls (2000) examined effects of tabloid newscast styles on audience information processing. Do such practices influence audience perceptions of the trustworthiness of news? The researchers hypothesized that participants would rate tabloid newscast stories as more arousing, would exhibit higher levels of skin conductance (an indicator of arousal), show reduced heart rate, and recall more information from tabloid stories, but would also rate standard reporting more informative and believable (pp. 583–585). They tested a combination of 80 students and nonstudents at a major university in the Midwest. Results showed that participants reported being more aroused when watching tabloid news stories. Physiological measures confirmed audience arousal was significantly higher for tabloid versus standard story versions. However, these same participants found standard versions of stories more informative and believable. Compared to predicted outcomes, subjects also found tabloid stories to be less enjoyable (pp. 591–593). The researchers argued that results supported the contention that newscast audiences "both recognize and distrust tabloid journalism" (p. 595).

One of the fundamental questions in news research is how different media influence perception and memory of news. Walma Van Der Molen and Van Der Voort (2000) compared children's recall of news for television, print, and audio media and tested three assumptions regarding "the observed superiority of television news" (p. 5). They questioned television's superiority over print, particularly if photographs were included as part of printed news. They also tested the audio channel as a factor in helping to reinforce print news stories. Finally, the researchers assessed whether a child's reading ability, or lack thereof, might contribute to superior recall of television news. A total of 192 fourth and sixth graders from six schools in The Netherlands participated in the study. Results indicated that television news stories produced the highest recall. There were no differences between the text-only and text-with photo versions, or between print and audio news versions (p. 16). The researchers concluded results reinforced findings from previous research showing "television . . . to be the most effective transmitter of news information" (p. 21).

What elements of a newscast story about disease prevention are of greatest importance to audiences? Cooper, Burgoon, and Roter (2001) examined "cues that prompt viewers to actively or passively process television news stories about prevention topics" (p. 228). Their approach was anchored in **expectancy value theory,** suggesting that audiences pay attention to story content that interests them, particularly those regarding health issues. The researchers predicted relationships between audience beliefs about health and attention paid to health-related newscast stories. They tested 458 adults selected from court jury pools in Baltimore. Results showed "personal relevance" (p. 236) as well as "novelty, shock value, and the absence of exaggeration" (p. 237) to be the most important audience beliefs in helping to predict attention paid to health-related news stories. As a practical recommendation, the researchers suggested "health advocates should make a special effort to emphasize the relevance of information to the lives of viewers" (p. 236).

SURVEYS

Readers may recall from introductory and other chapters the mass communication perspective known as **cultivation theory.** This theory characterizes television as a powerful cultural ambassador, particularly for those individuals who represent its heaviest consumers. Cohen and Weimann (2000) utilized this theory in an effort to determine what kinds of television genres have what kinds of effects on television viewers. A total of 4,840 Israeli students from 150 schools and 350 different classes in "Jewish schools supervised by the Israeli Ministry of Education" participated in the survey. Results showed that "the higher the viewing of news, the higher the level of trust and help and the lower the fear of being exploited and the fear of victimization" (p. 108).

What do television news reporters perceive as changes in the way stations emphasize news coverage? Coulson, Riffe, Lacy, and St. Cyr (2001) examined television news reporter perceptions of city hall coverage in the face of increasing market pressures toward sensationalism or tabloid news practices at the cost of providing viewers with important information about local public affairs. City hall news reporters working for television affiliate broadcasters in 214 U.S. television markets participated. Results showed participating reporters averaged ten years in the profession, with 60 percent of respondents indicating their station provided routine coverage of city hall, though 54 percent felt not enough reporter time was given to coverage of such issues. In addition, only 28.1 percent of respondents felt other reporters considered coverage of city hall "most important" (pp. 85–86). Reporters in smaller markets more often felt their station provided adequate coverage of local government (p. 87). The researchers concluded that results suggest smaller television markets with fewer broadcast television facilities "seem to be the places where local television news is doing the best job of covering city hall" (p. 90).

Sotirovic (2001) examined the audience effects of watching television news stories about crime. The researcher argued that audience preferences for crime policies, such as preventive or punitive approaches, could be informed by distortions in crime-related news coverage. Surveys were administered to 395 randomly selected adults from a U.S. state in the northern Midwest. Results indicated "media use patterns" contributed 2.4 to 12.4 percent to audience beliefs about crime policies. More specific to television news, results indicated "Fear of crime also is related to higher use of simple media content and television crime and local news" (p. 321) though individuals having more direct experiences with crime were less affected by television news content. Among conclusions, the researcher argued, "people who are more exposed, and pay more attention to, complex media content, represented by the traditional hard-news media format, are likely to have more-complex thinking about crime" (p. 324).

SUMMARY

Some trends can be distilled from the content analyses presented in this chapter.

- Differences may exist in journalistic decision-making processes among the major broadcast and cable news divisions or organizations.
- Conglomerate ownership of television media has resulted in cross-promotion between traditionally distinct programming genres. Television news divisions now include stories of questionable journalistic value designed to promote programming events in entertainment divisions of the same organization.

There is reason to suspect that professionals in the world of television news share more in common than they differ across affiliate, broadcast network, and cable network levels. The "sameness" prevailing in other television genres such as action-adventure dramas, situation comedies, or reality programming is a form of homogeneity also clearly apparent in television network news. This homogenization is due, in large part, to a departure from the traditionally sacred nature of network news divisions such as ABC, CBS, and NBC, where revenue generation was a low priority. These organizations were annual loss leaders, but are now forced by ownership to compete and perform at levels comparable to entertainment divisions in the same network. Further, these divisions now cooperate in cross-promotion, particularly on the part of news in advancing ratings efforts on the part of entertainment programming. Such trends may or may not contribute to the ongoing and stereotypic depictions of race and gender in television news, both in the United States and apparently abroad. Clearly, this area of news research suggests programming trends consistent with other television genres.

- African Americans, compared to all other race and ethnic groups, are overrepresented as perpetrators of crime compared to national crime statistics.
- African American suspects may lose their fair day in court as a function of violations of antiprejudicial guidelines established by legal practitioners.

You may remember that television news is perceived as the most credible source of information for many viewers. Therefore, how the news portrays, distorts, and reinforces social roles and stereotypes in society becomes an important consideration. Some researchers who document such findings suggest that such practices may be unintentional on the part of news organization personnel, and that such practices are borne out of years of doing journalism certain ways and represent deep-seated racial bias reflecting larger race and class struggles.

- Television remains the preferred medium for news, particularly for younger generations.
- Stories with high levels of personal relevance garner the most attention.
- Stories are encountered and filtered by preexisting cognitive schema for such things as race, gender, and crime.
- The most frequent American television news viewers may develop a distorted view about risks in the larger world, compared to audiences who watch less news or viewers in at least one other country who apparently take some measure of comfort from such information.
- Audiences that engage more complex news narrative structures, correspondingly, approach issues like crime in more complex ways. Clearly, content, form, and context may inform such perceptions.
- Television audiences both recognize and distrust tabloid and sensationalistic storytelling practices.

Much work remains in these and related areas of news research. Compared to some areas of inquiry, such as media violence, sample sizes remain relatively small when conducting research on news audiences. Larger samples are desirable in order to lend more credibility and weight to findings. In addition, the relationships between variables in news research remain relatively small and account for little in the way of the bigger picture. If, as some of the research summarized here suggests, audience ratings are a primary goal in network and local television news, then the day-to-day professional practices seen to fuel such efforts may have wandered from traditional journalistic values and principles concerning the function and role played by news organizations in a free society. These factors appear to contribute to everyday decisions concerning what stories are considered newsworthy, what stories get covered, how they get covered, and what stories eventually make it to air. This is a dynamic and robust area of inquiry for future research.

REFERENCES

Bae, H. (2000). Product differentiation in national TV newscasts: A comparison of the cable all-news networks and the broadcast networks. *Journal of Broadcasting and Electronic Media, 44*, 62–77.

Cann, D., & Mohr, P. (2001). Journalist and source gender in Australian television news. *Journal of Broadcasting and Electronic Media, 45*, 162–174.

Cohen, J., & Weimann, G. (2000). Cultivation revisited: Some genres have some effects on some viewers. *Communication Reports, 13*(2), 99–114.

Cooper, C., Burgoon, M., & Roter, D. (2001). An expectancy-value analysis of viewer interest in television prevention news stories. *Health Communication, 13*, 227–240.

Coulson, D., Riffe, D., Lacy, S., & St. Cyr, C. (2001). Erosion of television coverage of city hall? Perceptions of TV reporters on the beat. *Journalism and Mass Communication Quarterly, 78*, 81–82.

Dixon, T., & Linz, D. (2000). Overrepresentation and underrepresentation of African Americans and Latinos as lawbreakers on television news. *Journal of Communication, 50*(2), 131–154.

Dixon, T., & Linz, D. (2002). Television news, prejudicial pretrial publicity, and the depiction of race. *Journal of Broadcasting and Electronic Media, 46*, 112–136.

First, A. (2002). The fluid nature of representation: Transformations in the representation of Arabs in Israeli television news. *Howard Journal of Communications, 13*, 173–190.

Grabe, M., Lang, A., & Zhao, X. (2003). News content and form: Implications for memory and audience evaluations. *Communication Research, 30*, 387–413.

Grabe, M., Zhou, S., Lang, A., & Bolls, P. (2000). Packaging television news: The effects of tabloid on information processing and evaluative responses. *Journal of Broadcasting and Electronic Media, 44*, 581–598.

McAllister, M. (2002). Television news plugola and the last episode of *Seinfeld*. *Journal of Communication, 52*, 383–401.

McCombs, M., & Reynolds, A. (2002). News influence on our pictures of the world. In J. Bryant & D. Zillmann (Eds.), *Media Effects: Advances in Theory and Research* (pp. 1–18). Mahwah, NJ: Erlbaum.

McCombs, M., & Shaw, D. (1972). The agenda-setting function of mass media. *Public Opinion Quarterly, 36*, 176–187.

McLeod, D., & Detenber, B. (1999). Framing effects of television news coverage of social protest. *Journal of Communication, 49*(3), 3–23.

Oliver, M. (1999). Caucasian viewers' memory of Black and White criminal suspects in the news. *Journal of Communication, 49*(3), 46–60.

Radio-Television News Directors Association & Foundation. (2000, September 14). *Code of ethics and professional conduct: Radio-Television News Directors Association.* Retrieved December 9, 2003, from http://www.rtnda.org/ethics/coe.shtml#.

Radio and Television News Directors Foundation. (2003). *2003 local television news study of news directors and the American public.* Retrieved December 1, 2003, from http://www.rtnda.org/ethics/2003survey.pdf.

Sotirovic, M. (2001). Affective and cognitive processes as mediators of media influences on crime-policy preferences. *Mass Communication and Society, 4,* 311–329.

Tuggle, C., & Huffman, S. (2001). Live reporting in television news: Breaking news or black holes? *Journal of Broadcasting and Electronic Media, 45,* 335–344.

Walma Van Der Molen, J., & Van Der Voort, T. (2000). The impact of television, print, and audio on children's recall of the news: A study of three alternative explanations for the dual-coding hypothesis. *Human Communication Research, 26,* 3–26.

ACTIVITIES

1. Today's multichannel news industry affords an opportunity to see how different countries and cultures cover the same news stories. This activity asks you to isolate one major story in the news, perhaps a story about U.S. politics, or foreign military involvement, or an international news story of considerable import so as to find its way in a number of international television news agendas. To do this you will need to gain access to television newscasts from different countries, or different cultures within countries. For example, you could isolate a major story on a dominant U.S. cable news network, as well as the same story on one or more of the Latino or Hispanic networks increasingly available by means of cable television. You will also want to sample television programming from other countries, including Western broadcasts such as the BBC as well as major Arab or Asian programs. You will have to exercise a bit of initiative and energy in this task by preparing in advance so that you can secure a video record of breaking or continuing news stories. Another way to consider accomplishing this task is to pursue Internet websites for various networks, both domestic and international. Often, major stories are included as web-linked video files. Once you have your stories, analyze how each different network treats the story. Because of language limitations, you may be forced in some instances to analyze the story as told by means of video and other visuals, in terms of what is emphasized, what experts or spokespersons are consulted, and so on. Compare and contrast the treatment of this story on the various networks chosen for this exercise. Summarize your findings. Compare your findings to the work performed by others on this same activity, perhaps for the same or different stories. What generalizations can you provide based on your collective findings?

2. Acquire one or more major metropolitan dailies, preferably the morning newspaper(s), for a weekday of your choice. The same day, make arrangements to videotape at least two local or regional evening newscasts in your television market. Perform a content analysis on your video samples in order to answer the following questions. How many news stories were contained in the major news segment of each newscast? How many stories were international, national, regional, or local in scope? How does this compare across the stations you analyzed? How many of the stories on each newscast were timely or breaking stories? How many were soft news, or stories that could be aired most any day? How many stories overlapped between the stations you analyzed? How many stories aired on each newscast corresponded to stories in the morning newspaper? Summarize your findings. To

what extent do you think local television newscasts do a good job of providing local television viewers with important information about the world in which they live? Compare and contrast your findings with others who may have performed the same task.

3. Videotape a weekday version of your most preferred local evening newscast. Ideally, you should perform this activity during a time when a major story does not dominate local reporting. Analyze each story in the newscast. Is the story one read by an anchor? Is the story a video package produced by a reporter that very day, or is the story a video package produced by a local reporter days in advance? Is the story a package that might have been produced by someone or an organization other than the station or channel? Is the story a live remote feed from a field reporter? Is the live remote relevant to the story being told? Do any of the stories help to promote or advance other programming efforts on the part of the station, or maybe their affiliated network? How many stories actually air during the newscast? How many of these are actually hard or timely news? How many of these stories could be aired most any day of the month or week? Basically, your goal is to try and break down the local newscasts and assess its value in providing news and information of value to local television viewers. Compare and contrast your results with others who may work on this activity.

QUESTIONS

1. Some of the research summarized in this chapter indicates that tabloid or sensationalistic approaches to news production abound and audiences both recognize and mistrust these methods of news communication. Why, in light of such findings, do you think television news operations persist in these practices?

2. Content analyses of U.S. television news confirm the overrepresentation of African Americans as perpetrators of crime. Corresponding audience analyses find evidence that such proposals prime cognitive perceptions leading to negative racial stereotypes. Why, despite advances in some areas of equal rights, do you think this practice persists in such a large and potentially influential part of the television industry?

3. Do you think that television news sets the agenda for what people think is important in their world? Do you think television news not only sets the agenda, but also influences what people think in terms of issues in their world? Why or why not? Be sure to use personal examples in your response.

ADDITIONAL READINGS

Allen, C. (2003). Gender breakthrough fit for a focus group: The first women newscasters and why they arrived in local TV news. *Journalism History, 28,* 154–162.

Bennett, W. (2001). *News: The politics of illusion.* New York: Longman.

Gant, C., & Dimmick, J. (2000). African Americans in television news: From description to explanation. *Howard Journal of Communications, 11,* 189–205.

Leshner, G., & Coyle, J. (2000). Memory for television news: Match and mismatch between processing and testing. *Journal of Broadcasting and Electronic Media, 44,* 599–613.

Powers, A. (2001). Toward monopolistic competition in U.S. local television news. *Journal of Media Economics, 14*(2), 77–86.

Rada, J. (2000). A new piece to the puzzle: Examining effects of television portrayals of African Americans. *Journal of Broadcasting and Electronic Media, 44*, 704–715.

Silcock, B. (2002). Global news, national stories: Producers as myth makers at Germany's Deutsche Welle television. *Journalism and Mass Communication Quarterly, 79*, 339–352.

Stempel, G., Hargrove, T., & Bernt, J. (2000). Relation of growth of use of the Internet to changes in media use from 1995 to 1999. *Journalism and Mass Communication Quarterly, 77*, 71–79.

Vavrus, M. (2000). From women of the year to "soccer moms": The case of the incredible shrinking women. *Political Communication, 17*, 193–213.

Walma van der Molen, J. (2001). Assessing text-picture correspondence in television news: The development of a new coding scheme. *Journal of Broadcasting and Electronic Media, 45*, 483–498.

■ ■ ■ ■ ■

CHAPTER FIFTEEN

TELEVISION AND PRESIDENTIAL POLITICS

Some argue that television took center stage in the U.S. political arena during the 1960 presidential race. The televised debates between candidates Kennedy and Nixon created political drama previously unseen by the American electorate and very likely influenced the outcome of that election. In 1976, Jimmy Carter was the first presidential candidate to employ a full-time creative advertising director to manage his successful television-intensive campaign. We now take for granted the interdependence between political campaigns, elections, and the electronic media, particularly television. Many are concerned about this development and warn that the high price of today's typical campaign for a major political office makes difficult the ability for you and me to participate in political life in important ways—that grass roots democracy is no longer a reality for American voters. Between 1976 and 1996 campaign costs to run for the U.S. House of Representatives jumped from $73,000 to $680,000 and from nearly $600,000 to $3.8 million to run for the U.S. Senate (Pew Charitable Trusts). The television industry has profited handsomely from political campaigning. One source estimated that paid television political advertisements resulted in more than $308 million to ABC, NBC, and Viacom/CBS station groups during the 2002 campaign season (Alliance for Better Campaigns, 2003). These factors have helped to contribute to increasing levels of distrust and cynicism on the part of the American voting electorate.

Think a moment about the role the mass media, and television in particular, may play in your own political socialization. Do you think television provides you with the kind of information necessary to make informed decisions about political candidates and causes? Does television provide balanced or biased coverage of major political candidates and issues? How does television news cover important political events like presidential debates? What have been the prevailing trends in political campaign advertising? Does such advertising emphasize candidate image over substantive treatment of important issues? What about the special case of negative campaign advertising? Finally, how do these various practices impact on the perceptions and behaviors of voters? What factor or factors contribute to how voters feel about political candidates, issues, and ultimately how they choose to participate in politics? These are among the questions asked by researchers whose work is summarized in this chapter. A search of the recent research revealed three main areas of investigation: news and politics, political advertising, and political knowledge. They provide the organization for this last chapter examining relationships between media, audiences, and effects. Research employing content analyses, surveys, and experiments are combined under each of these individual areas.

NEWS AND POLITICS

You will recall from the previous chapter that the majority of Americans receive their information about the world from television, and a majority of those who do believe that television news does a credible job of gathering and disseminating information. Those long-term trends have tremendous implications in terms of the political socialization process. Television news serves a major role in providing voters and future voters with information pertinent to making informed decisions about the political world. How good a job does television news do in terms of providing voters with such information? Larson (1999) examined how national evening television news covered public opinion about the 1996 U.S. presidential election both in terms of reporting about recent polls and "people-on-the-street" interviews (p. 135). The researcher content analyzed weekday evening news programs during the traditional fall campaign period by ABC, CBS, and NBC. Results were based on analysis of 110 stories aired about the campaign during that period, 68 of which were primarily reports about recent public opinion polls and the remaining 42 were interviews featuring voters on the street (p. 137). Almost 90 percent of all poll-type stories embraced traditional "horse race" themes reflecting the latest poll results, an interesting finding in light of the fact that the 1996 race concerned the dominant incumbent Clinton versus the Republican candidate Dole. The most prevalent topic for voter-one-the-street stories was campaign issues (pp. 138–139). The researcher concluded, "Public opinion about issues was practically absent from poll reporting but not from people-on-the-street statements. . . . People-on-the-street reporting enhanced the quality of television's coverage of . . . public opinion" (p. 142). The same researcher (Larson, 2000) compared the three broadcast networks in terms of coverage and found NBC reported more public opinion as well as more voter-on-the-street stories in what the researcher perceived to be an effort to reflect so-called "average" voters' views (p. 23). In related work, Craig (2000) examined trends in CBS television network news reporting of poll results between 1968 and 1996. Results from an extensive content analysis revealed stories about poll results more than tripled during the nearly 20-year time span. Moreover, the poll stories moved from the lower rungs of story order to consistently within the top two or three (pp. 34–35). Not surprisingly, there had also been a consistent increase in reporting prescribing what a particular candidate *will do, should do,* or *needs to do*" (emphasis in original) (p. 35) based on most recent poll results.

Many other chapters have included reports of meta-analyses of existing research literature. Such studies provide a useful milestone in assessing what we know about a particular branch of mass media study, how powerful any trends in findings may be, and what appear to be fruitful venues for future research. D'Alessio and Allen (2000) performed such an analysis of studies examining **news bias** coverage of U.S. presidential elections since 1948. Research on news bias examines whether one political candidate or party receives unfair amounts or types of journalistic coverage. The researchers' meta-analysis was based on 59 studies and examined how much time or space was devoted to coverage of one candidate or political party over another. The researchers found, for television, "a ratio of about 47.3 Republican minutes for every 52.7 Democratic ones—a preponderance almost certainly undetectable by the audience" (pp. 146–147). Statement bias is the study of how news gatherers and disseminators strive or do not strive to balance statements promoting one political party or candidate versus another. The researchers found that television network news reflected a pro-Democrat statement bias (p. 148). Overall, the researchers concluded, "TV network news coverage of presidential campaigns reveal a very small, if not completely consistent, liberal (or at least pro-Democratic) bias" (p. 149).

News bias in coverage of presidential politics may be more complex than the simple frequency with which each political candidate or party are represented. Bias may also be a function of the language and style with which presidential politics are covered by news media. Just, Crigler, and Buhr (1999) examined journalistic tone and coverage of the 1992 U.S. presidential campaign for various media, including both network and local television news outlets. The researchers based their content analysis on a fairly extensive collection of news stories, candidate interviews, and political advertising. Results indicated that direct quotes from presidential candidates comprise 5 percent of newspaper, 16 percent of television network, and 20 percent of local market television news (p. 29). Newspapers focused 70 percent of the time on policy issues, compared to 51 percent for television interview programs, 49 percent for network television news, and 38 percent for local television news (p. 31). Television interview programs and, naturally, paid political advertisements were the most consistent source of information about where candidates stood on various issues (p. 32). Finally, journalists and candidates were equally cynical about government institutions, as "journalists tend to demean politicians, while candidates, not surprisingly, praise the electorate" (p. 37). From a related slant, Mullen (1999) examined how contentiousness, the use of hostility and aggression in reporting, is reflected in the visual and auditory techniques of news reporting. The researcher content-analyzed story language and 163 visual images of a sample of ABC, CBS, and NBC presidential news coverage of then President Clinton (p. 163). Results indicated that story language, that used by both reporters and by President Clinton, were more contentious than noncontentious. Visual analysis revealed more complex relationships. Overall, visuals were less contentious, but the powerful nature of visuals impacted the "overall perceived contentiousness of the news story" (p. 169).

Few of us would underestimate the potential influence major televised presidential debates have on helping to frame public perceptions of major candidates.

■ ■ ■ ■ ■

BOX 15.1

WATCH THE PRESIDENTIAL DEBATES AT THE LEAGUE OF WOMEN VOTERS WEBSITE

The League of Women Voters (LWV) is an organization dedicated to encouraging grassroots voter involvement in the political process. Their website provides an electronic resource for voters, educators, and researchers (www.lwv.org). Traditionally, the LWV has sponsored the televised presidential debates and now provides a video archive of the presidential debates from 1976 through 1988. Research summarized in this chapter suggests that journalistic coverage of these debates may emphasize some things at the expense of other important themes and thus provide a distorted impression for those who do not have a chance to watch these important moments in U.S. political life. One of the best ways to form your own opinions about this controversy is to watch some of these debates and decide yourself. Check out the presidential debates video archive at www.lwv.org/elibrary/video/debates.htm.

How well a presidential candidate performs can influence voter behaviors and election outcomes (Benoit & Wells, 1996). Indeed, the debates may actually be the solitary influence for some voters (Owen, 1995). Despite their prominence and potential influence, there are those in the voting public who do not or cannot watch presidential debates. Some must rely on media coverage of such events. How good a job do the media do in covering presidential debates? This was the focus of a study by Benoit and Currie (2001). The researchers content-analyzed U.S. presidential debates in 1996 and 2000 and studied whether media "reflect the nature of those debates" (p. 31). Results indicated that news coverage for both 1996 and 2000 debates emphasized verbal attacks between candidates significantly more they the actually occurred during televised debates. News coverage of the 1996 also emphasized candidate personalities and character more than such themes were actually advanced during the debate (p. 34). The researchers suggested television news coverage of media debates "over-represent attacks (and defenses) . . . at the expense of acclaims" (p. 36). They concluded that news coverage of presidential debates has "the potential to foster the inaccurate impression that the debates are mostly negative (when in fact debates are mostly positive)" (p. 37) (see Box 15.1).

POLITICAL ADVERTISING

Are there trends in the language used in presidential campaign advertising? Ballotti and Kaid (2000) examined 1,267 television advertisements between 1952 and 1996. They suggested four central themes prevail in such advertising: activity, certainty, optimism, and realism. They discovered that activity themes using words such as "work, change, start, and moving" (p. 264) were reinforced every "1.15 words per ad" (p. 263). Certainty type words such as "is, be, leadership, all, whole, shall, and world" (p. 265) appeared very rarely in any commercials. The same trend was seen for optimism words such as "prouder, better, work, confidence . . . and working" (p. 265). Realism words such as "to, be, his, man, am, let, for themselves, are, son, from him, live, father's, president, states, have, has, and in" (p. 266) appeared every 36 words per commercial. The researchers concluded that realism and activity themes are most prominent in presidential television advertisements, with less realism and more certainty themes over the period of the 44-year span.

Another way to think about and organize presidential television advertising is in terms of image and issue differences. Image advertising often conveys and promotes the intangible or psychological dimensions for a product, service, or, in this case, a presidential candidate. Issue advertising is simply what the term means, a presidential advertisement promoting the candidate's position on one or more issues. Johnston and Kaid (2002) content-analyzed a large sample of advertising for presidential candidates to explore different production and style techniques used to promote either image or issues. The researchers analyzed a total of 1,213 advertisements, broken down into 35 percent with predominant image appeals and 65 percent issue oriented (p. 286). Results indicated that image advertising dominated campaign advertising during the 1970s and 1980s, but there was a strong return to issue-oriented messages during the 1990s and in 2000 (p. 295). In terms of language and style, image advertising was generally positive in tone and designed to advance the candidate's cause. In contrast, negative messages including attacks on the opponent were almost exclusively found in issue advertisements (p. 296). Trends over years indicated that language used in image advertising, "is not designed to create fear or stir emotions" because the researchers found "issue ads do" (p. 298), in part reflecting findings that most arguments in issue advertisements are emotional, rather than fact based.

Because political advertising is often criticized for being less than factual, for being negative, for promoting images over substance, and for misleading voters, the major U.S. television network news divisions have come to practice a form of "adwatch" as part of news featured aired during presidential campaigns. An adwatch is a news package or feature where television viewers are provided with a critical framework for encountering political advertising. Tedesco, Kaid, and McKinnon (2000) examined how ABC, CBS, and NBC covered presidential campaign television advertising for the 1996 election. Their content analysis examined both advertising aired during primary and fall races. They discovered the majority of network adwatch features focused on negative advertising, in part because negative advertisements for the period in question outnumbered positive themes three to one (p. 546). Most of these adwatch features were aired as part of larger, "routine campaign reports" (p. 546). During the fall campaign period, 76 percent of these adwatches "were treated as priority agenda items and appeared within the first 10 minutes of the news" (p. 547). These results were generally consistent for all three-television networks. President Clinton's advertising was analyzed about twice as often as candidate Dole's. Compared to the 1992 campaign season, the researchers concluded that overall network coverage of the 1996 presidential race was less, but overall adwatch content increased.

One of the criticisms of content analyses in general, and specific to political advertising, is the potential difference between what is analyzed and what targeted audiences actually see or hear. Many content analyses presented in this and previous chapters imply that audiences are actually exposed on an equal basis to the range of media analyzed. In reality, advertising exposure schedules vary significantly as a function of many factors. Specific to political television advertising, some paid political advertisements are aired repeatedly and some receive little or no exposure. However, these messages may be counted equally in terms of the images they represent and potentially convey to targeted members of the voting population. Prior (2001) recognized this problem and took into consideration rates of exposure for television political advertising. The researcher compared advertisement tone for both Republican and Democrat advertising during the 1996 presidential election against the actual frequency and estimated exposure for such advertising in one major metropolitan area. A total of 132 political advertisements were analyzed (p. 337). Results indicated that 49.1 percent of all advertisements produced by Republicans were negative, but 89.7 percent of those actually aired in the specific market were negative (p. 340). Overall, "Democrats relied more strongly on one type of ad—the comparative ad. . . . Republicans were more one-sided in their choice of tone, using 88% negative ads" (p. 341). The researcher recommended that future research tackle the problem of assessing similar trends in cable television and Internet services.

Political campaign strategists have long assumed that television advertising can play an effective role in influencing voters. One of the problems with measuring such effectiveness has been the inability to track, particularly for U.S. presidential races, large-scale television advertising schedules allowing one to speculate about potential effects on voters. Goldstein and Freedman (2002) utilized advances in computer tracking technology to document political advertising schedules for ABC, CBS, NBCA, Fox, and 25 cable networks (p. 7). Using the database provided by this new development, the researchers were able to examine "patterns of ad sponsorship, tone, geographic targeting, and timing" (p. 6) as well as perform different television market analyses for candidates Bush and Gore. Their analysis included the examination of over 900,000 political advertisements for congressional and presidential campaigns aired in 75 television markets. They noted an 82 percent increase in presidential television advertisements between 1996 and 2000 and a 59 percent increased in congressional races for the same period (pp. 8–9). The researchers were also able to examine differences across television markets, thus reflecting differences in political competition for the first time. Results showed that markets where Bush or Gore had clear and insurmountable leads had significantly less political advertising. Markets where the voting for both presidential and senatorial outcomes was less clear cleared substantially more political television advertising. Of these advertisements, "Fifty-seven percent of the Bush ads were either attack (30%) or contrast ads (27%), while the remaining 43% were promotional. In contrast, a full 80% of the Bush ads broadcast were negative (40% each attack and contrast), and only 20% were promotional" (p. 11). Analysis of message tone indicated positive themes during the early summer 2000 months, changing to negative or attack messages by August, followed by a mixture of positive and negative messages in early September. By late September the predominant tone of presidential campaign television advertising compared the qualities of the two candidates, followed by attack themes at the end of the campaign (p. 13). All together, the Bush/Cheney campaign aired 3 percent more television advertise- ments nationwide compared to Gore/Lieberman. (p. 15). The researchers concluded that advertising tone is a function of the degree of competitiveness between candi- dates and that message timing is critical and must be matched to voter perceptions at particular parts of the campaign season.

One of the more cost-effective means of communication during early presi- dential primary races has been the production and distribution of short-videotaped features of candidates. What characterizes the communication strategies in such productions? Parmelee (2002) interviewed the producers of "meet the candidate videos" for the 2000 primaries representing candidates Bauer, Bradley, Bush, Forbes, Gore, and McCain. These videos are typically short, around 10 to 20 minutes in length, and are designed to create first impressions of presidential candidates. The researcher employed **frame analysis** to inform his approach. Frame analysis is the study of a central idea or scheme that informs interpretation of a series of events. In this case, frame analysis was used to isolate a key or central idea in each candidate video. Video producers were interviewed utilizing qualitative techniques in order to determine frames used. Results indicated a number of frames used by various candidates. Videos for Democrats Bradley and Gore promoted leadership and values respectively. For Republicans, Bauer's video promoted former President Reagan's ideals. Bush promoted change, and both Forbes and McCain promoted values (p. 321). All six videos had in common the frame "I'm qualified to be president because the media say I am" (p. 321). The researcher concluded that the use of videocassettes in early primary races is an important component for estab- lishing initial, positive impressions of individual presidential candidates.

POLITICAL KNOWLEDGE

This section of the chapter reviews what we know from recent research literature in terms of how television coverage of presidential politics contributes to voter knowl- edge. For example, how does television coverage of campaigns contribute to voter preferences for presidential candidates? Shaw (1999) used data drawn from both the 1992 and 1996 U.S. presidential campaigns in an effort to answer that question. The researcher considered such factors as opinion polls, campaign events, and news media coverage. Results indicated favorable television coverage of presidential campaign events did influence voter preferences. The nature of those events also influenced voter perceptions. The power of results in this study was quite small, and the researcher concluded that any campaign event, and television's coverage of that event, made a difference in election outcomes.

To what extent is political knowledge and voting behavior a function of education level, or preferences for one news medium over another, or perhaps the amount of time spent with particular media? These were the kinds of questions examined by Eveland and Scheufele (2000) as part of a larger National Election Study conducted during the 1996 U.S. presidential campaign. The researchers based their approach on the **knowledge gap hypotheses.** The knowledge gap hypotheses suggest that in cases where mass media become a fully integrated component of society, people in these societies who enjoy higher levels of socioeconomic status acquire information at more rapid rates than those people of lower economic status. Furthermore, as these societies progress, this gap in information increases (p. 216). Data were generated from 1,714 surveys collected after the 1996 presidential election. Results indicated that a respondent's level of education was "clearly the strongest predictor of political knowledge" and "Television news is only weakly related to political knowledge at best" while newspaper usage "is somewhat more strongly related to political knowledge" but did not contribute to perceptions of candidates or political beliefs (p. 223). In terms of the knowledge gap hypothesis, results indicated that "television use could decrease preexisting gaps . . . between those with more and less education, while newspaper use can either decrease the gap or at least not increase it" (p. 228).

The same lead author and two other colleagues (Eveland, Seo, & Marton, 2002) studied differences in political knowledge as a function of exposure to television, newspapers, and online news sources. Their experiment utilized 59 subjects (p. 362) and demonstrated television and newspaper's superiority over Web-based political sources when it comes to recalling political knowledge; however, the Web was superior in helping subjects structure memory of political knowledge (p. 370). In short, more traditional media were found to be effective tools for learning about politics, but the Web may be more effective in remembering such knowledge.

Researchers in political communication have long assumed that voter knowledge and behavior is the product of a mixture of information gained, sifted, and utilized from both interpersonal and mass media sources. Little is actually understood about how this process occurs, or how interpersonal and mass media sources work together or independently of each other. Scheufele (2002) explored this process with data originally collected in 1990 by the Opinion Research Center. Variables such as age, gender, income, political interest, exposure to newspaper and television public affairs, interpersonal communication about politics, and political knowledge were analyzed (p. 54). The researcher found that "the relationship between television hard news use and political participation was stronger for participants who talked to others more frequently about politics" (p. 56), and concluded that individuals who pursue political information in television and other media were more likely to act on such information if they talked about politics with others.

Voter participation in U.S. presidential elections continues to decline. Fewer and fewer individuals are involved in civic activities. A general cynicism toward things political also prevails. Have media contributed to this development? If so, how? These questions were studied by Wilkins (2000), who noted previous research indicated distrust in U.S. politics had tripled to over 75 percent since 1975 (p. 570). Using survey research methods, the researcher interviewed 257 U.S. citizens living in the state of Texas and collected information on a number of variables, including levels of participation in both politics and civics, trust in politics, and media variables (p. 573). Results indicated a fairly complex interplay of variables. For example, Texans who were active in their communities were more likely to participate in politics. Interestingly, people who generally distrust politics were actually *more* inclined to participate in elections. Television played a role to the extent that there was a relationship between people who watch television news and their tendency to participate in political processes (pp. 575–577). The researcher concluded that targeting television as the culprit for declines in political participation on the part of U.S. voters was an oversimplification of more complex processes. Indeed, distrust and skepticism appear to play important roles in active, not passive, political life.

In related work, Weaver and Drew (2001) assessed the role, if any, that media played in voter intentions during the 2000 presidential election. In short, does how one votes in such elections depend on exposure to and attention paid to various mass media? Data were generated by means of survey completed by 516 respondents in the heart of the U.S. Midwest. Measures included telephone respondent estimates of time spent with print and electronic news sources (including the Internet), attention paid to presidential debates, interest in the presidential campaign, interest in selected campaign issues, and demographics. Results indicated that demographics such as gender and education level played significant roles in predicting knowledge about presidential candidates and campaign issues. In this study, males with higher levels of education demonstrated greater levels of political knowledge. Democrats were less knowledgeable, and Republicans were more so. Interestingly, those respondents more reliant on television news demonstrated lower levels of political knowledge but at the same time showed higher levels of awareness regarding where the major candidates stood on key issues (pp. 791–792). The researchers concluded that findings from their study were consistent with those from previous research that, despite general criticism of media coverage of presidential campaigns, television news influenced political knowledge in positive ways and likely contributed to actual voting behaviors.

We have seen in other sections of this book how news media serve to set agendas for what people think is important in their worlds. Indeed, some agenda-setting research has gone so far as to demonstrate that not only do news agendas tell us what to think about, but also may tell us what to think in terms of specific issues. Boyle (2001) provided an interesting twist on this perspective in his examination of something called **intermedia agenda setting,** where messages in one type of media may influence the agendas in other forms of media. Specifically, the researcher examined relationships between campaign and news agendas for the 1996 presidential campaign between Clinton and Dole. Content analysis was used to study messages in television campaign advertising, major network newscasts, and three major daily newspapers. These messages were studied for the issues promoted. A total of 24 issue categories were coded and included such topics as taxes, leadership, political processes, drugs, and the economy (pp. 29–31). Some results were predictable and consistent with other research reported in this chapter. For example, horse-race issues predominated network news coverage of political campaigns. In addition, some support was found for the argument that major party television advertising influenced the network news agenda, particularly for the political challenger whose message, by nature, is more aggressive (p. 39). Among implications, the researcher noted how in times of peace and prosperity, it is incumbent upon the challenger in a major political race to focus on issues in such ways as to curry interest and attention on the part of major news media.

SUMMARY

What can we conclude based on this recent research in the field of television and presidential politics?

- Television network news coverage of presidential races emphasizes public opinion poll results over campaign issues.
- Meta-analyses of news bias show that Democratic presidential candidates receive slightly more coverage time than their Republican counterparts.
- Network coverage of presidential debates tends to focus on moments of conflict between candidates, rather than candidate stands on issues.
- Emphasis on image- over issue-oriented presidential campaign advertising ebbs and flows over the decades such content has been monitored.
- Negative messages are a prominent feature of presidential campaign television advertising.
- Education level is an important factor in voter knowledge. Television coverage of campaigns does appear to contribute in small ways to preferences for presidential candidates.
- Voters who talk more frequently to others about politics rely more than others on political information acquired from television news.
- Television news coverage of presidential campaigns may contribute in positive ways to actual voting behavior.

REFERENCES

Alliance for Better Campaigns (2003). *By the numbers: For television industry, politics is the gift that keeps on giving.* Retrieved December 2, 2003, from http://www.bettercampaigns.org/standard/display.php?StoryID=274.

Ballotti, J., & Kaid, L. (2000). Examining verbal style in presidential campaign spots. *Communication Studies, 51,* 259–273.

Benoit, W., & Currie, H. (2001). Inaccuracies in media coverage of presidential debates. *Argumentation and Advocacy, 38,* 28–39.

Benoit, W., & Wells, W. (1996). *Candidates in conflict: Persuasive attack and defense in the 1992 presidential debates.* Tuscaloosa: University of Alabama Press.

Boyle, T. (2001). Intermedia agenda setting in the 1996 presidential election. *Journalism and Mass Communication Quarterly, 78,* 26–44.

Craig, R. (2000). Expectations and elections: How television defines campaign news. *Critical Studies in Media Communication, 17,* 28–44.

D'Alessio, D., & Allen, M. (2000). Media bias in presidential elections: A meta-analysis. *Journal of Communication, 50*(4), 133–156.

Eveland, W., & Scheufele, D. (2000). Connecting news media use with gaps in knowledge and participation. *Political Communication, 17,* 215–237.

Eveland, W., Seo, M., & Marton, K. (2002). Learning from the news in campaign 2000: An experimental comparison of TV news, newspapers, and online news. *Media Psychology, 4,* 353–378.

Goldstein, K., & Freedman, P. (2002). Lessons learned: Campaign advertising in the 2000 elections. *Political Communication, 19.*

Johnson, A., & Kaid, L. (2002). Image ads and issue ads in U.S. presidential advertising: Using videostyle to explore stylistic differences in televised political ads from 1952–2000. *Journal of Communication, 52,* 281–300.

Just, M., Crigler, A., & Buhr, T. (1999). Voice, substance, and cynicism in presidential campaign media. *Political Communication, 16,* 25–44.

Larson, S. (1999). Public opinion in television election news: Beyond polls. *Political Communication, 16,* 133–145.

Larson, S. (2000). Network differences in public opinion coverage during the 1996 presidential campaign. *Journal of Broadcasting and Electronic Media, 44,* 16–26.

Mullen, L. (1999). Television news and contentiousness: An exploratory study of visual and verbal content in news about the president. *Journal of Broadcasting and Electronic Media, 43,* 159–174.

Owen, D. (1995). The debate challenge: Candidate strategies in the new media age. In K. Kendall (Ed.) *Presidential campaign discourse: Strategic communication problems* (pp. 135–155). Albany: State University of New York Press.

Parmelee, J. (2002). Presidential primary videocassettes: How candidates in the 2000 U.S. presidential primary elections framed their early campaigns. *Political Communication, 19,* 317–331.

Pew Charitable Trusts. *Campaign finance.* Retrieved December 2, 2003, from http://www.pewtusts.com/ideas/index.cfm?issue=3.

Prior, M. (2001). Weighted content analysis of political advertisements. *Political Communication, 18,* 335–345.

Scheufele, D. (2002). Examining differential gains from mass media and their implications for participatory behavior. *Communication Research, 29,* 46–65.

Shaw, D. (1999). The impact of news media favorability and candidate events in presidential campaigns. *Political Communication, 16,* 183–202.

Tedesco, J., Kaid, L., & McKinnon, L. (2000). Network adwatches: Policing the 1996 primary and general election presidential ads. *Journal of Broadcasting and Electronic Media, 44,* 541–555.

Weaver, D., & Drew, D. (2001). Voter learning and interest in the 2000 presidential election: Did the media matter? *Journalism and Mass Communication Quarterly, 78,* 787–798.

Wilkins, K. (2000). The role of media in public disengagement from political life. *Journal of Broadcasting and Electronic Media, 44,* 569–580.

ACTIVITIES

1. Think about some of the prominent issues in your community. A number of possibilities come to mind, ranging from economic to education, or growth to the environment. Choose one of these issues for further study. Conduct a content

analysis of one week's worth (Monday through Friday) of local television news coverage, noting important items in order to answer the following questions. Perhaps you and others can choose different local television newscasts in order to expand your sample and to compare results once you have completed your individual analysis. What is the prominent issue in your community that you studied? How many stories were reported about the issue? What was the basic thrust of the story? Did reporters emphasize basic facts, conflict between various factions, expert opinions, politician opinions, person-on-the-street opinions, or other things in their coverage of the issue? What can you summarize at weeks end in terms of how the issue was covered by this local television news outlet? Compare your results to those generated by others who may have studied other stations.

2. Some research has shown that a number of factors contribute to how people vote for presidential candidates over their lifetime. These factors include their parents' political views, peer influences, and how they voted in their first national election. Interview at least five members of your family or close associates, ideally across a range of generations and ages. Ask them when they first voted in a presidential election, which candidate they voted for, and factors influencing their decision to vote in the way that they did. Then be sure to ask each individual about the role, if any, played by the media in the decision to vote for that particular candidate. Be also sure to ask them how they feel the media contribute, if at all, to their decisions to choose this or that presidential candidate in more recent years. What can you distill from your information gained from talking to these five people? Compare your ideas to those generated by others. Can you summarize the role you believe the mass media, and television in particular, play in an individual's behavior when it comes to presidential politics?

3. For years, mass communication researchers and political scientists argued that communication about politics was a combination of interpersonal and mass-mediated processes. Opinion leaders, it was argued, paid more attention to news about politics and shared and, therefore, influenced so-called opinion followers on political matters. Now some argue that such backyard communication is increasingly rare, and that the mass media contribute more and more significant roles in political socialization. Interview five individuals to test these ideas. First ask these individuals what they believe are the most important influences in helping them to decide about presidential politics. Then ask them to rank each of the items they describe from the most influential to the least influential. Compare your results to others to see if you can validate either more traditional or evolving perspectives regarding the role between interpersonal and mass-mediated process when it comes to political socialization.

QUESTIONS

1. Conservative critics of network television news have complained about a liberal bias when covering presidential politics. Liberal critics argue that the national television news media are owned and operated by major corporations and are therefore guilty of conservative bias. Research reported in this chapter suggests that a very slight democratic bias may exist, but certainly not one warranting extreme claims made by representatives of either political ideology. What do you

think? Provide at least three examples from recent television news coverage in order to justify your opinion.

2. Do you think you have ever been affected by television advertising for a presidential campaign? If so, how? If not, what other factors do you think contributed to your thinking about presidential candidates?

3. Some future-thinking individuals believe that television will occupy a less important role in future presidential politics. Indeed, there is mounting evidence that the Internet may play an increasingly important role and may represent something of a return to a form of grass-roots democracy. Search the Internet for recent examples of presidential candidate websites. Compare those sites to some of the findings from content analyses regarding presidential campaign advertising found in this chapter. What are the similarities you see between communication messages and strategies in the two media? What are the differences? What do you think the future holds in terms of these two forms of political communication?

ADDITIONAL READINGS

Bucy, E., & Newhagen, J. (1999). The micro- and macrodrama of politics on television: Effects of media format on candidate evaluations. *Journal of Broadcasting and Electronic Media, 43,* 193–210.

Holbrook, T. (2002). Presidential campaigns and the knowledge gap. *Political Communication, 19,* 437–454.

Jamieson, K. (2000). *Everything you think you know about politics—and why you're wrong.* New York: Basic Books.

Jamieson, K., & Waldman, P. (Eds.) (2001). *Electing the President, 2000: The insiders' view.* Philadelphia: University of Pennsylvania Press.

Moy, P., & Scheufele, D. (2000). Media effects on political and social trust. *Journalism and Mass Communication Quarterly, 77,* 744–759.

Snoeijer, R., de Vreese, C., & Semetko, H. (2002). Research note: The effects of live television reporting on recall and appreciation of political news. *European Journal of Communication, 17,* 85–101.

Agenda-setting theory The study of how news organizations decide what stories to cover and how such coverage influence audience perceptions of what is important in the world.

Attribution theory The study of how media influence audience perceptions about social attitudes and behaviors. The theory has been applied, for example, to the study of how exposure to pornographic media can affect audience perceptions as to the causes of sex-related crimes.

Coding Where typically two or more researchers examine and assign the same meaning to an identical element in media content.

Coefficient of determination The percentage of the variance explained by the interaction of two variables.

Cognitive developmental theory The perspective that children of different developmental stages process information about the world in qualitatively different ways.

Content analysis Systematic observation of elements in print, electronic, cinematic, and other media, usually by documenting the frequency with which such elements appear.

Content threads Patterns of print and electronic media consumption common for individuals within society.

Correlation coefficient A statistic conveying both the strength and direction of the relationship between two variables.

Critical television viewing Teaching children and adolescents strategies for demystifying television's industries, production techniques, and contents.

Cultivation theory A widely adopted theory of mass communication suggesting that television in particular is a powerful transmit-

ter of a consistent cultural perspective that comes to represent the same perspective for audiences engaging higher levels of media content.

Deductive thinking Using a hard and fast set of rules or principles and applying those rules to new situations.

Denotative signs Cultural signs shared in common by many people. A traffic signal is generally perceived as a denotative sign.

Dependent variable The variable influenced by the manipulation of one or more independent variables.

Eating disorder symptomatology Factors contributing to eating disorders.

Elaboration likelihood model A psychological theory of persuasion suggesting that there are direct and peripheral routes to cognitive processing of messages.

Empirical/empiricism Systematic observation in the physical or social world.

Ethnicity A fluid construct used to describe groups who share in common some combination of culture, history, race, religion, or language.

Ethnomethodology A branch of sociology where researchers study how people do everyday interaction.

Expectancy theory A theory of mass communication suggesting that exposure to media messages informs perceptions about people and places encountered in the real world.

Expectancy value theory The study of how audiences pay attention to story content of interest to them.

Feminist theory A perspective informing approaches in mass communication research exploring how media portray women as sex objects, in demeaning roles, and in inequitable power relationships.

Frame analysis How cognitive schema or beliefs inform the interpretation of future experiences, including media experiences.

Framing How media professionals use storytelling conventions and production techniques to emphasize parts of a story over other parts, and how those practices inform audience perceptions of the same story.

Gender constancy Acquiring gender personality.

Gender schema theory The study of how individuals perceive new information about female or male roles based on previous knowledge.

Gender studies The study of differences and similarities between women and men.

General affective aggression model/general aggression model The study of how media cue aggression-related knowledge stored in memory.

Hostile attribution bias The study of how exposure to frustrating social stimuli can trigger aggression.

Independent variable The variable or variables one manipulates in an experiment or measures in survey research.

Individual differences theory The study of how factors such as gender and age influence media consumption patterns and perceptions of content.

Inductive thinking Taking into account surrounding contexts and conditions in order to generate assumptions about social phenomena.

Inferential statistics Extending the characteristics of a sample to a larger parameter or population.

Intercoder reliability Typically mathematically derived measures of agreement between two or more coders of media content.

Intermedia agenda setting Where messages in one type of media may influence the agendas in other types of media.

Knowledge gap hypotheses The study of how classes of people in advanced societies acquire media-based information at more rapid rates than classes of people in lower economic strata.

Manipulatives Dolls or other toys that researchers have children use to help respond to questions.

Mass communication The process by which individual audience members engage in and give meaning to media contents.

Mass media Print, electronic, and filmic opportunities supported by multiple platforms for presentation and audience consumption.

Media effects A blend of mass-mediated and socially constructed meanings and behaviors for each audience member.

Meta-analyses Summary studies of previous studies.

Metacognition A branch of cognitive developmental psychology focusing on how children and adults think about thinking.

Method/methodology Systematic use of data collection tools.

Modeling theory The study of human behavior based on the guiding principle that behaviors can be learned given appropriate reinforcement conditions.

Mood management theory The study of how audiences pursue certain types of media content dependent on mood.

News bias Often applied to the study of balanced or inequitable news coverage of political candidates and campaigns.

Noninferential statistics Statistics used to report characteristics of a sample.

Parameter A characteristic of a larger population. Those households with cable television would be a parameter of all households with television in a given market.

Pearson product moment correlation A common correlation coefficient typically represented by the symbol r.

Persuasion theory The study of attention, perception, cognition, and attitude change.

Phenomenological sociology A perspective in social research where sociologists believe that what people say and do is a product of how they view the world.

Pornography Representations of sexuality used as fantasy material for sexual arousal.

Price elasticity The study of how demand for various products and services are influenced by pricing.

Priming theory A perspective suggesting that prior exposure to certain kinds of information will influence future exposure to similar information.

Probability level A statistic used to determine whether results generated for a specific sample are representative or subject to error.

Qualitative research Typically a process of deductive reasoning applied to the study of how people act and describe their actions in society.

Quantification/quantitative The practice of converting observed behaviors into numbers that can then be systematically analyzed using statistics.

Reliability The quality of measures used to collect data for variables.

Replicability The ability to duplicate methods, procedures, and outcomes of a previous study.

Sample Typically a smaller segment of a larger parameter or population.

Social learning theory A widely adopted theory of cognitive psychology credited to Albert C. Bandura and his colleagues. The perspective basically argues that people can model learned behaviors given an appropriate set of stimulus materials and reinforcement contingencies.

Social science/social scientific research The use of quantitative methods in the study of human behavior.

Statistic A numerical representation of an observation.

Stereotype Perceiving and engaging the world with a preexisting set of filters.

Stereotype threat Social stigmatization as a function of being type cast because of media portrayals.

Symbolic interactionism A branch of sociology wherein researchers see the self as on display for observation through each individual's presentation of roles.

Theoretical constructs Component parts of theories amenable to measurement by means of operationally defined variables.

Theory A body of beliefs, rules, or principles generally thought to be true.

Third-person effect A mass communication theory with the primary hypothesis that audiences perceive media effects as far greater for others than for self.

Triangulation Data analysis incorporating information derived from more than one method.

Uses and gratifications theory A prominent theory in mass communication research purporting that individuals have needs and wants that can be satisfied through media consumption.

Variables Organized sets, groupings, or classes of observations. Gender, education level, and hours spent watching television are all examples of variables.

AUTHOR INDEX

SUBJECT INDEX